Reflecting
GOD'S CHARACTER
in Your Business

Tim Voorhees
Joyce Avedisian-Riedinger
Mike Pendleton

*You reflect Christ in who
you are and what you do.*

Blessings,
Joyce

HIGH BRIDGE BOOKS
HOUSTON

Reflecting God's Character in Your Business
by Tim Voorhees, Joyce Avedisian, and Mike Pendleton

Printed in the United States of America
ISBN (Paperback): 978-1-946615-83-1
ISBN (eBook): 978-1-946615-28-2

Some names in the following case studies have been changed to protect anonymity of people who declined to be named in this book. Nonetheless, all company names in the book are those of real companies and in many cases the actual owners and managers of these companies have been named. The authors are very grateful for the contributions from the many prominent Christian business owners and managers who agreed to be profiled in the following chapters.

Some of the images in this book are stock photos that represent actual people and situations. Authors give all necessary credit to iStockPhoto.com.

High Bridge Books titles may be purchased in bulk for educational, business, fundraising, or sales promotional use. For information please contact High Bridge Books via www.HighBridge-Books.com/contact.

Published in Houston, Texas by High Bridge Books

Contents

Preface

DO BUSINESSES RUN WITH CHRISTIAN practices and principles truly enjoy greater prosperity? To answer this question, we first need to define what a Christian-run business is, understand what it does, and look at examples from Scripture and from the modern marketplace. This book examines these examples, observing how their leaders reflect the character of God while building businesses with God-honoring missions and identities.

Having a Christian mission involves so much more than simply introducing Christian practices into a business (e.g., prayer, peacemaking, or tithing). Having a Christian identity involves much more than simply listing and teaching biblical principles. We must first understand how God communicates His character and expects us to reflect His character.

While Christian business conferences and publications promote hundreds of books about Christian business, very few books attempt to communicate a fully realized understanding of business leaders' responsibilities to know God and reflect His divine character. This book seeks to fill a void among Christian business books by emphasizing how God communicates through covenants.

The fullness of God and the six main elements of God's relationship with man are reflected through Biblical covenants that teach us about the identity and mission of successful Christian-run organizations, including businesses. Christian business leaders often end up communicating the six elements of God's character more actively than they realize. When the authors interviewed the employees and associates of these Christian leaders, they discovered that these leaders have consistently understood and conveyed 1) God's revelation, 2) His purposes, 3) divine leadership structures, and 4) Christ-centered principles and priorities. These result in 5) a "quadruple bottom line," and 6) scalable business models. These six elements are explained in the following introduction and at the start of each of the six sections in this book.[1]

Knowing the six main elements of divine character helps leaders confront sin in their own lives and in the organizations they lead. Studying the biblical and practical application of these elements encourages repentance and fosters a deeper personal relationship with God and a conversion of the heart. Only then can leaders walk in the Spirit, follow Christ's examples, and embrace teachings from our Father. This book explains all these concepts in the context of covenants.

Teachings about biblical covenants reveal how believers who know God have a context for integrating His principles into business practices. Business leaders who understand the covenantal character of God know about the source of divine principles, the purpose behind the principles, examples of leaders who model the principles, teachings about the meaning of the principles, clear examples of blessings related to following the principles (or the negative consequences of neglecting the principles), and the deeper relationships and greater prosperity that can result from reflecting divine character through our relationships with others.

A covenantal perspective on Scripture helps us deepen our understanding of Christ: specifically, His character as the mediator of the new covenant, and the covenantal institutions overseen by leaders who respect the authority of Christ and His Church. This is most evident as Christ works through His Church to reconcile all things to Himself. God placed Christ far above all rule and authority, power and dominion, not only to be head over the Church (Eph. 1:21-22), but to reconcile all things—on earth and in heaven (Col. 1:18-20). Throughout the centuries, the Church has established covenants and maintained covenantal relationships by means of Christ's established Church discipline:

blessing the faithful and withholding blessings from the unfaithful. These principles of discipline are meant to encourage the peace and purity of the Church, encouraging its members to place their hopes in God (1 Tim. 6:17).

Christ works to reconcile all things, including all business leadership structures, to Himself by putting in place business leaders who heed church authority when stepping off the church campus to engage in the marketplace. Covenantal principles apply vertically in the believer's relationship with God and then horizontally in relationships with other believers. The same leadership structures that maintain peace and purity within Christian churches also apply to families and businesses run by Christians. This book explains how Christian-run businesses can learn from mature churches when applying covenantal teachings to maintain pure and peaceful relationships, while also honoring God and building productive teams.

When writing this book, the authors have been united in a desire to extend spiritual principles beyond the church campus to guide productive teamwork in the marketplace while bringing teamwork principles from the marketplace into the church. The authors believe that many church boards (as well as boards of related non-profit schools and ministries) can be run much more effectively if these organizations apply marketplace teachings from this book. Similarly, the for-profit enterprises in the marketplace can confront sin much more effectively when involving qualified church leaders on governance boards. This book seeks to equip spiritual leaders at churches to understand marketplace leadership teachings while also seeking to equip marketplace leaders to understand spiritual leadership teachings. As noted at http://www.reflectinggod.info/7LightSources, and as explained in the following chapters, spiritual leaders at churches (including chaplains, prayer meeting leaders, Christian worldview teachers, and trained peacemakers) can and should work with marketplace leaders (including

C-Suite executives, board members, and consultants) to shine light into darkness while encouraging God-honoring teamwork.

This understanding of covenant unites the three authors in their diverse approaches to Christian business. Joyce holds a Ph.D. in organizational development. Before helping to establish a successful telecom company, Mike earned degrees in business and law. Like Mike, Tim has degrees in business and law, as well as a vast amount of practical experience working with Christian business leaders. All three authors hold a firm belief in the authority of Scripture and the application of the biblical covenant model when helping business leaders reflect divine teachings about business success. Despite their diverse religious backgrounds—Joyce and Tim being dedicated Protestants, and Mike being a devout Catholic—all 3 co-authors have developed a profound understanding about how the covenantal perspective of Scripture can bring people together while fostering teamwork and mature accountability.

While contributing as an author in this book, Joyce also works to emphasize the value of translating covenantal principles into leadership and organizational practices and helps to equip business leaders to reflect love and holiness. Her goal is to encourage leaders to apply an in-depth understanding of Scripture and to integrate this understanding into their day-to-day business practices.

Mike, while continuing his life-long studies in management and organizational theory, spends his time writing about how there is only one book that has the best influence in business: The Bible. Mike's writing is fueled by a deep conviction that business leaders must understand the Bible in the context of modern management. The proof lies in the most successful and the longest-lasting organization ever built: Christ's Church. Mike has observed first-hand how the leadership principles seen in the Church have worked in business. He saw the fruit of this, not only in the financial success but also in the affirmation that team members feel when they fulfill a calling that honors Christ and realizes the unique, special, and incredible calling that God has created for each of them. His mission extends beyond the Church to every organization led by those who want to learn how to apply biblical principles to management and organizational theory.

Tim has spent 40 years advising wealthy clients, many of whom are founders and owners of Christ-centered businesses, as a lawyer and/or wealth manager. Even before writing his master's degree capstone paper on Christian business in the early 1980s, Tim sought to understand and apply biblical principles of business. When he was introduced to covenant theology through the works of theologians like Vern Poythress and Ray Sutton, he quickly found a framework for explaining why some theological systems lead us into a deeper relationship with Christ while other systematic theologies fail to do so. The covenantal framework articulated by Poythress, based on earlier covenant theologians' writings dating back to the early seventeenth century[2], can now guide 21st-century businesses, as explained throughout this book. Tim firmly believes that by integrating these biblical principles into business practices, Christian-run businesses can enjoy greater prosperity.

---

[1] http://www.ReflectingGod.info/4xBottomline

[2] See, e.g., www.Covenant.net/6Elements.

Executive Summary

EVERY SUNDAY, preachers assure listeners in the pews that they can experience abundance and enjoy great blessings if they are faithful. Congregants may leave the church services with much hope but many burdens. The business leader wanting to practice what is preached may feel defeated as he or she goes into the secular marketplace and tries to live out the Christian faith. Too often, the encouraging message proclaimed from the pulpit does not extend beyond Sunday morning and outside the church campus. Why?

This book will explain how the biblical values proclaimed from the pulpit are relevant to leaders seeking to create value in the marketplace. It will show how the blessings promised throughout Scripture are often given more to covenant communities than to individuals. The following chapters illustrate how reflecting Christ's covenantal character helps business leaders unite teams in productive efforts to improve results for shareholders, staff, clients, and the community.

Values proclaimed from the pulpit can inspire leaders to shine light into darkness by following biblical principles and reflecting the character of Christ. God's light illuminates festering sins such as greed, pride, anger, envy, lust, gluttony, and laziness. Each chapter gives examples of common sins in business organizations, shows how sinful behaviors are rooted in the seven deadly sins, and inspires believers to reflect God's character by rising above that sin. The authors focus on showing how leaders can triumph over the temptations and darkness that surround them every day by relying on the Bible as a victory manual.

To overcome darkness with light, Christians are called to imitate Christ's character through relationships that reflect the character of Christ to people around us. See, e.g., 1 Corinthians 4:16, 1 Corinthians 11:1, 2 Thessalonians 3:9, Hebrews 6:12, Hebrews 13:7, and 3 John 11.

Reflecting Christ's character[1] starts with understanding[2] and following Him.[3] The character of Jesus in the New Covenant reflects God as seen throughout covenants in the Old Testament. These covenants show a consistent pattern of six elements in the same sequence, as explained in endnote 4 at the end of this executive summary.[4] This book will explain the six covenantal elements with biblical references and provide practical examples of successful business enterprises defined by covenantal relationships

The six elements of the divine covenants will be explained with 16 chapters, as shown on the chart below. The chapters are organized into six sections that begin with a brief summary of how each section helps the reader reflect a different dimension of divine character.

The sixteen chapters are focused on translating common themes from Sunday morning sermons into practical advice to equip business leaders to make a difference each day. This book can better empower people to have a daily impact than can most traditional Christian business books. Throughout each of the sixteen chapters, the reader should see clearly how values proclaimed from the pulpit can translate into clear value evident on bar charts tracking bottom-line results. The values are made practical through a simple focus on shared mission, vision, and values, roles, goals, controls, work flows, and cash flows.

God lights the pathway for business success when leaders follow this covenantal model on individual, team and corporate levels. On an individual level, knowing the six main dimensions of divine character helps the individual draw closer to Christ.

SECTION ONE: REVELATION AND RESOURCES
Seeing How Divine Character Is Revealed through Covenants
Seeing Abundant Resources and Developing a Vision for Stewarding Them
SECTION TWO: TRANSCENDENT VISION AND VALUES
Knowing and Living Your "Why": Vision and Mission
Driving True Success through Commitment to Divine Core Values
SECTION THREE: HIERARCHICAL SPIRITUAL LEADERSHIP
Governing the Board to Speak with One Voice
Unifying the Management Team with Clear Roles, Goals, Workflows, Cashflows, and Controls
Developing Respect for Spiritual Authority through Training, Mentoring, and Discipleship
SECTION FOUR: ETHICS (CHARACTER QUALITIES)
Stewarding Time, Talent, Treasure, and Trust with Biblical Principles
Managing Staff with Biblical Principles
Managing Risk with Biblical Principles
Encouraging Peacemaking Based on Biblical Principles
SECTION FIVE: OUTCOMES (KPI)
Improving Shareholder Benefits
Optimizing Staff Benefits
Prospering Your Customers
Investing in the Community
SECTION SIX: SUCCESSION
Investing in the Future through Succession Planning

Knowledge of His revelation (element 1) and purposes (element 2) lead a believer to confess human weakness (element 3), ask for strength in following divine precepts (element 4), experience the blessings of obedience (element 5), and use blessings to extend the Kingdom through Christ-centered churches, families, and governments (element 6).

On a team and corporate level, believers can more effectively unite in building Christ-centered organizations when they are committed to identifying God-given strengths and opportunities (element 1); articulating divinely-guided purpose and mission statements (element 2); following spiritually mature authorities (element 3); honoring godly management principles and priorities (element 4); consistently committing to advance the well-being of key shareholders, staff, customers, and the community (element 5); and building succession plans to perpetuate values that make the enterprise successful (element 6). The call to action is for leaders to make a shared commitment to uphold these six elements of divine character.

Every chapter shows how following this covenantal model helps business owners and managers reflect God's character by overcoming darkness with light.[5] The 16 chapters each start with a case study that contrasts leading in light with succumbing to darkness. The case studies identify key issues, describe relevant biblical principles, and apply the principles to the issues in the case. The application involves "How-to Steps" for reflecting the light and suggests techniques and conflict management principles to confront darkness. Each chapter ends with questions that help the leader assess the extent to which their corporate culture bears the marks of God's covenantal character. Business owners and managers are encouraged to take the assessment tests and together commit to improving how they reflect the six elements of divine character.

In each chapter, you will see case examples of ways that light overcomes darkness caused by the seven deadly sins. From the case studies, the reader should learn how to spot core sins and overcome the darkness with light. Here is a brief summary of how darkness is confronted with light:

- In Chapter 2, read how Bill, who got fired from his job and was burdened by debt, tapped into six non-financial resources to develop a thriving business.
- In Chapter 5, read how Ben, the founder and leader of a growing international ministry, watched a few self-interested board members violate God's principles while hijacking the board and misappropriating donated property for personal benefit. Learn how a CEO can select a qualified board that upholds his or her values and affirms the strategic plan to prevent such a catastrophe.
- In Chapter 6, read how the SEC raided William's business and uncovered breaches in compliance standards

that shut down operations. See how the CEO can avoid being vulnerable to the SEC and other regulatory agencies.

- In Chapter 7, read how Nick, a co-founder of a growing business, was sorely dejected when his partner unexpectedly abandoned the business. See how a mentor stepped into the fray and helped Nick turn a disgrace into a blessing by rebuilding the business founded on God's principles and creating a prosperous enterprise.

- In Chapter 8, read about how Jerry built a multi-million-dollar business by championing God's stewardship principles but then risked losing everything to creditors. In deciding to move from success to significance, he sold his business to fund charities, but self-seeking financial advisers urged him to leverage his sales proceeds in aggressive investment portfolios. See how the seller of a company must not assume that expertise with building business value equips the seller to build value in an investment portfolio.

- In Chapter 9, read about how Nick, founder and CEO, built a prosperous business by transforming the secular business model in the construction industry into a Spirit-led business model and culture.

- In Chapter 11, read about how Tony, a committed Christian, received repeated negative and disparaging emails from a manager in his company. The ripple effect was to undermine respect for Tony, damage employee morale, and harm customers. See how the chaplain guided Tony on how to use biblical peace-making principles to shed light into the darkness.

- In Chapter 13, learn what biblical principles can create a positive environment for increasing employee engagement to overcome the staggering Gallup report that 70% of employees are disengaged at work. (*Disengaged* employees do the least to get by or actively undermine the mission and values of the company while *engaged* employees are enthusiastic and committed to the company.)
- In Chapter 14, read about how Marian, founder and CEO of Turbocam, dealt with an irate client who demanded a discount even though he did not fulfill his part of the contract. Learn what godly principles work for gaining long-term, loyal customers.
- In Chapter 15, read how a senior leader was driven by money at the expense of family, friends, and church activities, pulling his subordinates down with him. Learn God's principle of giving and how God entrusts money to us that should be invested in the community of a company for optimum results.
- In Chapter 16, read about Dr. Robert Clinton's study of biblical, historical, and contemporary leaders, which revealed that only one in three leaders finished well. Learn what six character qualities distinguish those who finish well from those who don't.

God's light and character can be experienced on an individual, team, and company level. If the leader is respecting God's teachings, the leader and people around him will enjoy the fruits of the spirit: love, joy, peace, patience, kindness, goodness, faithfulness, gentleness, and self-control.[6] When the leader allows God's spirit to guide him, people should see the unity of the Spirit through the bond of peace[7] and a glimpse of the Kingdom on earth.[8] As team members foster trust through committing to God's teachings, the business undergoes a realignment of principles, priorities, teamwork, productivity, and innovation. These fruits inspire people to know and reflect divine character qualities more actively.

This book will help you reinforce healthy behaviors, spot dysfunctional behaviors, identify core issues, apply scriptural truths to confront the issues, and build businesses where the leaders and team members walk in God's light. God's light can help each Christian business leader experience the fruits of the Spirit more consistently while building teams and organizations that enjoy God's abundance more fully.

When a business person leaves the church campus after hearing the pastor preach about God's light, the darkness can be overwhelming. Light has come into the world, but the people prefer darkness for their deeds are evil.[9] Take heart! This book will show you how to respond to the seven deadly sins by practicing divine virtues. You will see how you can reflect covenantal character to build productive teams. Most important, you can apply the teachings on the following pages to effectively unite with Christ and fellow Christians while experiencing the fruit of the Spirit in abundance.

---

[1] Ephesians 5:1.

[2] Philippians 3:10-12, 1 John 4:7.

[3] See John 10:27, 12:26, and 21:8, John 4:7.

[4] For example, the six elements of the Biblical covenant are evident in the stories surrounding these business relationships in Scripture. The stories surrounding each passage below shows how the Biblical characters, 1) appreciated God's revelation

and resources, 2) respected divine purposes, 3) honored authority, 4) followed Biblical principles, 5) realized blessings, and 6) extended divine influence. At www.ReflectingGod.info/Business6Elements, see a summary of how the above six elements apply to the following business structures:

Limited Partnership	Sarah and Hagar (Genesis 16:1-6)
General Partnership	Johoshaphat and Abah (2 Chronicles 1:8)
Buy-Sell Agreement	Abraham buying land from Ephron (Genesis 23:10-20)
Employer-Employee Relationship	Jacob working for Laban (Genesis 29-30)
Lender to Borrower	Bond-servants (Nehemiah 5:5)
Corporation	Local Church (Hebrews 13:7)
Family Business	David and Solomon (1 Chronicles 28:11-12)

[5] See, e.g., Psalm 74:20.

[6] Galatians 5:22.

[7] Ephesians 4:3.

[8] Matthew 6:10.

[9] John 3:19.

Section 1

Revelation and Resources

Seeing How Divine Character is Revealed through Covenants

Seeing Abundant Resources and Developing a Vision for Stewarding Them

As noted in the Introduction, God reveals His character through covenants. Leaders maintaining a covenantal relationship with God will seek to reflect His divine character through their lives while uniting with others in covenantal relationships. Both the leader's personal relationship with God and his or her relationships with others can reflect the six elements of the covenant. Chapter 1 gives examples of how leaders in biblical history and successful Christian business leaders prayerfully unite with Christ to discern divine opportunities. Mature Christian leaders develop their strengths while properly managing the weaknesses and threats that can undermine strengths and opportunities. Teachings about a personal union with Christ in Chapter 1 are applied to business organizations in Chapters 2 through 16. Chapter 2 shows how Christ-centered leaders and teams can identify six types of non-financial resources available to every person to build productive enterprises and realize financial rewards, the seventh and, arguably, the least important resource. Readers, regardless of their financial net worth or business experience, will see the practical implications of Deuteronomy 8:18: "[God] gives you the ability to produce wealth, and so confirms his covenant."

Chapter 1

Seeing How Divine Character Is Revealed Through Covenants

GEORGE WAS AN INTELLIGENT and polished wealth management adviser who grew wealthy by promoting himself (pride?). He charged higher fees than other professionals but paid staff members at less than market rates (greed?). When clients preferred working with other local advisers, George criticized his competitors with unfair attacks (envy?). When Christians around George questioned his behavior, he attacked them with very negative emails copied to associates (anger?). While avoiding accountability, George maintained the nicest office and perks (gluttony?). He convinced enough people that he was producing quality work product even though George's staff knew that he was often too disengaged to really care about the clients' needs (laziness). He somehow got his secretaries to support his behavior even when they were clearly wrong; this made people wonder about his relationships with female staff members (lust?). These behaviors (7 deadly sins?) continued while George held himself out as a leader in his church.

George always interpreted contracts in his own favor. When a staff member or vendor seemed to have a better deal, George simply delayed payment or refused to perform. He pushed matters to the point of being sued before relenting. Parties grew tired of the brinksmanship and often let George negotiate more favorable deals. Whereas Psalm 15 teaches Christians to keep an agreement even it if hurts, George kept agreements only if they did not hurt him.

People around George were not happy, and his team was often dysfunctional. Why did George's dark behavior continue while efforts to shine light into the darkness were so often thwarted? Very simply, George attacked or marginalized staff members who quoted from Scripture, offered to pray with George, or proposed that conflicts be resolved by a peacemaker who was accountable to church elders (and the church discipline process). In short, George successfully kept God's light from shining through the means of grace described in Christian theology (and described at the end of this chapter). George was too often like the wicked described in Psalm 73 and haunts of darkness too often surrounded George because he did not respect God's covenant (Ps. 74:20) and he avoided accountability to a church that respected God's covenant.

How does respect for God's covenant allow God's light to shine into the darkness? Paul answers this question in 2 Corinthians 4:4, 6. He writes, "The god of this age has blinded the minds of unbelievers, so that they cannot see the light of the gospel that displays the glory of Christ, who is the image of God. For God, who said, "Let light shine out of darkness," made his light shine in our hearts to give us the light of the knowledge of God's glory displayed in the face of Christ."

The radiance of God's glory is seen in the face of His Son, who is the exact representation of God's being and who sustains all things by his powerful Word (Heb. 1:3). Christians are called to follow the Son's example (Eph. 5:1) and participate in the divine nature (2 Pet. 1:4). The light of the knowledge of God's glory, displayed in the face of Christ, is the light that should shine in our hearts (2 Cor. 4:6) and through our deeds (Matt. 5:16).

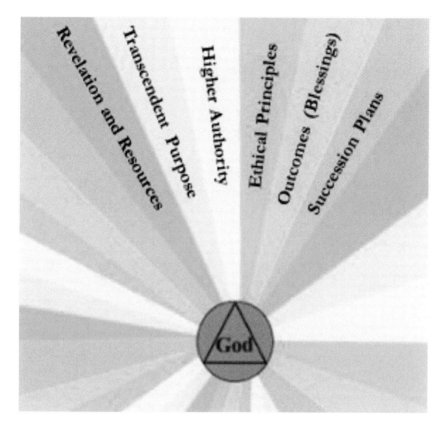

Christ sustains all things by his powerful Word (Heb. 1:3 and Col. 1:17). Teachings about Christ radiating His glory and divine nature can be explained using the covenantal sequence revealed throughout Scripture. Covenants have six elements that consistently display God's character: (1) revelation of resources, (2) transcendent purpose, (3) hierarchy of authority, (4) ethical principles [respected with Christ's help], and (5) blessings rather than curses. These blessings are leveraged around the world and across the generation to expand the Kingdom through a divine (6) succession plan.

These six dimensions of God's character are evident both in personal relationships and corporate relationships. A mature Christian seeks to reflect what natural law and Scripture teach about divine revelation, purpose, authority, ethics, blessings of obedience, and succession. Mature Christian leaders can reflect these characteristics through organizations. God has ordained three main covenantal institutions that give divine authority to the leader: the church, family, and government. (See www.ReflectingGod.info/3Institutions.) Most important, Christ has authority over the church that is given to mature elders. These elders are encouraged to maintain mature leadership over two other primary institutions: the family and the government. These three institutions are called to reflect the above six elements of divine character by upholding core values, such as are reflected through the 50 Bible verses summarized in six areas at the following link: http://ReflectingGod.info/CoreValues.

A fourth institution in the Scriptures is the business enterprise. A business lacks the covenantal authority given by God to the church, family, and government; however, a business will often adopt Spirit-led leadership structures from mature families and churches or from governmental leadership structures when directive management is needed. For these reasons, a business may reflect the covenantal character of God well enough that people regard it as the fourth covenantal institution in Scripture. When the business is led by mature Christians, it will typically reflect all six elements of divine character seen in Christian churches and Christian families. Of course, a business can follow divine teachings without being led by a Christian, but surveys of successful businesses around the world and across the centuries show that the business leaders, either intentionally or unintentionally, apply teachings likes those in the 50 Bible passages mentioned above and, therefore, reflect aspects of God's covenantal character.

In America, where 95% of people say that they believe in God and 80% claim to be Christians, the core business values from Scripture are readily accepted. Sadly, the reality inside business enterprises will often differ from the lofty rhetoric about God-honoring principles. Countless relationships fall into a deep dark abyss between Christian rhetoric and the actual business practices of fallen Christians who operate businesses. Resources are squandered, reputations are damaged, and teams are undermined when non-Christian behaviors go undetected or unconfronted because of the darkness. Too often, the employee or consultant who tries to bring light into the darkness encounters strong resistance and becomes the target of personal attacks. Why? "Light has come into the world, but the people preferred darkness, for their deeds were evil" (John 3:19).

Any reader in the marketplace, whether working for a for-profit business or non-profit organization, can probably recount examples of money or powerful individuals being exalted instead of God. Such idolatry undermines teamwork and demoralizes the business culture. When members of a business team see that their efforts are spent accumulating money or aggrandizing an individual, it undermines the desire to build strong and productive business relationships. The brief outline below suggests how this book will help believers identify and confront disruptive sins while shining God's disinfecting sunlight into the darkness that festers too often when Christ's followers are silenced or marginalized.

Reflecting God's character begins with knowing God and succeeds through efforts to make God known. Each chapter of this book encourages Christians to overcome past challenges and prevent future problems by knowing God more intimately. Intimate knowledge of God involves listening deeply, being in continual conversation with the Holy Spirit, and obeying His leading. The Spirit speaks through wise counselors, scripture, and circumstances to inspire the correct application of biblical truths to all types of challenges in the marketplace. Wise application of divine truths enables leaders to live out godly love and justice through their business and personal lives.

Knowing God

Believers know God's character through the means of grace: preaching of the pure Word of God, prayer, and sacraments. Praying Scripture back to God instills an understanding of His attributes and plan. Hearing biblical teaching opens the listener's eyes to dimensions of the image of God (imago Dei). Partaking of biblical sacraments establishes a mature relationship between the believer and the covenant community church. When the church properly administers baptism and communion sacraments, the church can maintain the peace and purity of the body, explained in the endnote at the end of this chapter.

Seeking a relationship with our Creator through the means of grace reveals His Trinitarian character. The believer finds principles in God's Word, sees the principles modeled by Christ, and learns to apply principles to particular situations with counsel from the Holy Spirit. The Holy Spirit guides and comforts the believer as God's law is applied to confront all areas of darkness. A personal relationship with God, Christ, and the Holy Spirit helps individual believers and covenant community church leaders identify core spiritual issues, discern facts, and apply relevant biblical teachings when making all types of decisions.

GRACE

Word. All discussions about the Christian Lord and Savior begin with His Word

Prayer. Application of God's Word to the lives of individuals requires personal and corporate prayer

Sacraments. Churches baptize members into the covenant community church and maintain peace and purity in the church through administration of the Lord's Supper.

Business leaders who turn to God through the means of grace experience His light. In this way, "God is a lamp to our feet and a light to our paths" (Ps. 119:105). Moreover, reflecting God's character allows light to overcome the darkness. This is a key theme throughout this book.

The disinfecting power of God's light begins in the heart of each believer. Godly preaching encourages the believer to practice active repentance. In God-honoring environments, Christians feel safe to confess weaknesses and trust that Christ will help them honor teachings about His law and His character.

If God's light is obscured, such as when the whole counsel of God (Acts 20:27) is not preached or prayers are not in harmony with Scripture, the light will be significantly diminished or extinguished. Even though Christ's love has come into the world, darkness can still prevail because people like darkness when their deeds are evil (John 3:19).

Darkness can cloud our knowledge of God in many ways, but the common denominator is that some words, actions, or thoughts contravene God's holy character. Such sinful behaviors tend to have a basis in the seven deadly sins highlighted by the church fathers. It is not difficult to find anger, greed, laziness, pride, lust, envy, and gluttony in the work environment.

Making God Known

Making God known involves living in ways that reflect all dimensions of His character. Divine character is made evident as individuals acknowledge how God is the source of all wisdom and resources upon which a successful enterprise is built (e.g., Prov. 24:3-4.) For example, the SWOT[1] analysis affords unique opportunities to unite executives in praying that God reveals opportunities, protects against threats, leverages strengths, and helps the faithful overcome weaknesses.

Opportunities and strengths highlighted during the SWOT analysis are some of the abundant resources revealed by God. Believers can make God known by using these resources in harmony with a transcendent purpose and mission as reflected through a hierarchy of spiritual authority that respects godly principles and priorities. Such faithfulness can lead to blessings that allow businesses to expand and make God known throughout larger regions or across more generations. The remaining pages of Chapter 1 give examples of how God is made known by business leaders who reflect six elements of divine character.

When reviewing the six ways that God's character is reflected by business owners and managers, you should see how God's covenants with Adam, Noah, Abraham, Moses, and David follow a pattern that is reflected later in Christ, the foundation of a New Covenant (Heb. 4:15). Each of these Biblical figures entered into a covenant with God after, 1) observing how God is the source of all revelation and resources; 2) seeing a divine purpose that guided personal vision, values and mission; 3) heeding God as He spoke, often through prophets or priests; 4) accepting that God is the source of ethical precepts; 5) understanding how faithfulness to divine precepts leads to blessings; and 6) seeing how God encourages use of His blessings to extend the Kingdom. These general dimensions of covenantal relationships are made evident in covenantal institutions and reflected by Godly leaders through business enterprises.

ELEMENT 1: Revelation/Resources

The creation covenant in Genesis reveals the vast array of resources created by the Father for His children. God stores up abundance for those who fear Him (Psalm 31:19). The New Covenant reaffirms covenants seen throughout the Old Testament. Christ, the mediator of the New Covenant, came that believers might live abundant lives (John 10:10).

Followers of Christ come to understand God's covenantal relationship with man through the means of grace. A team of believers committed to covenantal truths can encourage one another in cultivating God-given resources, such as the unique calling, skills, and abilities that God has given to everyone. Prayerful development of these gifts can reveal many resources needed to build a successful enterprise. It is usually not difficult to identify how team members have been blessed with many non-financial resources, such as emotional passions, spiritual insights, intellectual capital, physical talents, social networks, and professional skills. Experience working with successful individuals and families teaches that wise use of non-financial resources to serve others can lead to great financial blessings.

Developing God-given resources requires work and faithfulness. Consider, for example, the parable of the talents. In Matthew 25:14-30, a rich man delegates wealth management responsibilities to his servants. He gives five talents (a substantial amount of assets) to the first servant, two talents to the second, and one talent to the third. Two of the servants double the investments by respecting the master's stewardship principles; however, the third servant hides the money in the ground and earns nothing. The rich man returns, rewards the two who made money, but severely punishes the servant who did nothing. The parable inspires each person to identify God-given gifts and maximize returns in His service. God expects returns commensurate with the gifts given. The servant who received one talent was not condemned for failing to reach the five-talent goal; he was condemned because he did nothing with what he was given. The parable should inspire everyone to see how God encourages the wise development of the gifts that He has bestowed.

ELEMENT 2: Transcendent Vision/Purpose/Mission

In Element 1 (above) we see how an individual has 7 types of resources to steward. This stewardship is focused through Element 2 as a clear vision, purpose and mission direct the use of emotional passions, spiritual insights, intellectual capital, physical talents, professional education, social networks, and financial capital.

A leader, while praying for vision, focuses first on articulating a personal calling that should evolve into a purpose statement. The business-planning process requires that business leaders develop shared purposes and, ideally, help one another fulfill heartfelt purpose statements. Shared purposes often coalesce into a mission statement that guides strategic planning. Having a clear and compelling mission may be the single most important predictor of success in the planning process; however, this process of creating an effective mission starts with leaders seeking personal direction and an understanding of God's call.

The purpose, mission, and vision from God must be connected to the inner being. God's law is an important connector. In Psalm 1:1–3 we learn, "Blessed is the one ... whose delight is in the law of the Lord, and who meditates on his law day and night. That person is like a tree planted by streams of water, which yields its fruit in season and whose leaf does not wither—whatever [he does] prospers." The importance of law is emphasized by King Solomon in Proverbs 29:18. He writes, "Where there is no vision, the people perish: but he that keeps the law, happy is he." (To see definitions and more information about the relationship of purpose, mission, and vision, please see the glossary at http://www.ReflectingGod.info/Glossary.)

A leader must always strive to communicate a steady vision. While statements of purpose and mission or summaries of dreams may morph in response to new circumstances, the vision must act as a guiding light to keep family members, business partners, and advisory team members united. The planning team leader should help refine statements of vision in a way that inspires clarity and consistency. The leader can help develop the type of vision that prompted Leonardo da Vinci's wise comment that, "He who is fixed to a star does not change his mind."

The story of Nehemiah shows us that vision begins as a concern that God puts on our hearts. God gave Nehemiah a concern for the broken walls in Jerusalem and a picture of what could be and should be—to rebuild the broken walls. To gain support and commitment around the vision, Nehemiah communicated the vision as a solution to a massive problem so that people's minds and hearts were aroused enough to respond to the call. See how Nehemiah's prayer at the start of the chapter begins with affirming God's revelation and vision and then communicates the remaining four elements of the covenant, as outlined below.

ELEMENT 3: Higher Spiritual Authority

Throughout Scripture, God has put in place prophets, priests, and kings to do His will and make Him known. In Old Testament times, God revealed His Scriptures to man and allowed men to draw close to Him through the guidance of the leaders who united in holy councils (e.g., Psalm 89:5-7). Under the New Covenant, any believer can have a personal relationship with God through Christ, the mediator.

Christ equips mature leaders to reflect His character. Such leaders are trained to hear God as He speaks through prophets (Scripture) and wise (Spirit-led) counselors[2]. These leaders, like Moses and the capable men in Psalm 89 and Exodus 18, are often called to adjudicate conflicts. Successful companies and family businesses will usually have mature leaders who know how to identify problems and apply God-honoring principles to resolve them.

While a leader put in place by God may have much authority to "lord it over" people who depend on him or her, servant leadership is the only leadership model that works. The Christian leader starts by identifying the people to serve and the process for serving them effectively. The servant leader supports people on her team by praying for their needs and reflecting divine truths into their lives. In this way, the servant leader is much like the godly prophets, priests, and kings seen throughout Scripture.

As part of element 3 in the planning process, mature leaders can assemble teams focused on realizing both lofty dreams and foundational details. As the planning team leader works to articulate all elements of the plan, he or she will see how the group's purposes, missions, and dreams (discussed as part of element 2) may evolve in response to changing strengths and weaknesses of team members, to new opportunities, or even to threats in the external environment (discussed as part of element 1).

ELEMENT 4: Ethics

Successful companies have shared values. Values can be both unchanging principles, like the Ten Commandments, and priorities that honor God. Because both principles and priorities can be ranked to indicate which should most influence decisions, a values statement provides clarity about which decision-making criteria have the most value.

Leaders use values statements when making decisions. For example, profits may be a major priority but only if there is no violation of a divinely given principle, such as what the fourth commandment teaches about taking the seventh day of the week off to worship God.

Businesses often talk about following value statements, but very often revenues, profits, and bank account balances become the focus of the business enterprise to the exclusion of values that foster strong relationships. Why is developing ranked and quantified goals so hard to do and so seldom done?

Businesses need regular (weekly, monthly, or quarterly) meetings to communicate consistent *principles*, clarify changing *priorities*, and unite leaders around shared objectives. This commitment to consistent meetings is a logical extension of Hebrews 10 teachings about not neglecting to gather together in Christ-centered fellowship.

ELEMENT 5: Outcomes: Benefits of Planning

Faithfulness to these covenants yields rewards. See, for example, Deuteronomy 8:18. Moses writes, "But remember the Lord your God, for it is he who gives you the ability to produce wealth, and so confirms his covenant, which he swore to your ancestors, as it is today." Solomon writes, "Commit to the Lord whatever you do and your plans will succeed" (Prov. 16:3) New Testament authors teach that "you reap what you sow" (Gal. 6:7) and that "God is the rewarder of those who seek Him" (Heb. 11:6).

The measure of success from God's perspective centers on relationships that benefit everyone in a business directly and indirectly. This can translate into a quadruple bottom-line that measures benefits for customers, employees, owners, and the community. The community encompasses vendors, competitors, and the broader spheres in which business takes place.

Success derives from excellence in providing an exceptional customer experience, creating products and services, managing sales and marketing, and cultivating leaders who build strong people in a healthy culture. God-driven companies operate differently and better because they are based on His business model, which yields His results.

ELEMENT 6: Succession Plans

Leaders can leverage the success of the enterprise around the world and across the generations. This can happen as a result of consciously and intentionally laying a firm foundation by implementing the first five elements of covenantal planning: clarifying the revelation/resources, pursuing the transcendent vision/ mission, heeding higher spiritual authority, affirming ethical precepts, and witnessing the fruits/outcomes of following and honoring God. Faithfulness to the covenant can lead to bountiful outcomes that are leveraged through element 6: Succession plan.

Succession plans identify godly criteria for selecting, equipping, training, empowering, and rewarding successor owners and managers. This involves establishing a clear pathway into the future that will guide and inspire members of the team as they leverage resources and replicate successes.

Conclusion

Believers know the radiance of God's glory through a relationship with Christ. This relationship is deepened through the means of grace. Mature believers learn to radiate God's light and reflect this light into relationships. Teams guided by God's light can define plans to develop resources, follow a clear mission, respect leadership, honor biblical precepts, experience God's blessings, and extend divine influence.

A written plan with the six elements that reflect God's character enables leaders to stay focused on reflecting all six dimensions of God's character. Faithful connection to God's character results in personal and corporate rewards as well as protection against the seven deadly sins, which are so prevalent in business.

Covenantal planning is a blueprint for success God's way. Encouraging knowledge of God helps each member of a team see how and why he or she can pursue what pleases God. As a godly agenda is established, wise, strategic planners can articulate this plan using the language of business, referring to concepts such as goals, strategy, culture, tactics, and objectives.

As explained throughout this book, faithfulness to God fuels alignment, productivity, and performance. God's business model motivates people from the inside out, bringing true engagement and commitment. Growing inner commitment manifests with consistent improvement in outer results. When creating a culture guided by God's light, leaders make shareholders, customers, employees, and members of the community excited every day about making a contribution to honoring God. Businesses committed to God's light can experience the "quadruple bottom line" discussed in section 5 of this book while providing a clear and joyful alternative to the dark business culture described previously. [3]

At www.ReflectingGod.info/Survey, please indicate your level of agreement with the following five statements:

My leadership team seeks to use God's Word to shine light into darkness.

not true	1	2	3	4	5	*very true*
	○	○	○	○	○	

My advisers help me apply God's law to confront pride, greed and other deadly sins.

not true	1	2	3	4	5	*very true*
	○	○	○	○	○	

My managers learn how people in covenant community identify resources, pursue a mission, respect authority, uphold ethical precepts, encourage blessings, and extend the Kingdom.

not true	1	2	3	4	5	*very true*
	○	○	○	○	○	

My company encourages managers to develop servant leadership skills, following Biblical patterns, in family, church, and/or government roles.

not true	1	2	3	4	5	*very true*
	○	○	○	○	○	

My key advisers seek wisdom through God's Word and prayer in church communities that administer sacraments to maintain peace and purity.

not true	1	2	3	4	5	*very true*
	○	○	○	○	○	

1 The SWOT Analysis is taught in most business programs. It involves analyzing the internal strengths and weaknesses of an enterprise as well as external opportunities and threats. For a more complete summary of how the SWOT Analysis guides business leaders, see www.WOTSMOST.com.

2 We can hear God when we know God. We know God through doctrines and means of grace. Means of grace involve preaching of the Word, prayer, and proper administration of the biblical sacraments to maintain the purity and peace of the church body. Proper administration of the sacraments establishes a foundation for peace (by suspending communion rights when a member, as determined by Spirit-led elders, is rebellious) and a method for growing a church in a peaceful matter (by baptizing people into a covenant community church with members committed to maintaining peace and purity).

3 See Appendix 3 for more details about how Scripture affirms the need for a clear, written plan.

Chapter 2

Seeing Abundant Resources and Developing a Vision for Stewarding Them

BILL GOT FIRED from his job. He had a load of debt and many financial concerns but, more importantly, he had six types of resources that are more valuable than money. He asked his closest friends to meet with him about a plan to develop his 1) *calling and passions*, the most important of his resources. These friends were part of Bill's inner circle because they had a desire to seek 2) *deep spiritual insights*. Prayer support from these friends helped Bill to identify and develop his 3) *intellectual property*, 4) *physical talents*, and 5) *social network*. This helped Bill to communicate in the marketplace the value of his 6) *professional skills* as he built his new business.

Orders began to come in. Bill did not use debt, but he carefully invested earnings back into his company. By developing non-financial resources, Bill watched his business grow over 30 years to the point where it generates more than $20 million of annual revenue. By developing six types of non-financial resources, Bill acquired much of the 7th resource: financial capital. In this way, Bill showed how non-financial resources, contrary to popular opinion, can be much more valuable than financial resources.

All the business owners featured in this book started with few or no financial resources. Marian Noronha had nothing when he came from India to found Turbocam. Don Flow pursued his calling first as a student at Francis Schaeffer's L'Abri Fellowship before going to work at the bottom level in the car industry. Nick Goldmann began his company with little more than a truck and a commitment to prayer. In the early days, he often slept in his truck as he worked at job sites. Despite their lack of financial resources, each man had six other God-given resources that are more valuable than money:

1. **Passion from God and a sense of calling**: The men maintained close friendships and working relationships with associates who shared a commitment to knowing God's Word.

2. **Insights found in the Christian faith**: The light that shines out of darkness has shined into believers' hearts (2 Cor. 4:6). Believers then have "new eyes" to see from God's point of view (2 Cor. 5:16).

3. **Intellectual property:** With prayerful support, these young business owners opened their eyes to new trends, new opportunities, and new ways to build unique niches and create value in the marketplace.

4. **Physical strength**: They were blessed with good health, and they were good stewards of this blessing from God by taking care of their bodies and minds.

5. **Social networks**: The men engaged in community activities that progressively expanded their social networks.

6. **Professional skills**: Along the way, the men gained marketable skills while helping staff members acquire professional credentials as well.

The pattern above is seen in the life story of Marian Noronha. While at a Catholic boarding school in the 1960s, Marian developed a desire to have "ears that hear and eyes that see" (Prov. 20:12). This early faith matured into a deep knowledge of *revelation from God.*

Marian's purpose in the 1960s was to steward his savings well and build enough wealth to go to America. The purpose later matured into a corporate mission statement in 1993 and a family mission statement in 2004. In this way, revelation has been distilled into a guiding *purpose and mission.*

By 1975, Marian faced challenges that led him to the lowest point of his faith. This prompted him to find a church and listen to inspirational preaching on Christian radio. Marian found encouragement in the messages of Terry Virgo, Tim Keller, and John Piper. These pastors articulated the biblical message of God's relationship with man. Marian sought wisdom from godly leaders and developed a vision for providing spiritual mentoring through mature Christian leaders.

Marian's Christian leaders provided a variety of ethical teachings about stewardship, budgeting, debt, and employee-employer relationships. Marian sought the wisdom described in Ecclesiastes 3:12, the joy of work lauded in Ecclesiastes 3:22, the respect for God-given possessions seen in Ecclesiastes 5:18-20, and the balance of labor and the enjoyment of labor's fruits encouraged in Ecclesiastes 6:1-2. These and many related passages helped Marian and his associates to appreciate divine *ethics.*

Commitment to biblical precepts led to spiritual blessings. Marian was motivated by the vision of nations walking in God's light and the kings of the earth experiencing divine splendor (Rev. 21:24). Marian found inspiration in Isaiah 61 and Revelation 21 about bringing people into the Kingdom. Without setting growth goals, Marian confidently followed God's teachings in ways that led to greater abundance. His staff, customers, and community benefit while he produces benefits for himself as well. A "quadruple bottom line" was evidence of God's *blessings*.

Ultimately, Marian has been able to launch six new companies and transfer stock to successor owners. This leverages wealth across the generations from new owners who affirm the Christian values and embrace the corporate mission statement. This process affirms a God-honoring plan of succession.

By developing six non-financial resources, business owners featured in this book have created a foundation for teamwork and great productivity. The teamwork was based on shared purpose and servant leadership rather than on self-interested alliances. Through prayer, meditation, and listening to the Holy Spirit, team members were guided, inspired, and strengthened to hold to their ideals in the midst of adversity. Ultimately, although wealth accumulation was not a primary goal, these men became wealthy.

Let's explore what the Bible teaches about the six elements of God's covenantal character mentioned above.

1: Experiencing Abundance

Scripture reveals how God provides abundantly for His people (see John 10:10; 2 Cor. 9:8; Eph. 3:20; 2 Pet. 1:11). Teachings about abundance taught throughout the Bible are frequently misunderstood. Too often, preachers appeal to greed and materialism while implying that wealth is the God-given right of every person who supports the teacher's ministry. Such "health and wealth" teaching contravenes the clear instruction of Scripture. Consider how ancient believers were commended for their faith (Heb. 11:39) but went about in sheepskins and goatskins destitute, persecuted, and mistreated. They wandered in deserts and mountains, living in caves and in holes in the ground (Heb. 11:37-38).

Even when lacking in material wealth, the saints across the centuries have held firmly to their faith and trusted in the hope of Scripture. They had a vision of unity based on the righteous standards taught by the prophets. Solomon writes, "Where there is no vision, the people cast off restraint but blessed is he who keeps the law" (Prov. 29:18). The saints have trusted that respecting the law helps believers operate with one mind and one spirit while experiencing joyful relationships. Paul writes, "Then make my joy complete by being like-minded, having the same love, being one in spirit and of one mind" (Phil. 2:2).

Scripture encourages believers to find wealth in their rich relationships with the Lord and with fellow Christians. Knowledge of God's character can result in peace and other fruits of the Spirit to carry the poor and oppressed through the most trying situations. When the Christian knows the Lord, he can enjoy blessings "exceeding abundantly beyond all that we ask or imagine" (Eph. 3:20). The key is to have a deep understanding of God's character that 1) provides for all needs without undue reliance on material wealth and 2) encourages teamwork that results in productivity and the fruits of labor. In this chapter, we will use Scripture references and real-life examples to make these points clear.

2: Building a Productive Team with a Clear Mission

Genesis 45:16-28 illustrates God's abundant provision when His people are united around a clear mission. Jacob needed to help his family survive a famine, so he reluctantly sent his sons to Egypt to buy grain. Jacob waited far longer than expected for their return. When they ultimately came back, their carts were full of provisions. Jacob learned that his son Joseph was ruler over all the land of Egypt. This early story in Genesis shows how God provides exceeding abundantly beyond all that we can ask for or imagine when we trust him.

Jacob did not have a "divine right" to prosperity, but he had a mature mission to steward wealth for his family. Jacob exhibited the character qualities that Apostle Paul commended when teaching about wealth in 1 Timothy 6:17-19. Jacob was not conceited, nor did he fix his hopes on the uncertainty of riches. Instead, he was generous and ready to share.

God always uses circumstances to help us focus on the ultimate goal of developing spiritual maturity. There are always spiritual purposes behind any material blessings that God supplies or withholds. In the case of Jacob, God was carrying out prophesies dating from the time of Abraham to protect His people from the corrupting influences of the Canaanites. God used the famine and the move to Egypt to work out a divine plan.

Before the spiritual and economic blessings arrived, Jacob had doubts. The day before Jacob's sons returned from Egypt with abundant provisions and renewed faith, Jacob had been lonely, grieving, and fearing that those who remained behind might starve. He was at a point of despair when his sons returned with their good news. Then, Joseph was "revived" in Genesis 45:27 when his sons came back with their message of hope. Right after this, Jacob complained, "All these things are against me" (Gen. 42:36). Nevertheless, God was working all these things together for good for him.

3: Respecting Divine Leadership Teachings

Why did Pharaoh provide so abundantly for Jacob and his 11 sons? Pharaoh may have seen character qualities in them because of their knowledge of divine character. Clearly, Pharaoh was impressed enough with one of Jacob's sons, Joseph, to make him prime minister over all of Egypt. Although in rebellion against God, Pharaoh was used by God.

The Bible says, "The eyes of the Lord range throughout the earth to strengthen those whose hearts are fully committed to him" (2 Chron. 16:9). This strengthening can happen through somebody who does not follow God, but there is always a divinely-guided leadership process orchestrated by the sovereign Lord of the universe.

Throughout the Bible, God used prophets, priests, and kings to provide leadership. In the New Testament, God uses apostles, prophets, evangelists, pastors, and teachers to equip his people for works of service "so that the body of Christ may be built up until all reach unity in the faith and in the knowledge of Christ" (Eph. 4:11-13).

In the modern business world, business professionals typically do not turn to prophets, priests, kings, apostles, evangelists, or pastors for wisdom. Yet, spiritual insights of wise leaders may be the greatest resources available to a Christian business person. How can the business person know that divine wisdom is available through consultants, coaches, counselors, and others who would presume to provide godly counsel? This question is answered by looking at how the business owners featured in this book found wisdom. Chapter Six summarizes how successful business owners choose wise advisers.

4: Following Divine Principles

The link between following biblical principles and producing wealth is not automatic. The story of Jacob reflects what many successful business owners encounter. Most people who have led a successful business can remember times when there were doubts about covering payroll, making mortgage payments, or responding to competitive challenges. Many successful business owners have deep faith because they learned to rely on God and see how blessings came in accordance with His perfect timing.

In Chapter Seven of this book, we explain how divine principles foster teamwork and productivity. This productivity often leads to wealth. As the value of an enterprise grows, there are often financial dividends to supplement the rich relationships enjoyed by shareholders, staff, customers, and the community. These blessing are explained more in the "quadruple bottom line" discussed in Chapters 11-14.

5: Realizing Blessings

God often provides in totally unexpected ways, such as when new technologies create new markets. Jacob's sons returned from Egypt with new clothes and carts that were totally unexpected fruits of a mission to obtain grain. Jacob saw how our loving Father delights to bestow unexpected gifts on His children. Readers of Genesis see how these sons worked together through times of blessings and adversity, illustrating a healthy dependence upon one another.

6: Investing Blessings to Extend Influence

The knowledge of divine character was instilled in the early Jewish people like Abraham, Jacob, and Joseph. They had knowledge of Adam and God's covenant with him. While Moses had not yet come down from Mount Sinai to show how the Ten Commandments reflected divine character, Jacob clearly communicated elements of the divine covenant. For example, in Genesis 49, Jacob transmits a message to the next generation that includes elements of the Abrahamic covenant and earlier Adamic and Noahic covenants.

In the above six sections, we see how Jacob...

1. Affirms the family blessing of many sons in verse 1,
2. Gives a transcendent decree or purpose in verse 2,
3. Affirms a spiritual authority process in verse 10,
4. Declares principles of justice in verse 16,
5. Outlines provisions in verses 20, 26, 29, etc., and
6. Establishes the family's multigenerational ownership of the field bought from Ephron in verses 30-33.

These six elements of the covenant in Genesis 49 reflect the six elements described in greater detail in the Preface and Introduction of this book. These six elements form the foundations of multi-generational plans that can help any family business build wealth across the generations, as explained at www.ReflectingGod.info/EthicalWills.

The elements of biblical covenants are clearly tied to wealth accumulation throughout Scripture. For example, Deuteronomy 8:18 reads,

> But remember the Lord your God, for it is he who gives you the ability to produce wealth, and so confirms his covenant, which he swore to your ancestors, as it is today.

As this book shows, we remember our God by reflecting His character, and this character is reflected through six elements of covenant. When a Christian leader builds a team around the six elements, great productivity can result. Productivity produces value, which can be exchanged for money. This results in wealth and other benefits for staff, customers, shareholders, and the community.

Conclusion

Every individual is blessed with abundant non-financial resources. We can all turn to Scripture and wise counselors as we develop a more mature understanding of our 1) passions and calling, 2) spiritual insights, 3) intellectual capital, 4) physical talents, 5) professional skills, and 6) social networks. These non-financial sources of wealth can equip us to lead productive teams.

As opportunities arise to lead teams, we can learn from the covenantal principles that helped Jacob and his sons prosper. We must 1) discern available resources, including the six non-financial resources listed above, 2) crystalize a clear statement of purpose, mission, and values, 3) establish a spiritually-mature leadership structure that reflects God's character while helping people in an organization be heard, 4) follow clear ethical precepts/divine principles, 5) be open to blessings and acknowledge how they come from God, and 6) use blessings to extend divine influence around the community and across the generations.

At www.ReflectingGod.info/Survey, please indicate your level of agreement with the following five statements:

I choose prayer partners who are spiritually-mature and wise advisers.

not true	1	2	3	4	5	*very true*
	O	O	O	O	O	

My prayer partners help me see and leverage my God-given non-financial resources, starting with God's calling on my life and work.

not true	1	2	3	4	5	*very true*
	O	O	O	O	O	

My prayer partners guide me in developing a personal SWOT and Spirit-led plan.

not true	1	2	3	4	5	*very true*
	O	O	O	O	O	

My plans are tested against Scripture to confirm that they are in line with God's plans for developing resources.

not true	1	2	3	4	5	*very true*
	O	O	O	O	O	

I am committed to being a servant leader who enhances the well-being of all key stakeholders.

not true	1	2	3	4	5	*very true*
	O	O	O	O	O	

Section 2

Transcendent Vision and Values

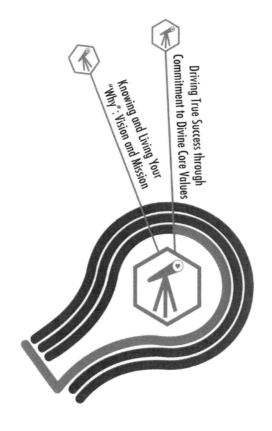

Knowing and Living Your "Why": Vision and Mission

Driving True Success through Commitment to Divine Core Values

VISION IS DEVELOPED as part of God's revelation. Divine revelation helps Christians understand the immutable character of God as well as His unchanging law.[1] Because vision is closely linked to God's unchanging revelation, it must remain constant. A steady vision helps leaders identify exactly where they want to go and what results they want. A vision provides leaders of an organization with a mental picture of the future they aspire to attain. What differentiates a Christ-driven business from a secular business is that Christian leaders prayerfully turn to God when defining the vision. They live the vision through God-honoring core values demonstrated by their decisions and behaviors. Moreover, the managers of a Christian business develop their personal purpose statements with a mature understanding of their personal vision and values. These personal and corporate statements of vision and values are aligned to guide leaders of an enterprise as they refine a statement of mission and execute objectives based on the mission. Chapters in section 2 show how a vision based on the covenantal character of God is most likely to inspire successful pursuit of personal purpose statements and corporate mission statements.

---

[1] See, e.g., Proverbs 29:18.

Chapter 3

Knowing and Living Your "Why": Vision and Mission

> *Where there is no vision, the people are unrestrained, but*
> *happy is he who keeps the law.*

— PROVERBS 29:18, NASB

A FRAIL, ELDERLY LADY encounters a car salesperson seeking guidance and honesty in selecting the right vehicle at a fair price. The salesperson sees an easy target and selects a car, not necessarily the most appropriate car, showing a higher ticket price than she requested. The lady attempts to bargain but is overcome by the forcefulness of the salesman, and she gives in. Later the same day, a shrewd, wealthy businessman encounters the same salesperson. He assertively describes what kind of car he wants and at what price, having done competitive price shopping in advance of his visit. The salesman shows him the sticker price, and the businessman insists on negotiating the price, or he will leave. The salesman relents on the price to make the sale, hoping for a repeat customer.

What was the mission and vision of this car dealership? Did it emphasize profit over customer well-being? Was the mission not adequately communicated and embraced by the employee? Were compensation and other policies not aligned with the mission to encourage respect for the mission?

The highly respected business author Peter Drucker defines a mission as "why you do what you do; the organization's reason for being, its purpose … what, in the end, you want to be remembered for. Every mission reflects opportunities, competence, and commitment." The mission may evolve as an organization faces new opportunities or threats or as leaders reassess their strengths and weaknesses.

The evolving mission must be defined in full view of a steady vision. Vision is developed as part of God's revelation. Divine revelation reveals the immutable character of God as well as His unchanging law (see, e.g., Proverbs 29:18). Because vision is closely linked to God's unchanging revelation, authors of strategic planning books frequently write that vision must remain constant. A steady vision helps leaders identify exactly where they want to go and what results they want. A vision provides a mental picture of the future that leaders of an organization aspire to attain.

Discerning a Vision Should Begin with Studying God's Revelation for His People

What differentiates a Christ-driven business from a secular business is that the leaders prayerfully turn to God when defining the Mission and Vision. Each leader is a steward fulfilling his or her unique purpose in a way that helps the organization realize its mission without compromising vision. The case studies presented in this chapter reveal the process by which that happens.

Leaders with a clear God-given purpose can unite around a mission that empowers all of them to focus their energy and achieve sustained high performance. Developing a clear vision and mission begins with at least one leader spending enough time clarifying his/her own purpose so that the leader can envision how others with complementary purposes might unite to pursue a compelling mission.

A leader focused on prayer can then inspire a team to unite in prayer. Nick Goldmann had a clear purpose to launch his company after praying to God for direction. At the start, Nick had nobody supporting his purpose, but he prayerfully joined with brothers in Christ with similar purposes. At the Serra Retreat Center, the men embraced a shared mission and vision to provide a Christian witness in the telecommunications industry. Chapters 7 and 9 explain how prayerfully following this revelation has led to great prosperity.

SERRA RETREAT 1998

Following God's Roadmap for Discovering a Vision and Mission

Proverbs 29:18 and Deuteronomy 5:33 reveal that without a vision and without following God's law, people go in all directions and their efforts are scattered and energy is dissipated and wasted. Alternatively, when people are aligned around a vision which reflects God's character and Word, they can prosper.

Throughout Scripture there is a clear link between respecting the Lord's commands and enjoying His blessings. We see repeatedly how revelation (element 1) is crystalized into a mission (element 2) that guides leaders (element 3) as they establish principles (element 4) that unite teams in a way that leads to blessings (element 5) and greater impact across time and/or around the world (element 6).

When we love the Lord, we obey His commands (see, e.g., John 14:15, 21). A divinely-inspired vision reflects divine laws that impede self-interest and other behaviors that undermine teamwork. There is a very close relationship between the vision uniting a team and the principles guiding team members. This is evident from the passage at the start of this chapter. "Where there is no vision, the people are unrestrained, but happy is he who keeps the law" (Prov. 29:18).

Discerning a vision should begin with studying God's revelation for His people. Each book of the Bible helps define man's covenantal relationship with God as well as man's relationship with three main covenantal institutions: the church, family, and government. Biblical principles for maintaining personal and corporate relationships apply to the operation of a business. A business leader can read Scripture and identify many commands that should guide his relationship with key stakeholders and encourage obedience to them among the individuals within an organization. A wise leader encourages obedience to these commands while helping team members enjoy the prosperity that results from leveraging strengths, capitalizing on opportunities, minimizing weaknesses, and guarding against threats that can undermine teamwork. Moses summarizes this link between obedience and prosperity: "Walk in obedience to all that the Lord your God has commanded you, so that you may live and prosper and prolong your days in the land that you will possess" (Deut. 5:33).

John 5:30 and Isaiah 55:8-9 focus on the importance of waiting on the Lord to discover His Grand Vision. Leaders with vision sometimes refer to their Big Holy Audacious Goal (BHAG). The process of discerning a divine vision requires listening, writing, and clearly communicating what the Spirit reveals. Each business leader has unique resources available for serving unique target markets. Applying God's teamwork principles to developing the resources requires careful attention to discerning relevant principles that can be communicated effectively to others. When the principles clearly come from God and clearly apply to the matters affecting the key stakeholders, a leader can generate great support. When godly leaders help one another guard against sin and follow a Spirit-led plan, the vision can be communicated persuasively so it genuinely moves and inspires people rather than having to be sold.

When leaders are guided by pride, greed, envy or other self-interested behaviors, the process of prayerful vision casting is thwarted. Why? All sins involve violations of God's commands. God does not regard the prayers of law breakers[1].

God gives us His light to illuminate a pathway toward a clear vision. We can understand God's road map when we turn to the light of Scripture and ask God to reveal idols that keep us from hearing His voice or seeing the reflection of divine character. God actively tries to share His light, but business leaders must struggle to see it in a business world that encourages too many dark behaviors. For, "people loved darkness instead of light because their deeds were evil" (John 3:19).

When leaders are guided by love for God and love for others, the vision becomes clear.

> "For My thoughts are not your thoughts,
> Nor are your ways My ways," says the Lord.
> "For as the heavens are higher than the earth,
> So are My ways higher than your ways,
> And My thoughts than your thoughts."
> (Isa. 55:8-9)

> By myself I can do nothing; I judge only as I hear, and my judgment is just, for I seek not to please myself but him who sent me. (John 5:30)

> Write down the revelation and make it plain on tablets so that a herald may run with it. For the revelation awaits an appointed time; it speaks of the end and will not prove false. Though it linger, wait for it; it will certainly come and will not delay. (Hab. 2:2-3)

Mark 12:31 is about loving thy neighbor. Christ's teachings about loving others relate to people having a mission and vision focused primarily on the well-being of customers, employees and other key stakeholders. This principle comes alive in seeing people as made in God's image (Gen. 1:26). This image has elements of covenantal relationships where people form bonds characterized by love rather than self-interested transactions.

> The second is this: "Love your neighbor as yourself."
> There is no commandment greater than these.
> (Mark 12:31)

Respect people as made in God's image (see Gen. 1:26).

In the following two case studies, a consistent theme is that the leaders who are Christ-centered pray and listen for the guidance of the Holy Spirit. In keeping with 1 John 4:1 and related passages, mature leaders test the spirits while seeking wisdom from Scripture and the counsel of prayerful people on advisory councils. Senior leaders invite input from mature Christian prayer partners who know God and know the marketplace. For example, leaders may meet regularly with a corporate chaplain or a Christian consultant who helps develop a plan and then commits to pray for realization of objectives in the plan. Prayer partners encourage accountability to the Mission and Vision as they help fellow leaders make the right commitments and then honor them. Leaders help create a culture of integrity when employees see that commitments are reinforced and sustained by behaviors, policies and processes aligned with the vision and mission. The result is greater benefits for shareholders, employees, customers, and the community—a quadruple bottom-line.

Flow Auto Case Example: Honoring God's Word and Character in Your Mission

Don Flow is President of Flow Automotive which employs 1500 employees in 39 franchises in 8 cities in Virginia and North Carolina. Don embraces the redemptive power of business in light of the teaching of scripture. His business philosophy is linked to his relationship with God ... God has graced him with abundance through every aspect of his life, and he in turn models this relationship with his customers, employees, and the community. Don explains, "It's about those three things [customers, employees, community]. We have to have a profit to do those three things, but profit is not the goal." His God-given vision and mission support the theological understanding that each person has inherent dignity and deserves to be treated with respect.

Flow Automotive Vision and Mission

Vision: An organization dedicated to creating life-long enthusiastic customers by delivering superior value and providing extraordinary personal service

Mission: To serve the total automotive needs of our customers

This vision and mission characterize Flow Companies *as a service company rather than a sales company* —employees serve customers while they sell and fix cars. For Don Flow, the mission and vision reflect an eternal purpose. Don prays on a daily basis that the way the company relates to customers and fellow employees will be a signpost to the Kingdom of God.

The mission and vision come alive operationally through core values, operating principles, and service standards. These values and principles are based on the golden rule. Employees are taught not to advantage themselves to the disadvantage of the customers and to treat customers like guests in their home. Don's core company values are also his professed personal values.

- Earning Trust: Always doing what is right for the customer. Doing what we say we will do, going the extra mile and caring for the customer as a "valued friend."
- Pursuing Excellence: Creating a high-performance organization. Affirming the dignity and contribution of each employee, challenging workers to excel, giving second chances, and collaborating in an "environment of truth, trust, and accountability."
- Providing More. Delivering superior value every day. Providing quality, service and affordable prices, continuous improvement of efficiency and productivity, and systematic innovation.

Don knows that serving God means more than selling cars through an organization that maintains integrity. Serving God through the retail automotive business requires a way of leading and operating radically different from the norm. In so doing he has fundamentally altered the accepted industry practices that many perceive as unfair and deceptive.

Don builds and sustains trust with the customer through a series of policies and processes including a no-haggle, one-price, used-vehicle policy, 'fix it right the first time' service guarantees, and an extensive customer follow-up program. The one-price process was first implemented in the early 1990s in stores where Don and his team noticed that the customers most at risk in a negotiation environment were women and minorities. They were paying more, on average, than other customers.

Don created an environment in which customers could confidently send their mother for service without preparation or worry.

To ensure that employees wholeheartedly serve customers and provide service beyond the expected industry standards, the New Employee Orientation program is built around the mission, vision, and values. The successful implementation of Don's vision and mission involves culturally and spiritually diverse people owning these practices at a deep level and thereby living the spiritual truths which underlie the vision and mission.

Realizing God's Promises in the Quadruple Bottom-line at Flow Automotive Companies

1. Customer: Enormous customer loyalty and satisfaction. Winner of "Best Auto Dealer: Winston-Salem's Journal Reader's Choice Award." Serve on numerous manufacturer boards in recognition of outstanding performance.

2. Employees: Known as a great place to work; high employee engagement and satisfaction; low turnover; employees cared for through such programs as emergency fund, college tuition for children. Received Triad's Best Places to Work Business Journal Award.

3. Community: Huge commitment to the community. Individual employees serve with a wide variety of non-profit organizations and are paid to volunteer in the community. They have received numerous community recognition awards for outstanding leadership.

4. Owners: Highly profitable; create over $1 billion in revenue and maintain projections to double in size in the next 10 years. Able to manage costs and implement processes better than competitors.

Turbocam Case Example: Receiving and Living a God Inspired Vision and Mission

Marian Noronha, founder and Chairman of Turbocam International, illustrates how a God-inspired vision and mission are related to realizing a quadruple bottom line, through excellence and generosity. (The Turbocam Group is a global turbomachinery development and manufacturing company with headquarters in New Hampshire.) Marian first felt a strong call on his life evolving from his experience as a church planter. In working with the poorest people in the church, the Holy Spirit revealed to him the need for jobs and wealth creation as an expression of the Kingdom of God. In 1982, at 28 years of age, Marian met with a group of fellow church planters at a Burger King who talked about what is successful and unsuccessful in church-based businesses. This meeting sparked his mission and vision for Turbocam. His initial mission statement was "Turbocam exists as a business to create wealth for its employees and support Christians in their service to God and to people." At a later time, when he met with trusted Christian members of the Fellowship of Companies for Christ, they corrected Marian by declaring, "If you measure success by creating wealth for Christians, you can miss God's purpose." Convicted by their godly advice, Marian rewrote the Mission Statement to its current form: "To honor God, create wealth for its employees and support Christian service to God and people."

Quad Aim

Turbocam Mission

Now Turbocam exists as a business for the purpose of honoring God, creating wealth for its employees, and supporting Christian service to God and people. Turbocam seeks to accomplish this purpose by achieving excellence in the manufacturing of turbomachinery parts. Turbocam develops five-axis machining and related technologies to satisfy the needs of customers for Quality, Price, Delivery, and Service.

Leaders at Turbocam explain the mission as follows: As we interact with our customers, suppliers, and employees we hold ourselves accountable to God's law expressed in the Bible. We are committed to integrity in our business and personal relationships.

Marian's definition of success is expressed on Turbocam's website: We would like to be a company that gives generously to help those in need, locally, nationally, and internationally. We can measure our success by the amounts that we donate or the time that we give. This is an inadequate measure—God has given too much to us for us to make vain comparisons. We can only give if we know that our earnings are blessed by God.

Marian asserts, "I started this company as a means of making a living, while also spreading the Good News of salvation through Jesus Christ. There are many ways to achieve "success" in business. I have learned that in a business, God comes first. God has blessed our efforts and made us a growing company with dedicated employees, loyal customers and many suppliers who enjoy being associated with us."

Reflecting God's Kingdom Through the Quadruple Bottom-line

Turbocam is one of the biggest companies in New Hampshire and has a reputation with customers, employees and the community for doing the right thing and for quality and excellence.

Turbocam leaders have held to a clear vision for helping their constituencies in the following ways:

1. **Customers**: Cummins a global company of 50,000 employees is Turbocam's biggest customer and closely reflects Turbocam's relationship with all key customers. The head of Components Purchasing exclaims, "everyone who works closely with Marian understands his mission and his faith. Marian's mission is focused on creating wealth for his employees and the community. He further explains, "The alignment of ethics and values between Cummins and Turbocam is tight and no one comes close to providing the service which Turbocam does." As a result, the relationship is a long-term true partnership. Cummins knows through experience that everything Turbocam does is in the best interest of Cummins. For example, when Turbocam makes an improvement in their facility to reduce costs, they always share the cost reduction with Cummins.

2. **Low employee turnover**: Only 30 out of 500 leave in a year and some of these leave voluntarily. There has been only one layoff since 1998. Even during industry

downturns in 1998 and 2008, there were no layoffs. As a result, Turbocam is one of most sought-after companies to work for in the state of New Hampshire.

3. **Community**: Thirty to fifty percent of employees are engaged in ministry and an overwhelming majority give financial support. For example, Turbocam partnered with a leper community in India and helped them make valves to sell to auto manufacturers. One division of Turbocam donated money to build a school in Nepal, and another department raised money to support the education and feeding of kids in Haiti. An expression of the culture of generosity at Turbocam is reflected in thousands of dollars donated each year by employees in donation boxes in the cafeteria earmarked for 10 different charities locally and in Haiti, Nepal, and India.

4. **Owners:** Revenue growth in the last five years is 100%. Profit growth is good but kept at just 5% because profits are invested to strengthen R&D projects, employee benefits, and charitable giving.

Partaking in the Fullness of God's Rewards

God's revealed mission when implemented by a godly leader builds a sustainable and healthy organization. A business which is a signpost for the Kingdom sets different and superior business and industry standards based on excellence, integrity, love, truth, and covenantal relationships. The result is a quadruple bottom-line which is the result of all key stakeholders being aligned around a shared mission and vision, trusting each other, and working as a team, including customers, employees, vendors, owners and the community. As everyone pulls in the same direction, productivity increases, waste decreases, and there is a win-win because everyone is empowered, enriched, and partakes in the wealth created.

Conclusion

Any American involved in the marketplace can identify companies like the one in the story at the start of this chapter. Too often employees have double standards because commitments and behaviors are not evaluated vis-à-vis a clear mission and vision. This happens when there is lack of clarity about the divine revelation and resources discussed in chapter 1 or a lack of effort to discern a divinely-inspired vision and mission using the process described in this chapter.

Why do leaders fail to seek God's light to illuminate the road to a clear vision? Too often there is a lack of commitment to seeing how God's commands should guide motives and behaviors. When the law is preached, sin springs to life (Rom. 7:9) and darkness is revealed. This can be an uncomfortable process unless there are qualified and loving chaplains, consultants and other prayer partners who can help the leader find hope in the darkness while illuminating a vision and mission statement with God's light. When employees see an earnest effort to reflect divine character through the vision, they are more eager to align their thoughts, words and behaviors with a clear mission for benefiting shareholders, employees, customers, and the community.

At www.ReflectingGod.info/Survey, please indicate your level of agreement with the following five statements:

Quiz 3

My mission and vision are articulated in written statements and embedded in strategy, leadership practices and company culture.

not true   1   2   3   4   5   very true

◯   ◯   ◯   ◯   ◯

My leadership team agrees on ranked and time-bound goals based on our vision and mission.

not true   1   2   3   4   5   very true

◯   ◯   ◯   ◯   ◯

My leadership team and key stakeholders are aligned around a shared corporate vision and mission.

not true   1   2   3   4   5   very true

◯   ◯   ◯   ◯   ◯

My vision and mission are communicated persuasively so they move and inspire people.

not true   1   2   3   4   5   very true

◯   ◯   ◯   ◯   ◯

My mission and vision are a revelation from God and reveal His Character and Word.

not true   1   2   3   4   5   very true

◯   ◯   ◯   ◯   ◯

---

[1] Hearing God's voice through prayer requires that the people praying first align with God's righteous standards. This entails affirming God's law and repenting of law-breaking attitudes and behaviors. The following passages explain more.

> We know that God does not listen to sinners, but if anyone is a worshiper of God and does his will, God listens to him. (John 9:31 ESV)

> If one turns away his ear from hearing the law, even his prayer is an abomination. (Prov. 28:9 ESV)

> The Lord is far from the wicked, but he hears the prayer of the righteous. (Prov. 15:29 ESV)

> If I had cherished iniquity in my heart, the Lord would not have listened. (Ps. 66:18 ESV)

> For the eyes of the Lord are on the righteous, and his ears are open to their prayer. But the face of the Lord is against those who do evil. (1 Pet. 3:12 ESV)

> Therefore, confess your sins to one another and pray for one another, that you may be healed. The prayer of a righteous person has great power as it is working. (James 5:16 ESV)

Chapter 4

Driving True Success Through Commitment to Divine Core Values

DURING THE KOREAN CONFLICT in 1957, the U.S. Army Corps of Engineers awarded Correct Craft a multi-million-dollar government contract to build 3,000 boats to support the U.S. military's efforts. As Correct Craft started to fulfill the order, government inspectors insisted on a bribe before they would approve the boats. Although the Meloon family—the founders of Correct Craft—needed to close the sale to keep the company from going bankrupt, they refused to give a payoff because doing so would violate their core values and mission, which was "building boats to the glory of God." Consequently, the inspector began rejecting boats the company made. At the end of the year, Correct Craft had delivered over 2,000 boats of which over 600 were rejected. The order cost the company more than it had made, putting it in debt. [1]

Because the Meloons did not view bankruptcy as a release from their obligations, they started the slow process of rebuilding the company and paying back the debts they owed. It took 19 years, but because of their commitment to stand behind their word, they repaid each of their creditors in full.

As modeled by the leaders of Correct Craft, a righteous leader is one who "keeps an oath even when it hurts, and does not change their mind" (Ps. 15:4).

In 2013, Ralph Meloon, former CEO of Correct Craft, was inducted into the National Marine Manufacturers Association's (NMMA) Hall of Fame. This award recognized his outstanding contributions to the recreational boating industry in the consistent practice of quality and innovation. His character and integrity were heralded.[2]

When a leader who chooses God's way demonstrates integrity of character, he finds favor with God and man (Prov. 3:4).

Rooting Company Values in Biblical Values

We define *core values* as the principles, beliefs, tenets, and priorities upon which an organization is based. Core values remain constant, are the essence of an organization's identity, and guide decision-making and behavior. Core values are the pathways for translating the mission into practice.

For core values to be effective in a company whose leaders seek to honor God, they must be rooted in God's Word and consistently and courageously modeled and enforced by the leaders and employees.

When the leader embraces a greater purpose that is not self-serving and models biblical truths such as integrity, creativity, excellence, and loving one's neighbor, he is shining God's light into his leadership and organization. Shining light builds trust and credibility. In turn, trust and credibility create the foundation for building teamwork, employee engagement and retention, raving customers, and a high-performance organization.

Embedding the Values in Day-to-Day Practices

The pathway to fulfilling the mission of the organization is for the leaders, employees, and the culture of the organization to be aligned around shared values. Behaviors and decisions must be aligned with the values and supported and reinforced by the strategies, structures, systems, staff, style, and skills in the organization.[3]

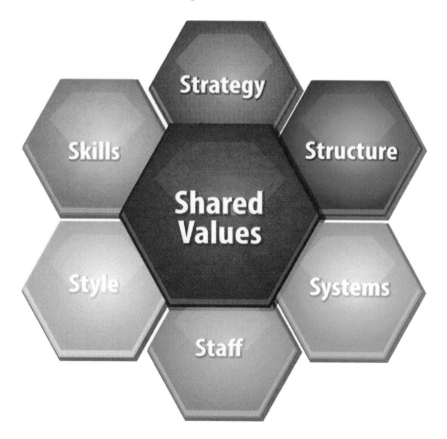

Correct Craft's values have been reflected through their over-the-top customer service. For example, a customer paid a dealer up front prior to delivery of a boat. Soon after Correct Craft had built the boat, the dealer went bankrupt before the customer received it. Nevertheless, Correct Craft delivered the boat even though they did not get paid. Relationships and doing what is right take precedence over expediency and profitability.

By doing what is right in the sight of God, Correct Craft has built a reputation of high performance and high trust. This reputation has given Correct Craft strong rapport with their customers as well as with companies they are pursuing as part of their strong acquisition strategy. Regarding a recent acquisition that occurred because of this high level of trust, current Correct Craft President and CEO Bill Yeargin said, "The owners wanted someone to buy their company whom they could trust to well manage their legacy and take care of their employees."[4]

The financial benefits of realizing their mission, "Building boats to the glory of God," are clearly evident today. Correct Craft is the third largest company in the marine industry, having earned approximately over $500 million in revenue in 2018.[5] The company is growing at an exponential rate in revenue and distributes into 70 countries. Between 2017 and 2018, Correct Craft increased its revenue and net income approximately by 25%.[6]

Don Flow of Flow Automotive explains, "It all starts with the value proposition: if we create value for customers, they will reward us financially. That starts with being a place of trust."

For example, Flow's core value of earning trust means treating each customer as a family member or valued friend. The value is reinforced and supported by "fixing it right the first time" service guarantees and an extensive customer follow-up program. The reward policy further reinforces this value because employee compensation is based on customer satisfaction scores as well as financial performance in the stores.

Likewise, Turbocam embeds their values and mission into day-to-day policies and practices. In living out their mission, Turbocam exists for the purposes of honoring God, creating wealth for its employees, and supporting Christian service to God and people. Honoring God is demonstrated through a variety of development opportunities used to build employee character and competence. All employees attend training to learn how to live out good character traits on the job and at home. Service to others is guided by the strategies, structures, systems, staff, style, and skills in the organization. Because character is a critical dimension of servant leadership, the employees measure success by the people they serve around them.

The rabbinical paradigm of discipleship is used to develop servant leaders. The organizational development director has established mentor learning communities of current and emerging leaders who meet regularly. They discuss real-time business transactions and relationships, asking the question, "How do I apply company values and biblical principles to this situation?"

True to their mission and values, Turbocam creates wealth for their employees and the communities in which they do business. They help local people to be self-supporting by enabling them to build businesses and by providing education and food for people in need. Their commitment to helping their employees create wealth was dramatically demonstrated in 1999 when no jobs were cut despite a 25% downturn in sales and in 2009 when sales dropped by 5%.

Building Win-Win, Covenantal Relationships

Then Jonathan made a covenant with David because he loved him as himself.

—1 SAMUEL 18:3

Values are sustained by win-win relationships (covenantal relationships) that are based on loving one's neighbor, working in the best interests of everyone involved, and keeping promises. They are also sustained by holding people accountable for living the values daily.

Win-win relationships, based on God's truth and grace, sharply contrast with transactional relationships that are based on quid pro quo, the prevailing norm in the business world. *Quid pro quo* means "an exchange of goods or services, where one transfer is contingent upon the other." A quid pro quo mentality frequently leads to broken relationships because it is self-serving.[7]

Win-win relationships is the fuel that fires Turbocam, Flow Auto, and Correct Craft. Their modus operandi with customers and suppliers is to develop long-term relationships and true partnerships with companies whose values are aligned with theirs. A long-term Fortune 500 Turbocam customer explains,

> We have a partnership in the truest sense of the word. People in our company think that talking to people at Turbocam is an extension of our business because we know that whatever Turbocam does is in our best interests. This is driven by Turbocam's CEO and founder, Marian, whose purpose is to ensure he is serving God and always doing right by his customers so they can continue growing.

Commitment to developing a true partnership is particularly evident when Turbocam develops a certain product the customer needs without an agreement. The level of trust is such that Marian knows the customer will support and protect them. Conversely, the customer knows Turbocam will support them no matter what the problem is, even if it is outside their product offerings.

Flow Automotive Companies builds win-win relationships with a foundation of grace and truth. For the past 50 years, Flow has defined itself by three principles:

1. A covenant with our customers to be a place that keeps its promises and is worthy of their trust. For example, "the fix it right the first time" service guarantee ensures promises are kept.

2. A community of people who work together toward a common vision.

3. A commitment to work toward the common good of every city where Flow does business. For example, the dealerships participate in community projects and give employees paid time off to volunteer in their communities. [8]

Confronting Spiritual Darkness

Leaders at Turbocam, Flow, Correct Craft, and other businesses with Christ-centered leadership routinely encounter spiritual darkness when trying to shine light through their companies. The inspector undermining Correct Craft seemed to have no qualms about violating anti-bribery teachings from Scripture. Why? The Bible tells us, "Light has come into the world, but people prefer darkness, for their deeds are evil" (John 3:19).

Because of dark behaviors, companies often struggle with engaging, motivating, and retaining their employees, suppliers, and customers. Darkness may fill an organization when one or more leaders rationalize a selfish emphasis on their personal compensation, power, or other idols. Too often, people within an organization complain about darkness but then reluctantly accept it as the norm.

To align faith and leadership, the leader must recognize evil and confront it. Darkness will grow worse unless the leader knows how to unite team members against the darkness in himself and in the team.

Unlike most companies with secular leaders, the companies with Christ-centered leaders attract, inspire, and retain their key stakeholders because they reflect God's light. The result is that they, and everyone with whom they interact, can enjoy prosperity (Josh. 1:8). The role of Christian business leaders is to develop effective ways to help their companies shine light into corporate darkness so that they can be faithful stewards.

Conclusion

What makes companies different and better is their respect for leaders who maintain unwavering commitment to God and His teachings. At Correct Craft and many other companies studied, leaders ask to be held accountable to moral absolutes and core principles (Prov. 28:20-21). With prayerful support, leadership team members are able to reflect Christ's divine character and the radiance of God's glory (Heb. 1:3).

If you are a business leader who wants to root your values in God's timeless spiritual truths, then make all decisions consistent with your core principles, cultivate win-win relationships, and embed Christ-centered core values in your company's policies, practices, and processes.

Hold yourself, your leadership team, and everyone else in your organization accountable for living them day to day. Only then can you overcome the darkness with God's light.

At www.ReflectingGod.info/Survey, please indicate your level of agreement with the following five statements:

My company's statement of core values is based on proven principles of the founders and timeless spiritual truths.

not true   1   2   3   4   5   *very true*
○   ○   ○   ○   ○

My leadership team makes decisions and behaves consistently with our core values.

not true   1   2   3   4   5   *very true*
○   ○   ○   ○   ○

My leadership team aligns our corporate culture with our core values.

not true   1   2   3   4   5   *very true*
○   ○   ○   ○   ○

My leadership team fosters trust by demonstrating character and competence.

not true   1   2   3   4   5   *very true*
○   ○   ○   ○   ○

My leadership team members hold one another accountable and enforce accountability throughout the whole organization.

not true   1   2   3   4   5   *very true*
○   ○   ○   ○   ○

[1] www.wakeboardingmag.com/blog/manufacturers/2009/07/16/

[2] http://www.nmma.org/press/article/18491

[3] Please see www.ReflectingGod.info/McKinsey7S for more information.

[4] Trade Only, May 26, 2015.

[5] Trade Only, October 18, 2018.

[6] Boating Industry, September 13, 2018.

[7] Quid Pro Quo agreements are contracts. With a contract, if one agreeing party violates his obligations, the contract is then considered broken. Both parties to the agreement can argue that the agreement should be terminated. Very often relationships end when agreements are terminated. With a covenant, however, both parties agree to respect the vision and values (or membership vows) of the covenant community while helping one another uphold agreements. Examples are seen in the three primary covenantal institutions (the church, family and government) where the organization continues to build strong relationships while multiple people work together to uphold commitments. If the covenant is breached by one party, other parties continue to fulfill commitments for the good of the community

[8] flowauto.com/history.aspx

Section 3

Hierarchical Spiritual Leadership

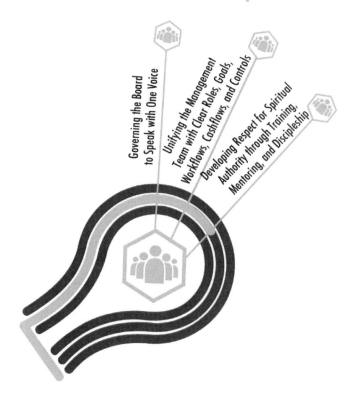

Governing the Board to Speak with One Voice

Unifying the Management Team with Clear Roles, Goals, Workflows, Cashflows, and Controls

Developing Respect for Spiritual Authority through Training, Mentoring, and Discipleship

THE COVENANTAL PLANNING PROCESS emphasizes the need for divinely-guided leadership. The governance process should help ensure that resources (explained in Section 1) are used according to a prayerfully discerned vision (explained in Section 2) that guides all six dimensions of covenantal planning (explained throughout the six sections of this book). The covenantal authority of the leader is executed through clear "roles, goals, controls, workflows, and cash flows." Chapter 5 explains how a visionary leader assembles a board that establishes roles and goals for key executives. Chapter 6 reviews how key executives use wise management training and mentoring programs to develop resources and encourage respect for established work flows. Executives also monitor key performance indicators (KPI) to spot and correct variances from objectives, i.e., to maintain corporate controls. Chapter 7 emphasizes the need for outside advisers who can help detect areas of darkness in an organization while helping managers unite team members around a plan guided by God's light. This keeps everyone in the company focused on combining the right team members and materials to improve the quadruple bottom line, as discussed in Section 5. As part of Chapter 7, the authors discuss the importance of monitoring cash flows using web-based dashboards and industry-specific performance metrics.

Chapter 5

Governing the Board to Speak with One Voice

BEN SPENT 30 YEARS building an organization that served churches globally. He held firmly to time-tested Christian beliefs and met often with his board members to pray for unity. The ministry thrived, but Ben felt growing pressure to expand his board of directors to include leaders from megachurches, parachurches, and other influential ministries that did not emphasize biblical orthodoxy as much as Ben. Gradually Ben brought on new board members who promised to help him maintain his core values while making the message "more relevant" to broader audiences.

As the ministry grew, Ben felt increasingly comfortable giving decision-making authority to the new board members. These new leaders thought they could keep expanding the appeal of Ben's original message by using allegorical interpretations of Scripture rather than the historical and literal interpretations underlying Ben's conservative views. Ben objected to the increasingly undefined teachings and the lack of commitment to equipping Christians to build the church as described in Scripture. As tensions grew, the new board members formed a quorum that fired Ben.

Soon, without a strong leader committed to core values, the ministry collapsed, hurting thousands of constituents, costing millions of dollars, and damaging the Christian witness of the ministry. Today a new board uses resources provided by donors from the first 30 years, but the new ministry, built around a shallow statement of faith, has not been able to grow or inspire interest in any new initiatives.

Ben suffered much anguish as he watched the new board fail to protect the valuable intellectual property and reputation for faithfulness developed over thirty years. Ben felt grieved that the new board did not respect the intentions of donors who contributed millions of dollars expecting that the ministry would remain faithful to its mission. Ben should have learned from the hundreds of for-profit and not-for-profit organizations that have "gone liberal," despite the founders assuming that the organization would remain faithful to God-honoring ideas proclaimed in the early years.

Examples abound of universities and not-for-profit charities forsaking the founders' commitments in order to attract donors, leaders, and new constituents.[1] Many additional examples exist of for-profit entities growing strong with Christian beliefs and practices before the organizations are sold to third parties who are more focused on money and power than on maintaining Christian values. The board of Ben's organization was compromised on a small scale like the big college boards have been compromised on grand scales.

The common denominator is a lack of commitment to the founders' vision and values. There was much rhetoric about this commitment to values based on the Creator/created distinction, but no real track record showing commitment to confessions of faith defining the Creator/created distinction. Too often boards trust rhetoric about maturity when bringing on new members but do not heed yellow and red flags. What should be done to protect Christ-centered core values?

Boards should often gather to actualize a vision which a godly leader has prayerfully developed. When two or three are gathered in Christ's name, the Spirit can lead.[2] The focus on honoring Christ encourages board members to lend time, as well as giving shareholders confidence that they can contribute assets. Shareholders may include donors who support non-profit organizations or banks and equity partners who support for-profit entities. Anyone would agree that a board can provide valuable leadership, but experienced board members can readily recite examples of board leadership going haywire.

What is the solution? Seminaries need to teach from much more mature and robust materials about Christian board governance. Boards need to insist that Christian board members have proper training in biblical and Spirit-led governance. Board governance consultants need to provide clear examples of how board members can be guided by mature preaching of the Word, prayer, and oversight from qualified church elders. This chapter seeks to teach lessons gleaned from well-run boards while cautioning leaders against repeating the mistakes of boards which failed to guide organizations effectively.

Lessons from past boards exhibit the importance of maintaining boards that 1) speak with one voice, 2) choose qualified and purposeful leaders, 3) maintain accountability, and 4) respond to danger signs.

Speak with One Voice

Leaders must heed Ephesian 4:3 and related passages, "being diligent to preserve the unity of the Spirit in the bond of peace." Much as Paul appealed to fellow believers in 1 Corinthians 1:10, board members should appeal to members in the name of our Lord Jesus Christ that they agree and quell division so that all can "be united in the same mind and the same judgment."

Agreement occurs when board members each recognize first principles from Scripture. Leaders must know the light of God's revelation. This light shines through three means of grace: preaching of the Word, prayer, and oversight from a church that maintains peace and purity through the proper administration of the sacraments. Preaching of the Word includes teaching about God's love and His holiness. Preachers explain God's holiness through commitment to the law (as well as Christ's modeling fulfillment of the law in Matthew 5:17). Preaching about commitment to the holy law of God addresses issues of leadership and governance (see, e.g., Hebrews 10:16 and 11:33). Preachers must, of course, emphasize transformation of the heart because no leader can honor the law apart from confessing weakness and knowing that through our weakness Christ displays His power (2 Corinthians 12:9).

Prayer applies God's Word to the matters at hand. Jesus emphasized daily prayer. For example, Mark records how Jesus, rising very early in the morning, "while it was still dark, departed and went out to a desolate place, and there he prayed" before he went out to preach among the people and in the synagogues.[3] Through prayer, people can repent of sins and experience the holiness that helps them see and hear the Lord. Isaiah explains the connection between holy behavior and listening to God. In Isaiah 51, he writes, "Listen to me, you who pursue righteousness, you who seek the Lord: look to the rock."[4]

Through prayer, leaders can see the Lord. In Genesis 32:30, Jacob called the holy place Peniel, saying, "For I have seen God face to face, and yet my life has been delivered." This holy quest to see God is reaffirmed in Hebrews 12:14, "Strive for peace with everyone, and for the holiness without which no one will see the Lord." Jesus makes this teaching foundational in the Beatitudes, where he says, "Blessed are the pure in heart, for they shall see God."[5]

Church communities can help believers understand the above passages even while living in the midst of a culture that often settles for moralistic therapeutic deism (MTD).[6] Prayer within mature churches emphasizes a biblical understanding of submission and repentance. Through community, leaders develop a shared understanding of God's revelation, purposes, and authority structures. This differs from MTD teachings that encourage individuals to develop their own morality apart from mature community.

Within a church community that maintains peace and purity through proper administration of the sacraments, board members receive teaching about the law and learn how the leadership vision is guided by God's moral law. Proverbs 29:18 shows the importance of scriptural teachings. "Where there is no prophetic vision the people cast off restraint, but blessed is he who keeps the law."

Each leader must know how to speak with guidance from God. When creating a personal board of advisers or prayer partners, one should choose wise leaders like pastors, elders, and godly men and women. Leaders may maintain a prayer journal to meditate on relevant Scripture when praying through difficult issues that arise. Across time, such prayer journals provide wonderful evidence of how the Lord of the universe is also a personal Father who answers prayers and draws His children close.

Choose Qualified Board Members Who Are Guided by God's Light and Purpose

"God is light; in him there is no darkness at all."[7] Board members must know the light of Scripture. Throughout biblical times there were seven types of mature leaders to whom the people often turned for guidance: Prophets, Evangelists, Pastors, Teachers, Counselors, Parents, and Peacemakers. In modern practice, people often turn to seven different types of leaders: The Chaplain, Counselor, Coach/Mentor*, Council (Board) Members, Corporate Prayer Leaders, Consultants, and Conciliators (Peacemakers). The roles of these seven modern sources of light are explained in the article "Light Sources."[8]

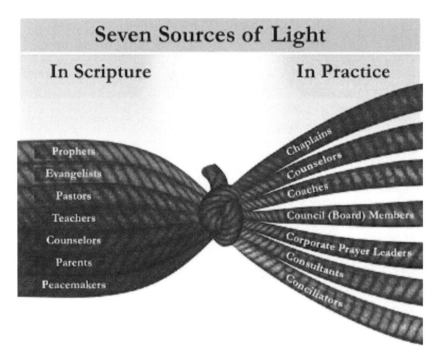

Seven Sources of Light

In Scripture

- Prophets
- Evangelists
- Pastors
- Teachers
- Counselors
- Parents
- Peacemakers

In Practice

- Chaplains
- Counselors
- Coaches
- Council (Board) Members
- Corporate Prayer Leaders
- Consultants
- Conciliators

Board members must know the Lord and His purposes for the resources bestowed on the organization. Leaders must have a mature understanding of stewardship, as explained in Chapter 8, which covers stewardship of Time, Talents, Treasure, and Trust. While a business may have great capital, expanding the business is not a goal by itself. Leaders of an organization should consider using its resources to build the institutions emphasized in Scripture and the confessions.[9]

Who should have a seat on the board? Jeff Bezos of Amazon has an empty chair at each board meeting where the imagined customer sits. Growing numbers of Christian companies involve a corporate chaplain in the governance process because the chaplain understands the concerns of the employees. Board members from outside the organization can speak for vendors, suppliers, and the community. Of course, a mature board also needs adequate representation from shareholders who are stewarding investments in the company.

Mature boards clarify roles. Often times the board will engage a consultant to translate biblical principles into behaviors for board members, confirm that board members have the right skills, bring fresh perspectives, expand constituencies, satisfy diversity requirements, and make sure that board members work well together. Consultants can help find board members who come from different disciplines, who maintain practical knowledge, and who know how to make connections to people with needed resources.

Board consultants can also help boards maintain a consistent purpose in keeping with Genesis 11:6: "If the people speak with one voice, nothing they plan to do will be impossible for them." Christian management consultant Doug Sherman recommends that board directives be written because, "Ideas are not clear until they are in writing."

Board members must also be spiritually aware individuals who know the insidious impact of darkness that apostle John addresses:

God is light and in Him is no darkness at all. If we say that we have fellowship with Him, and walk in darkness, we lie and do not practice the truth. But if we walk in the light as He is in the light, we have fellowship with one another, and the blood of Jesus Christ His Son cleanses us from all sin. (1 John 1:5-7)

Maintain Accountability

Boards must define accountability. They should create a clear statement of core values which mentions the principles that will guide the organization. "Where there is no law there is no transgression."[10] Where principles (moral laws) are made clear, people can see their transgressions and be held accountable for violations.

Standards of accountability must go beyond mere statements of principles. Good organizations understand that clear plans must be illustrated with budgets for CPAs, diagrams for engineers, checklists for MBAs, and narratives for attorneys. All must agree on cash flow projections, as Jesus reminds us in Luke 14:28: "For which of you, desiring to build a tower, does not first sit down and count the cost, whether he has enough to complete it?"

Principles must guide decisions. To confirm that principles guide a board member, have dinner with him/her and listen. Look at which church sermons influence the leader. Ask about the biblical worldview. One should not simply assume that board members consider biblical principles in their business decisions.[11]

While business founders must remain accountable to a board, wise founders avoid mistakes of previous leaders. A founder should not give up more than 50% of the voting control without careful consideration and adequate compensation. The founder should influence who on the board has voting power. Moreover, the founder needs to control bank accounts until there are good controls in place to insure proper use of cash. See the discussion in Chapter 6 about Controls.

Increasingly, boards can use assessment tests to review the many issues affecting their performance. One of these is the *Baldrige Perspective for the Board of Directors*, which helps boards of directors apply criteria for Performance Excellence to the governance process.[12] The Baldrige criteria have been developed by members of boards of companies recognized as Baldridge award winners. The award is named after Malcolm Baldrige, the U.S. Secretary of Commerce during the Ronald Reagan administration. This survey asks insightful questions in seven categories that relate to the six elements of the covenant model, as explained below. The questions help a board of directors assess the performance of the organization and target areas for improvement.

The following table shows how a board might reflect the character of God while using the Baldrige questions to evaluate a board. First, there is a review of the available resources, including human resources. Second, leaders focus on mission and concern for the customer. Third, upper management guides the leadership process. Fourth, leaders make principles and priorities relevant through a values-based and process-based planning system. Fifth they measure and improve results. Sixth, the organization leverages success as it grows. Of course, the Baldridge assessment questions cover only a subset of the issues reviewed in this book; however, the Baldrige questions can focus leaders on variables that apply to all types of successful organizations.

1R	Revelation and Resources	5. **Human resource focus:** How the organization empowers and involves its workforce.
2T	Customer-Driven Mission	3. **Customer and market focus:** How the organization builds and maintains strong, lasting relationships with customers.
3H	Higher Authority	1. **Leadership:** How upper management leads the organization, and how the organization leads within the community.
4E	Values-Based Planning	2. **Strategic planning:** How the organization establishes and plans to implement strategic directions.
4E	Process-Based Planning	6. **Process management:** How the organization designs, manages, and improves key processes.
5O	Measuring Outcomes	4. **Measurement, analysis, and knowledge management:** How the organization uses data to support key processes and manage performance.
6S	Leveraging Results	7. **Business/organizational performance results:** How the organization performs in terms of customer satisfaction, finances, human resources, supplier and partner performance, operations, governance and social responsibility, and how the organization compares to its competitors.

Emphasize God-Honoring Outcomes While Responding to Danger Signs

Despite the best intentions, a board can easily be seduced by idolatry. Boards need to beware of danger signs linked to idols of pleasures, pressures, possessions, and position.

The first danger is a focus on comfort—pleasures—rather than principles. Leaders often enjoy the comforts of success. Members of boards may convince one another that it is appropriate to spend corporate resources on personal financial rewards. This can be acceptable unless an idolatrous focus on the well-being of leaders undermines the commitment to customers, employees, and the community. Leaders need review by outside auditors or oversight boards. The apostle Paul warns of this danger: "When they measure themselves by themselves and compare themselves with themselves, they are not wise."[13]

The second danger is when leaders pressure one another to acquiesce to leadership teams' public statements even when it violates Christian principles. Many seasoned church elders can think of times when church leadership encouraged them to turn a blind eye to sin and make whitewashed public statements when a fellow elder was making bad business decisions or not upholding the high standards given to elders in 1 Timothy 3:2 and related passages.[14] Board members will use a variety of excuses not to "judge" a fellow board member accused of misconduct. Too often board members marginalize the accusers or question the judicial process to avoid pressures from outside to evaluate the character and competency of a fellow board member. Peer pressures cause boards and other leadership teams to overlook too many questionable behaviors.

The third danger is focusing on money—possessions—rather than Christ. Leaders need capital. Non-profit organizations need donors, members, and other constituents who provide financial capital, human capital, and other resources. For-profit entities need capital from bankers, investors, and other sources. The source of capital may often be people who, without knowing and supporting the values of the organization, want to influence those values. Leaders face pressures to compromise God-honoring values in order to satisfy constituents who lack the moral and spiritual principles affirmed by the organization's leaders.

Fourth is the danger of focusing on status—position—rather than Christ. Institutional reputations are "enhanced" by bringing on big name people. Companies hire prominent executives. Non-profits attract professors, authors, and other thought leaders. These prominent individuals are revered for their fame even if they lack moral and spiritual principles consistent with the organization they purport to serve. When an organization follows prominent leaders, they risk not following Christ. They succumb to John's warning about "the pride of life" which "comes not from the Father but from the world."[15]

Sunlight is the best disinfectant. When a board or other leadership team shows the danger signs of idolatry, a third-party consultant, qualified outside peacemaker, or oversight group must be available to review credible accusations of impropriety.

Leadership teams need a process to establish clear statements of values and then conduct regular meetings to spot deviations from the core values. Board must evaluate themselves but also involve third parties in spotting problems. For example, corporations may have a corporate chaplain who promises confidentiality to employees while gathering information and summarizing problems for management.

Leadership teams must look beyond rhetoric about vision and values. Much talk about church polity, doctrine, authority, and accountability may mask underlying problems. Prayerful leaders can often spot corrupt leadership, much like the Holy Spirt repeatedly warned apostles to stay away from various corrupt leaders.[16] The leadership process must be more about knowing and following Jesus.

Leaders must watch for cases where core values and vision become fuzzy or too abstract. When the core values are not clear, insidious forces cause organizations to drift from their original mission and beliefs. The changes seem too small to cause alarm, like the frog boiled in the kettle who was not alarmed by the gradual temperature changes.

Conclusion

How can you confirm that the board members know and follow the light? Engage chaplains, counselors, coaches/mentors, council (board) members, corporate prayer leaders, consultants, and conciliators (peacemakers) who know and prayerfully apply Scripture with oversight from qualified teams of elders.

When boards are guided by the light of Scripture, they can 1) speak with one voice, 2) choose qualified and purposeful leaders, 3) maintain accountability, and 4) respond to danger signs learned when they got burned.

Assessment Questions

Board members of Baldrige Award-winning organizations have affirmed leadership principles in the Baldrige Excellence Framework booklet, which includes the Criteria for Performance Excellence.[17] These principles parallel the elements of the biblical covenant, as indicated by the following list of six questions.

At www.ReflectingGod.info/Survey, please indicate your level of agreement with the following five statements:

My board members affirm our core values and maintain accountability to a church which embraces the historical and literal interpretation of scripture.

not true   1   2   3   4   5   very true
○ ○ ○ ○ ○

My board members affirm a statement of faith, mission statement, and core values based on scripture

not true   1   2   3   4   5   very true
○ ○ ○ ○ ○

My board members govern with one voice based on a shared understanding of God's revelation, purposes, and authority structures.

not true   1   2   3   4   5   very true
○ ○ ○ ○ ○

My board has third party audits and annual reviews of board members to ensure accountability to core values.

not true   1   2   3   4   5   very true
○ ○ ○ ○ ○

My board confronts and terminates board members or executives who disregard the mission, core values and statement of faith.

not true   1   2   3   4   5   very true
○ ○ ○ ○ ○

[1] www.ReflectingGod.info/GoneLiberal. In the article, Dr. Peter Jones gives the example of Wellesley College when reminding us again what huge pressures board members have to compromise. Harvard, Yale, and Princeton, as well as the many Wesleyan colleges (like USC, Vanderbilt, Northwestern, and Southern Methodist) have all gone liberal. Board members and leaders at these institutions typically defend their actions with vague "values-neutral" rhetoric that is always rooted in the "oneism" that Jones decries.

[2] Mathew 18:20

[3] Mark 1:35

[4] See also Acts 17:11.

[5] Matthew 5:8-9

[6] Notre Dame sociologist Christian Smith published a study of teen spirituality in America. Smith concluded that American young people today mostly practice a religion of "moralistic, therapeutic deism." See www.ReflectingGod.info/MTD.

[7] 1 John 1:5

[8] http://www.ReflectingGod.info/7LightSources

[9] www.ReflectingGod.info/3Institutions

[10] Romans 4:15

[11] See www.ReflectingGod.info/PrincipledDecisions

[12] www.nist.gov/baldrige/baldrige-perspective-board-directors

[13] 2 Corinthians 10:12.

[14] "Now the overseer is to be above reproach, faithful to his wife, temperate, self-controlled, respectable, hospitable, able to teach"

[15] 1 John 2:16

[16] See, e.g., Acts 16:6-7

[17] www.nist.gov/baldrige/publications/baldrige-excellence-framework/businessnonprofit

Chapter 6

Unifying the Management Team with Clear Roles, Goals, Workflows, Cashflows, and Controls

WILLIAM BUILT AN INVESTMENT ADVISORY firm that was respected throughout the community. He was a polished executive who oversaw a seemingly capable staff. A large network of community leaders respected him. Few people questioned him because he served as an elder at a highly regarded church. Investors and executives at his firm placed their trust in William since he assured everyone in his books, articles, and speeches that his firm maintained high standards of integrity.

William knew that not everything was run as required by compliance standards, but he delegated to managers who were charged with fixing the problems. This seemed like a reasonable solution to William until the SEC raided his business, uncovered numerous breaches of compliance standards, and shut down the operations. William, his family members, and fellow church elders were disgraced. What went wrong?

The above example about William is a composite of examples from several successful Christian-run investment firms that have run into serious problems. In every case, the Chief Compliance Officer (CCO) was not given adequate information or authority by the CEO. Problems came to light too slowly, and, as compliance beaches were observed, the CCO lacked authority to address the problems. The CCO told the CEO about the problems, but the CEO insisted that he had properly delegated responsibility for fixing the problems. In fact, the CEO was shirking his duties and failing to exercise adequate controls.

Section Three of this book emphasizes how the CEO oversees hierarchical leadership structures with input from a qualified board. Chapter 5 explains the role of the board in affirming a strategic plan for operationalizing the company's vision while upholding its values. After the board establishes the plan for the organization, managers in the C-Suite put in place systems to pursue the board's agenda for generating profits and enhancing the quadruple bottom line (as explained in Section 5 of this book), while seeking appropriate feedback.

In the 21st century, the C-Suite executives can have very technical roles but at the core, the roles have deep spiritual underpinnings. This is evident when studying how a successful modern business leader might apply the wisdom of Nehemiah, the ancient Jew who united a team of works around a clear vision and then operationalized the vision with clear roles, goals, workflows, cash flows, and controls.

Before studying the practical aspects of Nehemiah's leadership, we should first look at how he applied the means of grace. The book of Nehemiah has multiple references to the Torah. Nehemiah worked within the covenant community, which maintained peace and purity through the administration of the sacraments[1]. There are nine prayers in the book of Nehemiah, beginning with the prayer in chapter one that parallels the biblical covenant model perfectly.[2] God answers his prayer in practical ways as He guides Nehemiah's leadership throughout thirteen chapters.

Roles

Historians have confirmed that Nehemiah and his team rebuilt the wall around Jerusalem in 52 days despite fierce opposition. Nehemiah started with very few workers.[3] He articulated a clear vision to his brother, who agreed to help lead the workers.[4] He recruited the leaders of the city to perform the tasks.[5] Then Nehemiah appointed staff members to administrative functions within the city. This helped repopulate Jerusalem and surrounding towns with additional workers.[6] As Nehemiah inspired the workers to work within their roles, he called the leaders together and emphasized the roles of individuals in the plan.[7]

The head of any modern organization (usually the CEO) can learn from how Nehemiah managed the myriad management, financial, production, administrative, and other functions to achieve organizational goals. While the modern CEO may have some new challenges, a 21st century business leader also has access to many resources not available in previous centuries.

The Chief Executive Officer (CEO) may oversee four or more other "Chiefs." Most common are the Chief Operations Officer (COO) and Chief Financial Officer (CFO). Increasingly, companies have a Chief Information Officer (CIO) who maintains data processing systems as well as a Chief Compliance Officer (CCO) who monitors the myriad of regulations that impose external controls on an organization. Companies may have other C-Suite executives, such as those involved with customer care or customer experiences; however, the CEO, COO, CFO, CIO, and CCO roles are most common.

Goals

Nehemiah envisioned goals while still in Persia.[8] He developed a comprehensive set of goals to rebuild the wall once he arrived in Jerusalem and analyzed the situation.[9] While the vision was fixed, the goals could be modified in response to external opportunities and threats as well as internal strengths and weaknesses.

Nehemiah communicated success in achieving the goals, such as when the wall was halfway complete.[10] Instead of just listing goals as legalistic guidelines (like too many managers), Nehemiah communicated the goals broadly and with a sense of urgency.[11]

The modern manager has additional tools to communicate goals. Ideally, goals should be depicted with graphics, text, checklists, and numbers so that management team members can "quadrulate" what the team needs.[12] Some managers, such as lawyers, prefer textual summaries of goals; others, such as investors or shareholders, may prefer graphical bar charts to show results. CPAs may prefer specific numerical tables showing year-by-year after-tax income or growth in share value, and others, such as MBAs, may prefer checklists or project management reports. Much as Nehemiah's workers respected Nehemiah's vision, the executives working in the above roles must respect goals established and communicated by the board or the CEO.

A properly crafted strategic plan tracks achievement of goals in formats understood by shareholders, CPAs, MBAs, JDs and other members of the management team. Sample outputs are shown at the Reflecting God website.[13]

Workflows

Under Nehemiah's leadership, forty leaders and their crews worked shoulder-to-shoulder to rebuild the wall.[14] Some built large sections and others built smaller sections near their homes. Each worker was given tasks according to his available resources.[15]

Executives should be empowered to create and maintain uniform project management workflows that detail which staff members will complete specific tasks or projects by designed due dates. The modern company can communicate workflows much more effectively using project management software. Workers engaged in diverse endeavors can have confidence that a wise leader empowered with software will keep everyone working in unity with uniform completion dates.

Cashflows

Perhaps Nehemiah read King Solomon's wisdom (from 500+ years earlier) in Proverbs 24:27. Solomon wrote, "Prepare your work outside; get everything ready for yourself in the field, and after that build your house." Nehemiah carefully assembled needed resources, including written authorizations, timber for building,[16] capable workers,[17] and money.[18] He had backup plans when others ran out of money.[19] He was focused on preparation for his people, not on his own personal gain.

Nehemiah understood how work flows need to be linked to cash flow management (cash flows) covering the same time periods. Today, the intuitive process used by Nehemiah can be externalized with web-based dashboards that show how projects are completed with clear tracking of work flows and cash flows. Managers and consultants can link the project management results and data to key performance indicators (KPI) that focus all managers on realizing positive outcomes.

Analysis of comprehensive cash flows can be the best way to reveal irregular payments or deviations from desired results. Current, accurate, and fully integrated cash flow reports shine light on all financial activities. Accurate financial statements can be the sunlight in the sage's saying, "Sunlight is the best disinfectant."

Managers should meet regularly to discuss the cash flow reports and KPI graphics while clarifying what needs to be done. Plans must then be updated to reflect accurately how the team can best achieve its goals while maintaining positive cash flow. When all advisers use reliable web-based systems, adviser team members and clients can obtain a variety of timely reports. These "controls" help advisers monitor one another's performance and address problems promptly.

Controls

Controls are all about authority. Nehemiah found support from his leader, the king. Nehemiah asked that the king let him go, "to the city in Judah where my fathers are buried so that I can rebuild it."[20] Nehemiah did not Lord this authority over his people; instead, he created an atmosphere for people to speak up.[21] He put in place feedback mechanisms to solicit input about progress.[22] Nehemiah also had a contingency plan so that he could use his authority to respond to changing circumstances.[23]

Any successful business has managerial and financial controls that help managers hold team members accountable for duties and results. The accountability controls help ensure that all workers and advisers work within their roles. The controls must help reveal if employees are accomplishing the outcomes for which they have accepted responsibility or are acting in over-lapping or undisclosed roles. The best controls are depicted graphically in reports shared with all planning team members and stakeholders. Ideally, the reports should summarize the potential outcomes of the recommendations of all advisers in year-by-year after-tax cash flow summaries that integrate the cash inflows and outflows from all planning strategies.

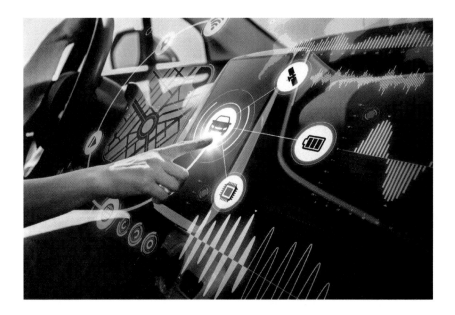

The best adviser teams use web-based project management software to track "who will do what by when." Designated members of management teams need to track all "to dos" on Next Action Checklists that clarify due dates for all COO, CIO, CFO, CCO. This checklist should be web-enabled to keep every adviser "on the same page." If managers and advisers review the checklists and forward suggested changes to the checklist, the checklist can be updated regularly, and the client can see clear progress toward fulfillment of all goals.

With good checklists and oversight from the person given necessary authority, management team members work together in unity, staff members focus on productivity, clients express high satisfaction, and shareholders achieve reasonable rewards. The community is strengthened when managers have clear roles and goals linked to well-defined workflows and reasonable cash flow reports. These processes work very well as long as one or more people in an organization have the necessary information and authority to address deviations from norms established in the strategic plan. A controls process is needed to spot and address problems if managers start to work outside their roles to achieve personal agendas rather than corporate goals. Moreover, controls help identify where work flows are neglected or where cash flow reports show variances from budgets.

Too often organizations fail to maintain proper controls. Then management team members fail to work together in unity, profits and productivity fall, and disunity festers. When management consultants are brought in to address the problems, they quickly observe the presenting problems related to disrespect for roles, goals, workflows and cash flow objectives. The deeper problem, however, is often more difficult to uncover.

When shareholders, staff members, customers, or members of the community see a problem in an organization, a qualified external consultant should be given the information and authority to assess and address the problem. The consultant must "peel the onion" to look behind defensive rhetoric, empty assurances, or diversionary tactics of those who are undermining the organization. Very often a consultant needs to schedule private interviews with people surrounding the organization's problems in order to spot the core problems. At the core of an organizations dysfunctionality and disunity there are usually several of the seven deadly sins.

The seven deadly sins are more common, insidious, and damaging than most managers care to admit. Greed very often causes executives to spend less money than they should on compliance while laziness causes them to spend less time on compliance matters. Arguably, greed and laziness caused all the problems that destroyed William's business described in the opening paragraph of this chapter. Of course, greed manifests in a myriad of other ways within an organization. It is very common, for example, for managers to inflate results or take credit for others' work in order to improve personal compensation.

While greed and laziness are two of the most common organizational sins, pride may be the most damaging. C. S. Lewis and other theologians call pride the greatest sin for good reason. A manager focused on exalting himself will tear others down in nasty emails, sarcastic comments, or other disruptive behaviors that destroy dignity. A self-interested CEO will advertise about his own skills and accomplishments while failing to acknowledge the hard work of people who contributed to his success. To protect a false image of honesty and integrity, a prideful leader will blame others using false accusations while giving the falsely accused no opportunity to address the injustice.

Gluttony, anger, envy, and lust also destroy organizations. How many companies fail to pay promised bonuses while executives enjoy first class flights, posh club memberships, over-sized executive suites, and other gluttonous perks? How many employees have had their reputations tarnished and career paths undermined because of angry outbursts or festering rage? How many managers have their success questioned or undermined by competitors or associates driven by too much envy? How many leaders have protected inappropriate behavior or engaged in dishonest cover-ups because of lustful urges spilling over into inappropriate relationships?

When the seven deadly sins are undermining productivity and dignity, how should the board or CEO respond? First, leaders must be sure that the strategic plan clearly communicates roles, goals, workflows, cash flows, and controls. Second, executives must be empowered to achieve the purposes for which they were hired. Third, everyone within an organization must have an appropriate appeals process. Hierarchical leadership is not just "top down." That is, leaders must not simply impose their understanding of God's character. Instead, each leader must listen to subordinates, especially those who seek to honor God. Often it is wise to have peer review committees or corporate chaplains who have a safe way to collect data (from shareholders, staff members, customers, and the community) and then tell the CEO or board about problems that need attention. If the CEO and board fail to listen, there must be an appeals process to a qualified third party, such as the CEO's church elders. Healthy churches maintain peacemaking processes so that leaders at the church can address accusations that the seven deadly sins are undermining relationships.[24]

Conclusion

When planning team members work together in unity, clients achieve their goals. Unified planning begins and ends with tracking details. We must confirm that advisers are working within their roles, achieving quantified goals, and responding promptly when control systems indicate problems. We must use the control systems to help clients and adviser team members have regular access to numbers, graphics, and paragraphs of text describing next actions necessary to achieve client goals. When planning teams respect roles, goals, and controls, clients consistently enjoy success in achieving their objectives and, perhaps more important, they experience much peace of mind.

At www.ReflectingGod.info/Survey, please indicate your level of agreement with the following five statements:

My business has clear roles for each member of the C-Suite.

not true   1   2   3   4   5   very true
○ ○ ○ ○ ○

My business has clear goals for each member of the C-Suite.

not true   1   2   3   4   5   very true
○ ○ ○ ○ ○

My business has clear workflows so that all projects are completed by the right person by the right date, with details in documents that are properly named, organized, and easily accessed.

not true   1   2   3   4   5   very true
○ ○ ○ ○ ○

My business has complete cash flow statements so that managers can confirm activities are profitable.

not true   1   2   3   4   5   very true
○ ○ ○ ○ ○

My business managers and compliance consultants have clear controls to verify that work is done properly.

not true   1   2   3   4   5   very true
○ ○ ○ ○ ○

* Workflows should be monitored with a web-based project management system; e.g., a virtual taskmaster

** Ideally, cash flow statements should be tracked with a web-based dashboard, such as by using QuickBooks.[25]

---

[1] The peace and purity of the covenant community church is clearly maintained in the New Testament through the administration of the sacraments. See, e.g., www.ChristianPeace.Institute/RC. In Old Testament times, sacraments were different, but they were still used to maintain holiness and other divine character qualities within covenant communities. According to Chapter 27 of the Westminster Confession of Faith, "The sacraments of the Old Testament in regard to the spiritual things thereby signified and exhibited, were, for substance, the same with those of the new."

[2] Then I [Nehemiah] said, "O LORD, God of heaven, the great and awesome God [Revelation] who keeps his covenant of unfailing love with those who love him and obey his commands [Transcendent Purpose], listen to my prayer! Look down and see me praying night and day for your people Israel. I confess that we have sinned against you. Yes, even my own family and I have sinned! [Hierarchy and Humble Submission] We have sinned terribly by not obeying the commands, decrees, and regulations that you gave us through your servant Moses [Ethical precepts]. Please remember what you told your servant Moses: 'If you are unfaithful to me, I will scatter you among the nations. But if you return to me and obey my commands and live by them, then even if you are exiled to the ends of the earth, I will bring you back to the place I have chosen for my name to be honored.' The people you rescued by your great power and strong hand are your servants [Outcomes]. O Lord, please hear my prayer! Listen to the prayers of those of us who delight in honoring you. Please grant me success today by making the king favorable to me.* Put it into his heart to be kind to me." In those days I was the king's cup-bearer [Succession/Inheritance] (Neh. 1:5-11).

[3] Nehemiah 7:4

[4] 7:2

[5] 2:16

[6] 7:3-5, 73

[7] 2:16-18

[8] 1:8-11

[9] 2:11-16

[10] 4:6

[11] 2:17

[12] Whereas engineers and managers can often derive accurate calculations by looking at three points of data (triangulation), the interpolation process can theoretically be improved by looking at four types of data (quadrulation).

[13] www.ReflectingGod.info/KPIreports

[14] Nehemiah 3:1-32

[15] 7:1-4

[16] 2:7-8

[17] 3:1-32

[18] 7:70-72

[19] 5:1-6

[20] Nehemiah 2:5

[21] 2:18

[22] 4:6

[23] 4:16-18

[24] See, e.g., the Book of Church Order of the Presbyterian Church in America.

[25] See, e.g., http://vfos.com/Dashboard/

Chapter 7

Developing Respect for Spiritual Authority Through Training, Mentoring, and Discipleship

NICK SAT DEJECTED in the living room of his house. A 10-year partner-ship and mentorship was over, and he felt sad and betrayed. His partner had just informed him that he wanted to divide their assets and go their separate ways. Nick had sensed something was wrong but ignored the signs. The two of them had often disputed over money and manage-ment philosophy, but Nick wanted things to work out. His partner had been his work mentor at a previous company and shown him the line-man trade. Nick had a tremendous amount of respect, admiration, and gratitude for him. Although he knew the relationship was over, he wasn't sure what to do next.

Nick loved the lineman trade and the brotherhood he had experi-enced in it. The trade was not known for the spiritual treatment of its workers, yet Nick was a devoutly spiritual man and yearned for a way to bring that to the workplace. The work of a lineman could be a dan-gerous one, and most companies cared little for safety and training, which often led to accidents and unnecessary risks. The trade was also filled with problems following drug and alcohol abuse. An "every man for himself" attitude resulted in poor treatment of subordinates and employees, which tended to create a nomadic group of linemen moving from company to company with no real home. Nick wondered and prayed about how this might change.

An old friend, Mike, stopped by and asked what the trouble was. After Nick explained, Mike suggested this may be a blessing in disguise since God works in mysterious ways. "Why don't you start all over with your half of the assets? We can form a new company and you can begin again," Mike said. "This time, however, let's dedicate the company to God and ask for His protection and care in all we do."

Nick agreed, and they were off on a journey that continues to this day. The two men discussed how best to make their vision happen and agreed that principles needed to come before personalities and that the principles to be used were the ones that our Lord laid out. They decided on the name HP (Higher Powered) Communications Inc.

In HP's early stages, a major dilemma was a lack of spiritually and technically qualified tradesmen. Unfortunately, the trade traditionally encouraged excessive drinking, drug abuse, and poor work habits, leading to down time, uncertainty, and lost profit. Early on, the partners discussed and committed to taking a long-term view of the business and training from within the company. The dream of a training facility and program was born. In the short run, HP would do everything it could to find and develop competent tradesmen, with good character high on the list of qualifications.

Before Nick and the early managers could address the problems in the industry, they had to agree that the principles laid out by the Lord would guide the organization, that the company would be dedicated to Him, and that all authority would derive from God's law and will for the company. The first question they would ask in all difficult situations would be, "What would our Lord have us do, and how does Scripture and His principles inform the decision?"

Both men discussed their previous bad experiences with other organizations and decided the primary cornerstone of the company would be treating employees like they themselves would like to be treated. "You shall love the Lord, your God, with all your heart, with all your soul, and with all your mind. This is the greatest and the first commandment. The second is like it: You shall love your neighbor as yourself." The whole law and the prophets depend on these two commandments."[1]

As Nick and Mike reflected on the greatest two commandments, they saw a need to observe how God worked through the people that they sought to lead. They believed that spiritual authority involved more than establishing a board (chapter 5) and putting managers in positions of control (chapter 6). They wanted an authority process that focused on watching what God was doing through each employee. Then they wanted to establish servant leadership by clarifying the spiritual authority process, listening to employees while showing principled concern for all, training groups of employees, identifying and mentoring existing and new leaders, and discipling employees one-on-one.

Clarifying Spiritual Authority

God's will is that spiritual authorities not lord it over those allotted to their charge but prove to be examples to the flock (1 Pet. 5:24). Like Jesus, the "Good Shepherd," managers should know the "flock" that they oversee (John 10:14, 27). If managers desire an organization guided by the Lord, they must institute principles of spiritual authority that encourage both "top-down" leadership, as managers listen to the Lord, and "bottom-up" leadership as managers listen to the people they seek to lead.

Strong spiritual authority only thrives when its leaders are first seeking the kingdom and God's will for people being led. This godly motive differentiates their organization from secular organizations. Many modern-day organizations believe in centralized, dictatorial management. This often results in one strong leader or a small group of individuals directing the entire company's activities with little input from lower-level managers and subordinates. Armed with this authoritarian disposition, the board—if there is one—is usually composed of "yes men." Such leaders use fear and anger as the primary management tools and motivators, and their organizations (both for-profit and not-for-profit) usually have very high turn-over, dissatisfaction, and unhappiness. Employees often feel like they have no voice.

On the other hand, godly organizations make sure that employees have channels for communicating with leadership. Senior leaders seek input from all sources with a defined group of decision-makers, preferably a board of high-quality individuals. Roles and hierarchy are clear, and job and performance evaluation regularly occur. Members of the organization have a strong sense of purpose and a spirit of cooperation combined with brotherhood and goal setting. This fosters open communication that drives the organization and motivates the employees.

In God-honoring organizations, leaders also have opportunities to teach their employees scriptural principles about respect for God and one another. God's law, especially the Golden Rule, should not only characterize the personal behavior of a leader but the group decisions of the company. This responsibility requires godly leaders to understand the authority structures modeled in Scripture. The New Testament reveals the mutual commitment between employers and employees:

> Slaves, be obedient to your human masters with fear and
> trembling, in sincerity of heart, as to Christ, not only when
> being watched, as currying favor, but as slaves of Christ,
> doing the will of God from the heart, willingly serving the
> Lord and not human beings, knowing that each will be re-
> warded by the Lord for whatever good he does, whether he
> is slave or free. Masters, act in the same way toward them,
> and stop bullying, knowing that both they and you have a
> Master in heaven and that with Him there is no partiality.[2]

When employers and employees both sincerely seek to do the will of God from the heart, this reflects God's character. Divine character is affirmed as managers show principled concern for all, train groups of employees, mentor existing and new leaders, and disciple employees, as explained in the remaining sections of this chapter. Moreover, as explained throughout Section 3, concern for employees fosters a culture of respect for godly principles (as explained in Section 4 of this book) and fosters improvement in key performance indicators, as explained in Section 5 and Appendix 3.

Listening to Employees While Showing Principled Concern for All

In Colossians 4:1, Paul reiterates the obligation of the employer to treat their employees with dignity and respect: "Masters, treat your slaves justly and fairly, realizing that you too have a Master in heaven." Of course, employees are not slaves, but Biblical teachings about master-servant relationships should apply in all organizations that seek to respect the Lordship of Christ.

A Christian company will reflect justice and fairness because the leaders' model is Jesus Christ: "We love because He first loved us."[3] Love involves obeying principles that Jesus commanded (John 14:15, 21). Love also entails showing sensitivity to others' needs and emotions. A godly organization will do what it takes to make love the cornerstone of their company culture while balancing love with justice. A caring culture forms when an organization's members exercise principled concern for one another.

Employers and employees must exhibit humility toward one another. Christian leaders must be humble and aware of their own failures in order to correctly identify others' flaws, according to Jesus in Mathew 7:4-5: "How can you say to your brother, 'Let me remove that splinter from your eye,' while the wooden beam is in your eye? You hypocrite, remove the wooden beam from your eye first; then you will see clearly to remove the splinter from your brother's eye."

Business leaders may find it more difficult when expected to act with love and humility toward others in real-life situations. High-stress, high-stake situations tend to make anyone grow irritable or uncaring. We can learn much when watching how Christian-led companies maintain cultures of love and justice in the midst of marketplace pressures.

HP's company culture of principled concern attracted qualified tradesmen in areas where similar companies did not. The company's culture also contributed to its employee loyalty, dedication, and commitment to the organization. It helped ensure the long-term spiritual and financial health of the organization.

At HP, and other companies studied for this book, leaders show an active commitment to serving the whole person. Some companies pay extraordinary medical costs not covered by insurance. Some businesses make loans to employees. Others pay for addiction recovery programs based on spiritual ideals that insurance companies and the government refuse to support. While many Christian-led companies encourage employees to have support systems through their families and churches, leaders consistently maintain programs to fill gaps when employees need help getting back on their feet.

Training Groups of Employees

Jesus modeled training at different levels. He chose and trained 70 people and sent them out to do preparatory evangelism in the towns he would visit (Luke 10:1). Then he mentored 12 men for three years. He "appointed twelve, that they might be with him and that he might send them out to preach ..." (Mark 3:14). Then Jesus drew Peter, James, and John into a more protracted leadership development as He discipled them to be the first great leaders of the church. See, for example, Mark 5:37, Matthew 17:1-2, and Mark 14:33. From Jesus' examples we see a broad circle for training, a more narrow circle for mentoring, and a smaller circle for in-depth discipleship.

Training focuses on teaching skills or types of behavior that build productivity, capacity, or performance (related to job). A good example is Turbocam's "Character First Training." This training differs from the deeper mentoring and discipleship relationships described in the following sections of this chapter.

Broad training programs often present opportunities for the senior leadership team to pass on their expertise and the values of the company. At the very least, training programs build unity and cohesion within the company. Trainers can also communicate a culture of concern. Trainees may begin asking: "Why do you care about me? Where do these principles come from? Where do you get your strength? Why are you always so positive? Why are you always smiling and happy?" Through the leaders, trainees see the law of Christ modeled. Without preaching, trainers can carry each other's burdens and, in this way, fulfill the law of Christ (Gal. 6:22).

Trainers cannot, however, apply Christ's law through their own strength or wisdom. The Holy Spirit must lead trainers as they apply God's law in making decisions. They must have a mature ability to listen and discern the leading of the Spirit. A Spirit-led trainer is characterized by a thirst for righteousness. These leaders seek opportunities to fellowship with others, thank God, and ask again for His protection and care for the entire company and the families of all assembled.

Love of divine law and love of employees have guided training programs at HP Communications and many successful organizations. Recognizing and following God's law is a wise business move and always bears long-term fruit, as seen in the training program examples at Turbocam and HP.

Turbocam emphasizes the whole person throughout the training process. Training focuses on building servant leaders and is led by the head of Organization Development. Everyone in the company goes through a "Character First" program. Each month a company leader presents a new character trait. During the ensuing month, each supervisor discusses the character trait with his own team members who dialogue about how to apply the character trait, emphasizing its importance to Turbocam and their customers. This training program is supplemented by mentoring and the discipling of small groups of potential leaders.

HP Communications training teaches character and competency as employees are trained to do aerial and in-ground placement of fiber optic cable and the related work required to build telecommunications networks. The work is difficult, often physically draining, and can be dangerous. The company developed the HP training center to respond to these challenges and dedicated it to God. As described earlier, the company initially intended it to build a qualified employee pool, but the program developed into much more.

HP took more than 10 years of planning to build the training center, but along the way, leaders discussed and nurtured their dream of a training facility, answering questions of where to put it, what would it look like, what were the training protocols, etc. They finally decided to locate the training center at the corporate headquarters. They set a date, assembled the company, and held a dedication for the training center, which presented another opportunity to rededicate HP to God. The training center became a hub where they equipped trainers to be role models, strengthening and unifying their company from the center.

Identifying and Mentoring Existing and New Leaders

The grid at http://www.reflectinggod.info/7LightSources/ explains how a mentor compares to a counselor, consultant, chaplain, coach (trainer), or other type of business adviser. The mentor is more focused on individual relationships than is the trainer and develops talents in a more holistic way through active engagement with assessing and encouraging refinement of talents and skills. Mentors often focus on developing the whole person as part of the succession planning process. The mentor may have a more general approach than a trainer because trainers tend to focus on development of specific skills.

When the mentor finds strength and courage in God and His principles, the mentoring process begins. This encourages joy of one-on-one relationships and the incredible opportunities it presents to us as Christians, whether we own a business or not. This model is the practical, real-life application of the Great Commission.

To enhance their understanding of mentoring and servant leadership, some leaders at Turbocam read and discuss a book by Jeremie Kubicek entitled, *Making Your Leadership Come Alive.* Kubicek personalizes people's understanding of servant leadership by asking questions like, "Who has had a positive impact on your life? What did they do for you?" He wants them to recognize that they are shaped by others who invested in them and realize they can do the same by serving others.

The mentorship dynamic between a mentor and a subordinate must be clear to allow efficient training. Servant leadership requires accountability since, ultimately, a quality job must be completed safely. At all times, the safety and value of human life must be paramount.

Mentorship at HP, Flow Motors, and Turbocam follow the pattern modeled by Jesus: life-on-life mentorship. Mentorship happens when two people meet on a regular basis, face life together, and learn from the experience. In these companies, the mentor is a leader who teaches their subordinates job skills and develops their character by modeling godly values. The next section offers concrete examples of actual training programs that have developed successfully.

HP Communications Inc. also models mentorship and discipleship. The company formed a central place to train linemen from all parts of the country. The training stresses safety and concern for each employee. Throughout the training, senior tradesmen rotate through the facility to teach and mentor, building a legacy of servant leadership through life-on-life mentorship. The training also includes leadership and team-building exercises to reinforce the concept "I am my brother's keeper." Trainers emphasize the idea that brotherhood and excellence are inexorably linked. Employees must work as a team to create an effective and unified company.

Flow Motors is another example of a company leading with a successful mentorship and discipleship model. At Flow Motors, mentoring takes place within the sales force and will be expanded to technicians. It happens in the context of the supervisor–employee relationship and career progression. The mentorship includes four stages. First are teacher-student relationships, where the manager teaches his subordinate how to do his job. Second is the coach–player relationship, where the manager coaches his subordinate on leveraging skills and applying company values in difficult situations. The third is the consultant–high-performer relationship, where the manager gives increased responsibility and authority to his subordinate to manage situations, providing guidance as needed. The fourth is the resource provider–all star player, where the manager provides resources to support his subordinate, who consistently executes well, makes good decisions, and takes effective action.

Turbocam is an example of a company where training led to Christian discipleship. At Turbocam, Mark, the senior organizational development leader, oversees a mentor learning community. Currently, he holds two classes of six staff members, all of whom either are or will be in leadership. Each class meets every other week for six months. The focus is on learning how to be a servant leader in the context of real-time business transactions and relationships. For example, when the mentees bring up a situation he is handling, Mark asks, "How do you apply company values to this situation?" The group discusses and thinks through the situation together.

Discipling Employees One-On-One

As the trainer's and mentor's involvement with the person being equipped grows, opportunities materialize to apply discipleship principles found in God's Word[4]. In the long run, that trainee becomes a trainer, and the protegee becomes the mentor, thereby repeating again and again the discipleship process modeled by Christ. Faithful discipleship multiplies servant leaders in a business, building a unified, God-fearing company.

Nonetheless, it is important to note that the depth and breadth of discipleship relationships will often extend beyond working hours and away from the business premises. Company leaders often need to work with pastors, priests, and chaplains to provide effective discipleship. Company leaders coordinate with good churches so that the church can provide spiritual care and oversight that company leaders may not be equipped or called to provide. Spiritual authorities can then teach what it means to apply the whole counsel of God (Acts 20:27) with oversight from the holy council of God (see, e.g., Psalm 89:7). God's Word and godly church leaders can then encourage Christ-like behaviors and attitudes as the person being discipled engages with people in churches, families, and other institutions apart from the business.

A company culture of principled concern is impossible without the discipleship model inspiring trainers, mentors, and disciplers.[5] The training relationship begins with imparting technical training, which can lead to a mentor and a subordinate forming a relationship that leads to discipleship.

Thus, over time, training and mentorship often matures into discipleship. As relationships go deeper, both the discipler and the person discipled can be mutually strengthened, both from a business and spiritual standpoint.[6] In the long run, this process is financially beneficial. From a human resource perspective, it reduces search and retraining costs.

Senior management is responsible for developing a system of training and mentorship that can lead to discipleship in an organization. Role models are integral at every level of an organization.

The process and necessity of discipleship is described in numerous places in Scripture. The first example, of course, is the model of Christ with his apostles, which shows how deeply discipleship reflects the purpose of God for relationships and organizations. We see how Christ is the Good Shepherd (e.g., in John 10) and how He embodies the best of what King David and other Biblical shepherds practiced, such as when David shepherded with integrity of heart and skillful hands (Psalm 78:72).

Discipleship examples from the Old Testament and the Gospels are seen throughout the New Testament. The apostle Peter exhorts leaders to exercise oversight, not for shameful selfish gain, but eagerly in order to provide an example for the flock. The reward is an unfading crown of glory. Peter goes on to explain that our earthly and immediate reward for humble servant leadership is grace.[7] In Titus 2, Christians are called to show themselves to be a model of a good works, and in teaching to show integrity and dignity. Other scriptural passages on mentorship to reflect and ponder include Proverbs 13:20 and 2 Timothy 2:1-26.

The natural outgrowth of those principles and others like the Golden Rule, as well as the proper work ethic, form the basis and foundation for the entire company. These principles, in turn, create a culture that fosters a solid mentoring and training program. Such a program nurtures unity within the organization. It also triggers healthy growth between members in the organization, as referenced in Proverbs 27:17 where it says, "as iron sharpens iron, so one person sharpens another." Such a program ultimately provides an opportunity for discipleship and spiritual unity.

The best practices from HP, Turbocam, and Flow Auto reveal an effective approach to management and discipleship, which we recommend to build a high-performing Kingdom company. Through life-on-life discipleship, leaders model and teach servant leadership and skills. This approach focuses on servant leaders making quality decisions and taking effective action in real-time business transactions and relationships. A company will thrive when its servant leaders develop servant leaders.

Conclusion

A diversified board of directors oversees managers who have a commitment to training and discipleship. Through the active evaluation of staff members, managers refine training programs that teach competency and character. With proper training, students are empowered to be effective managers. In this way, managers leverage training programs to build a spiritually essential enterprise.

At www.ReflectingGod.info/Survey, please indicate your level of agreement with the following five statements:

Quiz 7

My company has a clear understanding of the spiritual authority process.

not true 1 2 3 4 5 very true
○ ○ ○ ○ ○

The managers in my company listen to employees while showing principled concern for all

not true 1 2 3 4 5 very true
○ ○ ○ ○ ○

My company trains groups of employees to reflect timeless character principles.

not true 1 2 3 4 5 very true
○ ○ ○ ○ ○

My company identifies and mentors existing and new leaders.

not true 1 2 3 4 5 very true
○ ○ ○ ○ ○

My company provides an opportunity to disciple employees one-on-one.

not true 1 2 3 4 5 very true
○ ○ ○ ○ ○

---

[1] Matthew 22:35

[2] Ephesians 6:5-7

[3] 1 John 4:19

[4] For more information about biblical principles of discipleship, please see www.ReflectingGod.info/BiblicalDisciple.

[5] For descriptions of the roles of trainers, mentors, and disciplers (or disciple-makers), please see www.ReflectingGod.info/Glossary.

[6] Proverbs 27:17

[7] 1 Peter 5:1-5

Section 4

Ethics

Stewarding Time, Talent, Treasure, and Trust with Biblical Principles

Managing Staff with Biblical Principles

Managing Risk with Biblical Principles

Encouraging Peacemaking Based on Biblical Principles

SAINT AUGUSTINE WROTE EXTENSIVELY on the ranking of priorities and principles in his works on axiology. The Augustinian system of "graded absolutism" continues to inspire philosophers today as they define systems for making decisions. Christians in business can apply this wisdom as they establish and follow ranked lists of important principles and key priorities (management objectives). Chapter 8 summarizes key biblical principles about resource management and urges readers to develop ranked lists of priorities for stewarding time, talent, treasure, and trust. Chapter 9 offers principles for stewarding the most important resource in a business: the staff members. Chapter 10 suggests how businesses can assess and manage risks using biblical principles of risk management. Chapter 11 urges all business leaders to embrace biblical peacemaking as a way to foster peace and purity in relationships with others, themselves, and God.

Chapter 8

Stewarding Time, Talent, Treasure, and Trust with Biblical Principles

WHILE STILL IN HIS 20S, Jerry bought a small manufacturing business founded years earlier by his dad. Jerry's parents had encouraged him to get involved in the business from a young age, so Jerry was equipped with wisdom about how he could use resources for a focused purpose and share that purpose with trained managers with solid core values. The business prospered under Jerry's leadership.

As he watched his net worth grow substantially, Jerry realized that he could go "from success to significance" by selling the business and using much of the wealth to fund select charities. Jerry's advisers showed him how he could enjoy a secure retirement while giving more than $2,000,000 per year to underwrite Christian ministries. This plan inspired Jerry. He worked with a team of professionals to sell the business through a leveraged transaction financed by a large bank. At the closing of the sale, Jerry received tens of millions of dollars, plus a lucrative employment contract with the acquiring company. Advisers helped Jerry invest the money in leveraged real estate and various margined investments. Jerry made substantial commitments to use his big, new salary to fund charities.

Then the Great Recession caused stock and real estate values to fall, resulting in too little investment income to service debt. Jerry was forced to sell investments while fighting off lawsuits from banks and other creditors. The acquiring company refused to respect Jerry's commitment to treating employees well, honoring commitments, and delivering value to customers. Jerry found it impossible to work under the new management team and resigned. Without cash flow to honor commitments and weather the recession, Jerry's portfolios were decimated and his philanthropic plans thwarted. What went wrong?

Like too many business people, Jerry built substantial business value by following Christian stewardship principles, but then sold to a buyer who did not share those principles. The bankers encouraged a leveraged transaction despite Scripture cautioning against debt. The financial planners held themselves out as fiduciaries, but they made more money for themselves by encouraging Jerry to acquire assets with borrowed funds. The M&A brokers maximized fees by helping Jerry sell his company to the highest bidder—without considering whether the business buyer had the same core values which Jerry and his father upheld when they built the business.

Stories like Jerry's are common in the business press. Consider Maytag, the manufacturer of washers and dryers trusted by everyday Americans for decades. Frederick Maytag focused on quality, service, teamwork, and other God-honoring values, building a sterling reputation. His employees belonged to 30 churches that formed the spiritual foundation of the town in Iowa where Maytag built his factory. Then the Maytag company was sold through a leveraged transaction to buyers who focused on maximizing profits instead of maintaining core values. A reputation built across decades was lost in a few years.[1]

This rapid loss of wealth and reputation occurs when business owners sell to buyers who lack character. Usually the buyers will appear to have character and will claim to uphold scriptural values, but across time, variances from those values reveal otherwise: the buyers' convictions are in opposition to the teachings of Jesus. Too often the seller learns too late that the buyers have not studied the words of Christ and His prophets concerning stewardship of time, talent, treasure, and trust. The dangers are usually evident to any discerning observer who evaluates the acquiring company by examining its calendars (showing use of time), job descriptions (showing use of skills), bank statements (showing use of treasure or cash flow), and satisfaction surveys (showing treatment of trusting relationships).

Owners prosper because they know their businesses well, but they may not know the business of transferring a company to successor owners and managers. Finding successors with the same core values is difficult, so sellers compromise ideals or engage in wishful thinking when selling to a buyer who may have more cash than character. When the owner is offered millions of dollars to sell to a secular company, idolatry can cloud the decision-making process. Too often, businesses with God-honoring values are sold to companies run by managers who use time for secular ends, work according to job descriptions with secular purposes, and manage cash flow according to secular values, all while treating customers no better than secular companies would. These ends focus not on the Creator, but on position, possessions, and pleasure – man's creations.

Secular company leaders often intend to maintain quality, focus on service, and uphold other God-honoring values, but as Samuel Johnson observed, the road to hell is paved with good intentions. Secular companies may even borrow biblical ideas about stewarding time, talent, treasure, and trust. Although these ideals are revealed through common grace and general revelation, they seldom endure unless leaders know how Christ bestowed grace through special revelation. Unless leaders put trust in God's Word, they resort to empty rhetoric about core values, but fail to confront behaviors that undermine those values. In short, unless leaders know Christ as the source of divine truth, they may lack the confidence and conviction to maintain the core values required for trusting teamwork.[2]

When company leaders fail to reflect core values based on what God reveals about the character of Christ, God's light is obscured and sin festers in haunts of darkness (see Ps. 74:20). God's light can be maintained when God-fearing authority figures oversee healthy relationships. Otherwise leaders may focus on their own idols of power (position), money (possessions), and pleasure. Anyone within the company trying to focus on honoring God will often face strong peer pressure to quit using biblical language, turn a blind eye to greed, or tolerate bullying that is directed toward giving power or money to someone who does not respect God-honoring teamwork. A spiritual battle rages between employees who promote godly teamwork and those who seek personal idols.

Proper worship of the Creator provides fulfillment so that believers do not need to seek meaning through position, possessions, pleasure, or the power found in exerting control by pressuring peers or others. Reverent worship of the Creator begins with knowing God and His divine revelation. When someone seeks to follow God and enter into a personal relationship with Him through Christ, they can understand that He has given the believer resources to steward. Moreover, the Spirit of God helps the believer understand how divine revelation (e.g., Scripture) guides stewardship of assets.

I realize there's more to life than money. I also get joy from my possessions, position, and personal pleasures.

As suggested above, proper stewardship can be monitored by looking at use of time, skills, cash flow, and relationships. Scripture speaks about using all of our time for God's glory, but too often calendars show that Christians are not focused on building churches, families, churches, schools and other institutions that honor divine teachings and equip us to serve those whom God calls us to serve. God's Word also teaches how believers can discover their calling and pursue a job description with purpose. Too many resumes, however, show development of skills that exalt the individual but neglect strengthening communities that reflect God's character.

Scripture speaks more about money than many other topics, but too frequently, decisions about spending do not reflect biblical stewardship principles, as is evident from looking at checkbook registers or variances from budgets. The Bible also speaks often about stewarding the trust that people put in us, but how many church leaders receive negative reviews of the church campus when their employees, clients, and business partners are asked to assess faithfulness to Christian principles of business? In short, by looking at calendars, resumes, checkbooks, and satisfaction surveys, it is easy to see how Christians fail to honor God's teachings and reflect His light.

The following table summarizes biblical standards for stewardship as well as ways that believers can monitor their stewardship in practical ways. The goal is to guard against the idolatry that so easily compromises our wise use of God-given resources and undermines our reflection of God's creative character.

God-Given Resource	How to Steward this Resource	Where to Monitor Our Stewardship	Signs of Idolatry
Time	1 Cor. 10:31 – So whether you eat or drink or whatever you do, do it all for the glory of God.	Our calendars	Time spent on anything not glorifying God
Talents	Prov. 22:29 – Do you see a man skilled in his work? He will serve before kings; he will not serve before obscure men.	Our resumes	Projects pursued outside of our calling
Treasure	Matthew 6:20; 16:18 – But store up for yourselves treasures in heaven, where moth and rust do not destroy, and where thieves do not break in and steal.	Our checkbooks	Money spent that does not most effectively build the church.
Trust	Proverbs 15:1-2, 4 – Who may live on your holy hill? He whose walk is blameless and who does what is righteous, who speaks the truth from his heart.... who keeps his oath even when it hurts	Our client/ employee satisfaction surveys	Trust compromised by breached commitments

Scripture illuminates profound insights about using the time, talent, treasure, and trust God has given us. Where God's light is not reflected in our stewardship decisions, darkness grows and undermines unity in the body. Jesus reminds us,

Therefore, take heed that the light which is in you is not darkness. If then your whole body is full of light, having no part dark, the whole body will be full of light, as when the bright shining of a lamp gives you light. (Luke 11:33-36)

Christians should choose not to obscure light, permit darkness, and allow people in an organization to undermine stewardship through idolatrous behaviors. Idolatry compromises stewardship when immature or false Christians assume leadership roles in organizations without seeing how God's light shines through biblical stewardship principles. Too many leaders lack a biblical understanding about how stewardship principles can and should protect against the idolatry that undermines teamwork and obscures the path toward peace and prosperity.

Even when leaders have a mature understanding of stewardship, they are under constant pressure to form alliances with people who do not understand and pursue wise stewardship principles. Boards of Christian schools need to attract students, donors, and other resources, so Christian educational institutions routinely "go liberal." Owners of Christian businesses need expertise and capital, so the owners make commitments to generate cash; then, when revenues fall short of targets, owners justify protecting their own wealth by pressuring employees to work overtime instead of owning up to commitments.

Often budgets are prepared in reference to personal desires rather than stewardship principles. Even when budgets initially reflect objectives of a Spirit-led plan, team members tend to neglect commitments in budgets when a company lacks good internal controls to address budget variances. Regions or departments fight for resources, but managers do not know how to allocate resources or align incentives for resource development. When managers and workers are not aligned, people seek personal rather than corporate agendas, thereby compromising stewardship principles and undermining trust.

Teachings about stewardship become relevant when business leaders unite around a consistent plan and execute it with integrity. A wise leader develops a Spirit-led vision that is reflected through clear objectives, strategies, and tactics.[3] Objectives are carried out by employees with strategic initiatives based on each employee's purpose and calling. Employees have clear roles overseen by a manager or coordinator who sets clear goals. Employees and managers manage cash according to cash flow reports and manage time according to project management workflows. By coordinating team members with clear roles, goals, workflows, and cash flows, the manager or coordinator maintains trust.

Project Management Element	Resource to Steward	Relevant Biblical Teaching	Signs of Dysfunction
Roles	Talent	Ephesians 6:6 – Obey masters not only to win their favor when their eye is on you, but as slaves of Christ, doing the will of God from your heart.	Projects pursued outside of calling and apart from will of God
Goals/ Controls	Trust	In Donald Jacobs's book, *From Rubble to Rejoicing: A Study in Effective Christian Leadership Based on Nehemiah*, he refers to passages in Nehemiah when explaining how "a leader must assure that the planning gets done" (50).	Trust compromised through breached commitments to get work done
Cash Flow	Treasure	Luke 14:28 – Suppose one of you wants to build a tower. Won't you first sit down and estimate the cost to see if you have enough money to complete it?	Projects started without enough resources; people are spent because money cannot be spent.
Workflow	Time	Psalm 90:2 – Teach us to number our days, that we may gain a heart of wisdom.	Time spent on personal agendas instead of wise teamwork.

Leaders need to align staff members around a plan that coordinates the use of resources to achieve the corporate vision. A leader can use

roles, goals, controls, workflows, and cash flow summaries as tools to
align team members and reflect a Spirit-led vision. The leader must
heed wisdom from 1 Peter 4:2-6 and not let human desires interfere
with a planning process based on the will of God. The leader must guard
against idolatry. The leader must be ready to give an account to Him
who is ready to judge the living and the dead, looking beyond human
standards to develop a plan according to the Spirit.

Despite a leader's best efforts to address dysfunction in an organization, Isaiah 59:2-9 applies too often: iniquities separate us from God,
lips speak falsely, no one calls for justice, and no one pleads a case with
integrity. Team members may neglect their commitments, but then,
"[t]hey rely on empty arguments, they utter lies; the way of peace they
do not know. They have turned them into crooked roads; so justice is
far from us, and righteousness does not reach us. We look for light, but
all is darkness; for brightness, but we walk in deep shadows."

Roles, goals, controls, workflows and cash flow statements may be
based on human project management standards that deviate too much
from a Spirit-led vision. Even when the Spirit is guiding the planning
and the project management, employees may consider their deviations
from the managers too small to be of concern. Commitments are neglected, blame is shifted, excuses are proffered, and plans are undermined. Small sins have big impact. As C. S. Lewis writes in the
Screwtape Letters, "It does not matter how small the sins are provided
that their cumulative effect is to edge the man away from the Light."

To gain and maintain the abundant life Jesus promises (John
10:10), Christians should live in such a way that everything flows from
their relationship with God and be aligned with His will, commands,
and principles. If they are not accomplishing God's purposes in business and stewarding His resources according to the light of Scripture,
they are failing. To restore commitment to the abundant life, they need
to pray for wisdom to steward the abundant resources He gives them.

Conclusion

Jerry, the business owner in the introduction, built substantial business value by following Christian stewardship principles before selling to a buyer that did not respect what Scripture teaches. In retrospect, Jerry saw how the buyer's rhetoric about core values lacked substance. Moreover, Jerry sees how his advisers appealed to his pride and greed while encouraging the investment of sales proceeds in leveraged investments that lacked solid economic substance.

Had Jerry investigated his buyers and his business succession advisers more carefully, he would have seen the many signs of idolatry summarized in this chapter. He also might have seen how the idolatry would result in much pain, challenging his ability to maintain God-honoring relationships. Had Jerry worked with consultants to find a seller focused on developing a Spirit-led plan, he could have exercised greater discernment when looking for a Spirit-led buyer and bankers. As a result, Jerry might have protected his wealth and his legacy. More important, Jerry could have consistently maintained the Spirit-led and Christ-centered values that he successfully reflected for decades before.

At www.ReflectingGod.info/Survey, please indicate your level of agreement with the following five statements:

My calendar shows that I have set aside regular time for activities that
glorify God.

not true   1   2   3   4   5 *very true*
○   ○   ○   ○   ○

My resume shows that I am using my talents to pursue my calling and
steward resources for God's glory.

not true   1   2   3   4   5 *very true*
○   ○   ○   ○   ○

My checkbook registers show that I am spending money to build
God-glorifying businesses, families, and churches.

not true   1   2   3   4   5 *very true*
○   ○   ○   ○   ○

My employee and client satisfaction surveys show that I am fulfilling
commitments and maintaining trust.

not true   1   2   3   4   5 *very true*
○   ○   ○   ○   ○

My pastor and/or spiritual advisory board would agree that I am guarding against idols that undermine stewardship.

not true   1   2   3   4   5 *very true*
○   ○   ○   ○   ○

[1] www.ReflectingGod.info/Maytag.

[2] See: Kouzes, James M. and Barry Z. Posner. *Credibility: How Leaders Gain and Lose It, Why People Demand It.* Rev. ed. (San Francisco: Jossey-Bass, 2004).

[3] See www.wotsmost.com/

Chapter 9

Managing Staff with Biblical Principles

HP COMMUNICATIONS INC. was formed shortly after its founders discussed forming a new company owned by and dedicated to God as the ultimate authority. Early on, a small but committed group of employees assembled in a small retreat house and prayerfully dedicated the company to God, begging with complete abandon for His care and protection. Nick Goldmann led a small group that prayed for the strength to be a light in the darkness of the telecom business. The industry tended to be difficult, uncaring and sometimes brutal, but HP would attempt to be a stark contrast to those other companies. The employees asked the Holy Spirit to fortify, guide and strengthen them.

Senior leaders then met and agreed that employees should be stakeholders and partners in the enterprise and be given every opportunity to influence decisions that affected them and make full use of their natural, God-given talents. They also agreed that God should and would be the ultimate Director. Now came the hard work of implementation and daily commitment. They leadership team knew there would be many challenges ahead.

Identifying the Issues Faced by Nick

Nick loved the lineman trade and the brotherhood he had experienced in it and was unclear on how he should proceed. The trade was not known for the spiritual treatment of its workers, yet, Nick was a devoutly spiritual man and yearned for a way to bring that to the workplace. The work of a lineman could be a dangerous, difficult one, and often companies cared little for safety and training, which often led to accidents and unnecessary risks. The trade was also filled with problems from drug and alcohol abuse to an "every man for himself" attitude. Companies were extremely profit- and results-oriented, which led to poor treatment of subordinates and employees. These realities tended to create a nomadic group of linemen moving from company to company with no real home.

Nick and his managers had a commitment to learning and applying management principles like those in Section 3 of this book. Nick's leadership team also wanted to experience outcomes that would allow God's blessings to extend beyond shareholders to employees, customers, and the community, as described in Section 5 of this book regarding the Quadruple Bottom Line. The challenge, however, was to explain core principles to linemen and other staff members who might not understand management philosophies or have much involvement with shareholders, customers, or the community. The HP leadership needed to present ethical precepts that all employees could embrace with passion. Therefore, the leaders prayerfully focused on the following principles with leading from the Holy Spirit.

The company's foundational spiritual principles were those that all employees would know. All employees would recognize the principle that success begins with a prayerful relationship with God. Most employees would pursue an understanding of Godly values to form a foundation for healthy work, family, and community relationships.

Another foundational principle was that employees would maintain healthy vertical relationships or relationships with authorities such as God, pastors, or managers. Employees should respect and honor their supervisors. Likewise, managers should treat their employees with dignity, treasuring them as both a God-given resource and a person created in God's image.

Other foundational principles constitute the horizontal culture of brotherhood stemming from the Golden Rule, and these principles apply to all employees. Managers and leaders have a responsibility to train their subordinates by creating employee development processes. Employers nurture mentorship into godly discipleship.[1] Leaders also obey the Golden Rule by instituting employee care by providing health benefits, 401Ks, and other employee care systems. The Golden Rule applied to business does not stop there, however. It also should create a culture of teamwork and support within a business so each person desires to contribute to the whole team instead of just looking out for themselves.

These spiritual principles also apply to the company's Quadruple Bottom Line and its vision of benefiting each individual touched by its business. Business leaders should seek to involve their employees in the goals of the company through training and team building. They can also recognize employees' efforts by celebrating them through annual events. Customers should experience extraordinary customer service at a godly company driven by the Golden Rule. The company should also guarantee benefits to its shareholders and vendors as well. Finally, the company should be a nurturing community of families and churches. Every person the company affects should experience the benefits of scriptural principles.

The above principles, when encouraged in the hearts and mind, inspire a Spirit-led corporate culture. Commitment to the Golden Rule inspires actions that foster healthy teamwork and contribute to practical outcomes benefiting employees, customers, shareholders, and the community.

Upon entering most telecom companies, a person can quickly discern if spiritual principles are in practice. The unspiritual companies exemplify many negative similarities. Employees notice unreasonable authoritarian rules, lack of constructive guidance, and pervasive disrespect for managers. Opinions and input are suppressed, and there is little or no uplifting encouragement. Isolation and mistrust abound, communication is discouraged, and time off with family is frowned upon.

On the other hand, Nick dreamed of a situation at HP where employees had the opportunity to give input, suggestions, and opinion about how best to accomplish the mission and goals of the organization. He yearned for a place where management encouraged educational opportunities and frequently held employee training and departmental brainstorming sessions. He envisioned an environment where clear policies would be in place that foster positive, uplifting communications between staff members, vendors and clients and where management acknowledged religious holidays and family time.

The question is, practically, how does a company institute those principles? Do they make sense? Do they work? Nick wondered and prayed for an answer to how this might happen.

Clarifying Relevant Biblical Principles

One of most important guiding principles is "The Golden Rule": "You shall love your neighbor as yourself."[2] When we treat both employees and subordinates in the way we would like to be treated, the internal environment improves, and profound and drastic changes occur.

All of us want to believe we matter to the organization where we spend a good portion of our lives and commit to contributing to its mission. Healthy and spiritually grounded companies give opportunities for employees to influence decisions and the environment that affects them. They are given an opportunity to give input, suggestions, and opinions on how best to accomplish the mission and goals of the organization. Each employee has a unique insight and perspective to the operation of the company and can be a valuable asset. They should be treated as such, just as leadership would like to be treated, according to, "Do to others whatever you would have them do to you."[3]

Going a step farther, a company can actually help and encourage employees to discover, develop, and use their natural gifts on the job by being open to suggestion and asking for input. Many times, employees have hidden or unknown talents or gifts that management is unaware because it has failed to ask or get to know the staff that is the lifeblood of the organization. When management partners with and cultivates those gifts, everyone involved is benefitted. Listening to employees enhances innovation, productivity, and the health of the organization. Golden Rule is a guiding principle that will strengthen a company committed to God's principles: "Each one of you has received a special grace, so, like good stewards responsible for all these varied graces of God, put it at the service of others."[4]

Applying the Principles to the Facts Faced by Nick

As it related to employees and staff, Nick and his colleagues agreed that principles laid out by the Lord would guide the organization and that the company would be dedicated to Him. The men discussed their previous bad experiences with other organizations and decided the guiding rule would be that they would treat employees like they themselves would like to be treated, according to Jesus' words: "You shall love the Lord, your God, with all your heart, with all your soul, and with all your mind. This is the greatest and the first commandment. The second is like it: You shall love your neighbor as yourself. The whole law and the prophets depend on these two commandments."[5]

Despite the fact that these types of benefits were mostly unheard of in the construction industry, and that there would be higher cost and administrative burden, they agreed that their company would offer health insurance to employees, establish a retirement plan, encourage training, and emphasize safety programs. They would train and mentor the young men in the trade and offer advancement opportunities within the company, always taking safety very seriously. Instead of using harsh criticism and anger, they would use the tools of respect and consideration. They would mentor quality employees from inside the company and take a long-term view of human resources.

Finally, they agreed that when there were difficult times, the first questions would always be "What would Christ have us do?" and "What would Christ do under the same circumstances?"

The principles expressed a servant's heart, a pursuit of excellence, and attaining complete *customer satisfaction*. The leadership, however, consciously decided to be subtle, yet demonstrative, and let the actions of the company and its employees reflect God's character and principles rather than directly attribute His name in the mission statement. The senior leaders would lead by example rather than platitudes.

MISSION STATEMENT

HP Communications is a communications construction company committed to quality, efficiency, service and the highest standards of workmanship. Each of the many experienced craftsmen and members of the HP team make a personal commitment to excellence and customer satisfaction.

We at HP are problem solvers. We're not satisfied with just completing the job, we will design and build the best system to suit our customers needs. If problems are encountered, we will develop the best solution to remedy them.

Quality service and timely completion is what we strive for, every single day for each of our customers. The pursuit of excellence is at the core of everything we do at HP.

The HP team has a diverse array of very talented individuals that include journeymen linemen, splicers and maintenance technicians. The HP team also includes experts in the field of project management, administration, finance and law, all dedicated to giving our customers complete satisfaction.

This attitude started at the top of the organization and permeated every aspect of the company, creating an environment where the free exercise of religion could take place without coercion. Instead of promoting religion, the leadership is committed to practicing genuine humility in order to attract others to faith. Not surprisingly, this environment has led to many conversions within the organization.

Nick and his senior team believed that employee benefits were not only spiritually sound, they made good business sense. While health insurance, a pension plan, and disability insurance may be expensive for the company initially, they exhibit a care and concern for employees and also help attract and retain the best qualified talent. From a long-term perspective, the cost of training self-motivated employees results in loyalty and quality benefits that far outweigh the short-term costs.

Nick and his senior team also decided that educational opportunities, and departmental brainstorming sessions were also great tools to foster and develop the gifts and talents of the employee. If the organization cannot afford to pay for subsidizing educational opportunities, the company allows flexible work schedules to encourage the employee to advance their education. The company would have productive and well-structured departmental and companywide meetings to discuss how employees might be more productive and efficient, allowing an employee to exhibit talents while giving all participants a sense of belonging and ownership.

Regular training is another great tool used by HP to help the employee develop on-the-job competence, character, and confidence. HP uses cross-training within departments, which gives an appreciation for what others do in the work place and fosters mutual respect and admiration for fellow employees, as well as helping create shared goals. It also has very positive team building aspects and enhances communication. The end result is a horizontally cross-functional team which fosters healthy competition and oneness.

Every Monday morning Nick or a senior manager holds a company-wide training meeting for all tradesmen and field personnel. It is a great opportunity for the trainer and the trained to develop mutual respect, exchange ideas, and build and develop the long-term project of a positive corporate culture. It also gives an opportunity for company legends and champions of safety, leadership, and humility to be passed through the ranks, building a spiritually positive verbal tradition and culture.

Leadership also agreed that another essential ingredient is putting policies in place that ensure and foster uplifting communications between staff members, vendors and clients. One of the most important places to start is with e-mail, texting, and phone conversations. Everyone understands that e-mail and text, while efficient, can be easily misinterpreted and misunderstood. They can never replace the purity and value of face-to-face communication. All non-verbal communications should have the utmost tone of respect and acknowledgement of the dignity of the receiver of that communication. They established clear and consistent guidelines concerning communication and dispute resolution processes as described more fully in Chapter 9, "Ethical Relationship Principles."

One of the most important aspects of a manager's function may be resolving conflicts and disputes, which is essential to the unity and peace within an organization. All conflict resolution should be guided by Matthew 18:15-16:

> If your brother sins [against you], go and tell him his fault between you and him alone. If he listens to you, you have won over your brother. If he does not listen, take one or two others along with you, so that every fact may be established on the testimony of two or three witnesses. If he refuses to listen to them, tell the church. If he refuses to listen

even to the church, then treat him as you would a Gentile or a tax collector.

By far, sitting down face-to-face with your brother is always the preferred form of communication, followed by a phone conversation and finally, an e-mail, text, or letter.

Time off and an acknowledgment of religious holidays was also an important ingredient to the plan at HP. Nick and his team knew that can and does have a tremendous positive impact on an organization. They agreed that encouraging family time and celebration of religious holidays not only honors God and inspires the employee but also demonstrates that the leadership seriously values honoring God and practicing one's faith. It is not just lip-service, walking the talk is an essential part of leadership and creates a healthy spiritual environment within the work place. When the organization supports and fosters family time, the employee can tell that the organization has its corporate priorities in order: God, family, and work. HP has gone and continues to go to incredible lengths to support and be flexible with employees.

The annual Christmas extravaganza is just one great example. The company gives away literally millions of dollars in bonuses that night, and thousands in gifts and raffles that bring excitement to all attendees. Employees and their families are flown in from all over the US to a luxury hotel for an entire weekend of celebration. Nick and senior staff spend the entire night going from table to table in a room filled with more than 2,000 people, thanking staff and greeting family members. Needless to say, employees are truly grateful, and there is no shortage of joy and recognition of the birth of our Lord expressed.

Benefits of Implementing and Committing to Godly Staff Management Principles

As of this writing, HP has stayed true to the founding principles and flourished with more than 700 employees and with a true brotherhood and care for its employees, vendors, and customers. The brotherhood and commitment to excellence is pervasive throughout the organization. A tour of the corporate headquarters is all that is needed to confirm the spirit of the organization. Each department glows with gratitude, competence, and determination to excel. Employees are happy and content. Industry wide, HP is known to have the best training, employee benefits, and true concern for staff. There is no shortage of resumes and applications, trade professionals are lined up to be hired, and turnover is almost non-existent. The company as a whole has completed projects that other firms complained couldn't be accomplished and wouldn't dare attempt. Their standing in the telecom construction industry is unparalleled with both competitors and customers. It is known throughout the trade that if you have a tough job, HP is the place to go. In short, they have accomplished the truly miraculous time and time again through the application and commitment to biblical principles.

Conclusion

The backbone of any organization is the staff. Managing staff and providing leadership in an organization is sometimes overlooked but is essential to an effective, efficient organization. Many organizations reflect sound godly principles to the outside world of customers, vendors, other business associates and sometimes even competitors. They fall short, however, in the treatment of its own employees. In short, many companies practice sound principles externally but forget the importance of practicing them internally. The fruit of practicing sound staff management principles is bountiful and, yet, many organizations leave it out or give it less than its due. In many ways, the internal management principles are the spiritual engine to the organization and determine the long-term success of the organization. Will the company pull together in the difficult times? Will staff go the extra mile when needed? Will they stay for the long haul? With the proper God-inspired management tools, companies will flourish and answer those questions with a resounding "Yes!"

While HP Communications is not entirely unique, they are extraordinary. Most organizations can only dream of what HP has done, but they have certainly not done it alone. Nick, in particular, has availed himself of many mentors, collaborators, and outside experts over the years. The company does not hesitate to take suggestions and advice from qualified and trusted people outside the organization and process it internally with senior staff. Nick has said many times that has been an invaluable piece to the management puzzle, advice which leads directly to the topic in Chapter 10: Managing Risk with Biblical Principles.

At www.ReflectingGod.info/Survey, please indicate your level of agreement with the following five statements:

Quiz 9

My company gives opportunities to people to influence decisions that affect them.

not true   1   2   3   4   5   *very true*
          ◯   ◯   ◯   ◯   ◯

My company helps each staff member discover, develop, and use his/her natural gifts on the job

not true   1   2   3   4   5   *very true*
          ◯   ◯   ◯   ◯   ◯

My company provides training to help all staff members develop their competence and character.

not true   1   2   3   4   5   *very true*
          ◯   ◯   ◯   ◯   ◯

My company has e-mail policies in place to help ensure positive communications with staff members, vendors, and clients.

not true   1   2   3   4   5   *very true*
          ◯   ◯   ◯   ◯   ◯

My company respects and honors employees with time off and encourages family time and celebration of religious holidays.

not true   1   2   3   4   5   *very true*
          ◯   ◯   ◯   ◯   ◯

---

[1] For descriptions of the roles of trainers, mentors, and disciplers (or disciple-makers), please see www.ReflectingGod.info/Glossary.

[2] Leviticus 19:18.

[3] Matthew 7:12

[4] 1 Peter 4:10

[5] Matthew 22:35

Chapter 10

Managing Risk with Biblical Principles

CALEDONIAN BANK, an established institution with a 44-year history, filed for bankruptcy after the Securities Exchange Commission (SEC) alleged non-compliance with securities laws. The government froze the assets of more than 1500 customers, resulting in massive withdrawal requests from depositors. The SEC later softened initial accusations, but bank officers had too little time to show why they believed they were exempt from the regulations that led to the SEC claims. District Judge William Pauley III at the Southern District of New York slammed the U.S. securities regulators for how the freezing order against Caledonian affected the bank and its depositors.

In the published testimony, the judge asked the SEC lawyer, "The bank collapsed because of your actions, didn't it?"

"Yes, your honor," the lawyer responded.

"It's stunning," the judge replied. "It's incredible government overreach."[1]

Many honest citizens are surprised to see how easy it is to unknowingly violate regulations or fall victim to unfounded accusations from regulators. Complex regulations like those promulgated by the SEC are also found in a myriad of other government agencies, including OSHA,

NLRB, DOL, FINRA, CFPB, CFTC, FTC, and the IRS. These abbreviations are not equally well-known and regulations promulgated by these organizations may be even more obscure or arcane. Rules that may be known only to a few rule-makers may be the basis for cease and desist orders, lawsuits, or other government sanctions against businesses that have no awareness of their infractions until too late.

Government attacks on businesses are often most troublesome when religious expression is curtailed. Too often the DOJ and local judicial bodies take action against businesses for alleged violations of rules regarding religious discrimination when a manager affirms the role of prayer, Bible study, chaplaincy, or other religious practices in the workplace. Addressing how these regulations can undermine anyone, Ben Carson commented in his speech at the National Prayer Breakfast that "our taxation system [is] so complex – there is no one who can possibly comply with every jot and tittle of our tax [system]. If I wanted to get you, or you, I could get you on a tax issue. That doesn't make any sense."[2]

A Christian is called to respect the government and its laws.[3] Traditionally, American citizens could know basic laws and have confidence that courts would adjudicate fairly. Now growing regulatory risks weigh on the minds of business leaders more than other routine risks, and business leaders often fear that administrative courts will not adjudicate matters efficiently and effectively. This chapter seeks to help business owners understand regulatory risks along with the traditional risks keeping business owners awake at night. The following paragraphs explain risks related to 1) administrative regulations, 2) lawsuits, 3) hazards covered by insurance carriers, and 4) bad cash flow planning.

Managing Administrative Risks

When America was founded, a minimalist government gave maximum freedom to families and religious institutions (e.g., churches) to establish their own governance, often according to the laws of God. As government has grown from representing less than 10% of the GDP to representing nearly 40%, government regulations have also increased.[4] Now the risks of not complying with government regulations are some of the greatest risks faced by American businesses, especially if they lack the money and staffing to confirm compliance with regulations.

In 1983, Harvard University's legal historian Harold Berman wrote a brilliant book on how the evolution of legalistic regulations can destroy freedom. In *Law and Revolution*, Berman blames a quiet but relentless legal revolution that has been underway for a century: the burgeoning dependency on administrative law. Voters have limited abilities to make decisions based on moral principles, so they grant growing decision-making powers to executive bureaucracies that write regulations and enforce them through administrative law courts. American life is increasingly governed by tax courts, workers compensation bureaus, health care agencies, and myriad other regulatory bodies. The self-government under God, as advocated in Scripture, is replaced with government control.[5]

In 1 Samuel 8:6-21, believers are cautioned that a secular king creates secular adjudication and secular regulations. Samuel was deeply troubled when he heard the people of Israel demand, "Give us a king to rule us!" Samuel prayed, and God answered, "Go ahead and do what they're asking. They are not rejecting you. They've rejected me as their King. From the day I brought them out of Egypt until this very day they've been behaving like this, leaving me for other gods. And now they're doing it to you. So let them have their own way. But warn them of what they're in for. Tell them the way kings operate, just what they're likely to get from a king."

So Samuel delivered God's warning to the people asking him for a king. He said, "This is the way the kind of king you're talking about operates. He'll take your sons and make soldiers of them—chariotry, cavalry, infantry, regimented in battalions and squadrons. He'll put some to forced labor on his farms, plowing and harvesting, and others to making either weapons of war or chariots in which he can ride in luxury. He'll put your daughters to work as beauticians and waitresses and cooks. He'll conscript your best fields, vineyards, and orchards and hand them over to his special friends. He'll tax your harvests and vintage to support his extensive bureaucracy. Your prize workers and best animals he'll take for his own use. He'll lay a tax on your flocks and you'll end up no better than slaves. The day will come when you will cry in desperation because of this king you so much want for yourselves. But don't expect God to answer."

But the people wouldn't listen to Samuel. "No!" they said. "We will have a king to rule us! Then we'll be just like all the other nations. Our king will rule us and lead us and fight our battles."

Samuel relayed what they had said to God. God told Samuel, "Do what they say. Make them a king."

American voters have responded to environmental, educational, financial and other social problems by voting to give government leaders more power. This power is used to implement regulations that drive up costs of operating businesses as company owners are increasingly expected to bear tax costs and regulatory compliance costs. As taxes and other expenses diminish profits, growing portions of the capital base and labor force are committed to generating wealth for the government. A typical American now works to pay taxes from January first until mid-April (Tax Freedom Day[6]). Thus, many business owners spend over four months of every year serving the secular government due to the added costs that businesses are expected to bear.

When paying taxes and other costs to secular authorities, Christian business owners can seldom focus on building churches, families, and other institutions that honor Christ. Nor do the regulations help a Christian steward the wealth provided by God. Too often people managing resources fail to heed biblical principles about the stewardship of wealth.[7]

How can a business avoid the excessive costs that accompany governmentally imposed regulations? Obviously, if business leaders apply self-government and behave responsibly, society will require fewer regulations, and asset owners will not have to spend as much time complying. If voters see that businesses are governing themselves responsibly, they will be less inclined to empower administrators to govern through regulation. Of course, many view this solution as too idealistic.

As a second solution, businesses can lower compliance costs or contest unfair regulations by going to court. Hobby Lobby gave American Christians an excellent example when they successfully fought medical insurance regulations all the way to the Supreme Court.[8] More recently, the Supreme Court ruled in favor of a Christian baker who refused to make a cake for a couple that did not affirm a biblical understanding of marriage.[9]

The third and possibly most reasonable solution is for company owners to work with compliance consultants to confront sinful attitudes that prevent them from respecting the law of the state. Business owners or managers can easily rationalize disobedience when laws seem too bureaucratic, oppressive, or misfocused. Good compliance consultants can help managers look for the good behind governmental regulations and respect how God put authorities in place for our good.[10] Wise consultants can often find efficient and cost-effective ways to honor regulations while cautioning business owners against sinful tendencies to rationalist disobedience.

The above three solutions help executives manage compliance costs. By hiring qualified consultants and training staff members, business leaders can address compliance concerns in practical ways. Nonetheless, leaders must also stay attuned to spiritual dynamics while guarding against laziness, greed, and other deadly sins that may darken the heart and contribute to an environment that disregards compliance standards. Sometimes the costs of complying with regulations consume all company profits. Until—or if—voters reduce costly regulations, businesses have the option of operating non-profit organizations that can be exempt from many taxes, religious discrimination rules, and other regulations. This solution is discussed more in Appendix 5 of this book.

Managing Lawsuit Risks

Christian business owners face large risks of losing God's wealth through lawsuits. Litigation costs Americans more than $100 billion per year. All types of businesses are vulnerable now that over 100 million cases are filed in US state courts every year.[11]

Traditionally, law was based on Judeo-Christian substantive, relational, and procedural principles. Judges sought to honor God by encouraging fairness without destroying relationships. That landscape has changed as litigants turn to secular judges rather than the religious leaders who once adjudicated many conflicts. When surveying "Christian companies," observers now find many unhealthy board-level conflicts over control, ownership, cash flow, and management. These problems fester year after year even when church elders are involved. When surveying people involved with conflicts in probate, bankruptcy, and family law, as well as superior and federal courts, 80% of the parties in business conflicts identify themselves as Christians while paying little attention to biblical cautions about litigation. 1 Corinthians 6:7 and related teachings about Christian peacemaking are ignored. What's the solution? Christians must turn to Scripture and church history.

Francis Schaeffer explains that there have been titanic shifts from the old medieval understanding of law to the modern philosophies of jurisprudence. He writes,

> Christian educators, Christian theologians, Christian lawyers—none of them blew the loud trumpets until we were a long, long way down the road toward a humanistically based culture. Where were the Christian lawyers during the crucial shift from forty years ago to just a few years ago? Surely the Christian lawyers should have seen the change taking place and stood on the wall and blown the trumpets loud and clear. A nonlawyer like myself has a right to feel somewhat let down because the Christian lawyers did not blow the trumpets clearly between, let us say, 1940 and 1970. [12]

Judges historically applied a God-centered understanding of law. The essay at www.ChristianConciliation.Services/History summarizes how Jewish congregations and Christian churches have maintained Christian judicial processes for 3,500 years. John Whitehead, author of the *Second American Revolution*, shows how the Biblical teachings applied in Christian courts later informed the common law of England and America. Whitehead writes,

> Blackstone, a Christian, believed that the fear of the Lord was the beginning of wisdom. Thus, he opened his Commentaries with a careful analysis of the law of God as revealed in the Bible. [13]

A classic Christian understanding of law emphasized restoring relationships. Legal procedures and substantive law emphasized fairness, keeping with the first commandment to honor God, the fifth commandment to respect authority, the seventh commandment to not slander, and the ninth commandment to not bear false witness. By respecting the Ten Commandments and the many relational precepts they embody, Christian judges could shine light into conflict, confront sin, and illuminate the path toward peace.

How can Christian justice be restored? Christians need to heed 1 Corinthians 6:7 and resolve matters through the church instead of through secular courts. Moreover, Christians need to hire attorneys who will be guided by the Spirit, focus on truth, and avoid tearing down relationships in the quest to shift blame or win a victory by compromising the truth. (For information about attorneys who provide legal defense for Christian businesses, please see the Christian Business Legal Defense Association website at www.ReflectingGod/CBLDA.)

Managing Hazards with Third-Party Insurance

Proverbs 27:12 says, "The prudent see danger and take refuge." It is reasonable for the business owner to think through the consequence of a fire, theft, or other casualty and then minimize the risk through property and casualty insurance. Likewise, a business owner needs to consider the risk of death or disability and then guard against these risks through life and health insurance. Risks can and should be shared among parties who are equipped to manage the risks.

Of course, many risks cannot be anticipated. James warns, "Now listen, you who say, 'Today or tomorrow we will go to this or that city, spend a year there, carry on business and make money.' Why, you do not even know what will happen tomorrow. What is your life? You are a mist that appears for a little while and then vanishes. Instead, you ought to say, 'If it is the Lord's will, we will live and do this or that.'"[14]

Given the uncertainty of life and business, it is not realistic to use insurance to protect against all risks. Business owners can also use a variety of asset protection trusts. For example, in California, company owners can allocate a substantial portion of their wealth to Private Retirement Trusts (PRTs) that can be protected from creditors.

A more thorough discussion of the concepts in this section exceeds the scope of this book. For more information, please contact the authors.

Managing Cash Flow Risks

An effective strategic plan should explain concepts with diagrams, checklists, narratives, and cash flow summaries. Perhaps the most important planning component is a year-by-year (or month-by-month) projection of revenues and expenses. Discussions about cash flow force decision makers to evaluate reasonable assumptions in light of strengths and opportunities, as well as weaknesses and threats.

Business owners and investors often get caught up in excitement over a proposed plan without evaluating the costs in clear cash flow projections. Jesus warned against this problem in Luke 14:28-30: "Suppose one of you wants to build a tower. Won't you first sit down and estimate the cost to see if you have enough money to complete it? For if you lay the foundation and are not able to finish it, everyone who sees it will ridicule you, saying, 'This person began to build and wasn't able to finish.'"

To avoid developing financial projections for an endeavor that might not be finished, Christians need an "abundance of counselors"; "Plans fail for lack of counsel, but with many advisers they succeed."[15]

Conclusion

Would following the above four risk management strategies have helped Caledonia Bank avoid its sudden and tragic demise? We cannot know for certain. We do know, however, that the hundreds of business owners consulted during the drafting of this book routinely use strategies from this chapter to minimize risks.

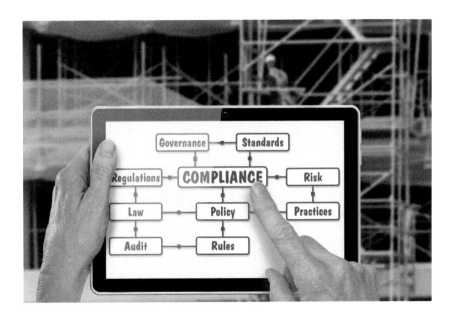

All of the above strategies presume prayerful awareness of threats, as well as awareness of the strength that proceeds from applying of God's Word. We need the Holy Spirit to warn us of our blind spots to hidden risks. We also need the full armor of God and the faithful support of mature and prayerful friends as we guard against compromising our own principles when facing risks as business managers.

The risks summarized in the above sections can seem daunting. We must prayerfully rely on the promises of Scripture: "For God has not given us a spirit of fear, but of power and of love and of a sound mind."[16]

At www.ReflectingGod.info/Survey, please indicate your level of agreement with the following five statements:

Quiz 10

My business hires compliance consultants and/or maintains compliance procedures to help confirm that we follow all government regulations, even when we disagree with them.

not true   1   2   3   4   5   very true

My business managers continually evaluate threats to the business and take protective actions (Prov. 27:12)

not true   1   2   3   4   5   very true

My business managers count costs through a careful budgeting process before undertaking new projects (Luke 14:28-30)

not true   1   2   3   4   5   very true

My strategic planning process does not presume upon tomorrow but instead develops realistic projections and contingency plans (Jas. 4:13-15)

not true   1   2   3   4   5   very true

My strategic planning process involves wise counselors who can help me assess risks and respond appropriately (Prov. 15:22)

not true   1   2   3   4   5   very true

[1] See www.ReflectingGod.info/CaledonianBank.

[2] See www.ReflectingGod.info/BenCarsonSpeech.

[3] e.g., 1 Peter 2:17 and Romans 13:1.

[4] www.usgovernmentspending.com/percent_gdp

[5] http://tinyurl.com/LawRevolutionBerman

[6] https://en.wikipedia.org/wiki/Tax_Freedom_Day

[7] See, e.g., Proverbs 27:23, Proverbs 21:20, and Proverbs 27:12

[8] https://en.wikipedia.org/wiki/Burwell_v._Hobby_Lobby_Stores,_Inc.

[9] https://www.christianitytoday.com/news/2018/june/jack-phillips-masterpiece-cakeshop-wins-supreme-court-free-.html

[10] Romans 13:4

[11] http://www.instituteforlegalreform.com/issues/lawsuit-abuse-impact

[12] Schaeffer, Francis. *A Christian Manifesto.* (Wheaton, Crossway Books, 1981) 47.

[13] Quoted in Devins, Neal. "Book Review of The Second American Revolution." *Faculty Publications.* (William & Mary Law School Scholarship Repository, 1985) 540.

[14] James 4:13-15

[15] Proverbs 15:22.

[16] 2 Timothy 1:7

Chapter 11

Encouraging Peacemaking Based on Biblical Principles

AS A COMMITTED CHRISTIAN, Tony sought to reflect God's light at work. He believed in maintaining a culture of peace at the office, but he was frequently bombarded by negative emails from a manager. Frequently, there was no clear solution to the negative statements in the emails. When Tony would ask for a personal meeting to clarify the source of the negativity, he would receive even more negative emails from managers who confused the facts, made wrong assumptions, copied other staff members in embarrassing ways, and otherwise sowed discord and doubts among staff members. The manager would criticize Tony and act like nobody else was at fault. He saw that the managers sending the emails were trying to undermine respect for Tony among other staff members even though Tony was simply trying to find a positive way to respond to the negative and false email exchanges.

Tony, wanting to help unite staff around God-honoring communication and planning principles, knew that he was being persecuted for righteousness' sake. Fellow staff members told Tony to disregard the emails because they were clearly based on the manager's need to protect his own turf while indulging in greed and pride, but Tony could not drop the matter: the disruptive email communications clearly hurt clients, damaged morale, and undermined respect for the manager who was supposed to be leading Tony's team. Tony asked his corporate chaplain what to do.

The chaplain reminded Tony that God is light. Tony's chaplain took Tony through passages in Scripture showing how light has come into the world and there will be no end to the increase in Christ's government and peace.[1] The chaplain could see why Tony encountered such resistance to his calm and well-intentioned efforts to promote peaceful teamwork based on truth. Simply put: people often prefer darkness where evil deeds can continue without confrontation.[2]

Within organizations, darkness is often evident in many types of communications. Since the mid-1990s, darkness has been documented extremely well in negative email exchanges. The author of a negative email may not have a positive agenda except protecting his own turf. Selfish motives often form the foundation for an altar where relationships are sacrificed to protect greedy, proud, envious, angry, lustful, lazy, and gluttonous desires or behaviors. Those observing the negative emails see that the seven deadly sins fester in darkness so long as the negative email sender refuses to have accountability to Christians who sincerely seek to shine light into darkness.

What should a Christian do to shine light into a dark environment? The process begins with the Christian maintaining a mature relationship with Christ (self-management) and encouraging company-wide commitment to ethical principles based on the character of Christ. God gives employees and employers opportunities to practice biblical behaviors when faced with conflict. In fact, peacemaking helps people see the wisdom of maintaining a mature personal relationship with Christ through biblical theology, Gospel teaching, preaching, and conversion, as well as a mature relationship with Christ's bride through membership covenants, leadership training, discipline, and evangelism. In short, teaching about peacemaking helps believers develop a more mature relationship with Christ and His Body, which is defined by the nine marks described at www.9Marks.org.

Apart from mature relationships with Christ and His church, selfish desires are undetected and/or unconfronted. Conflicts arise when selfish individuals seek to steal resources from co-workers or other shareholders in a business, whether it be money, donors, databases, buildings, fixtures, ideas, intellectual property, etc. Fortunately, churches around the world and across time have shown how Christians trained in biblical peacemaking can detect, confront, and resolve the conflicts before relationships are destroyed and teams are undermined.

Ken Sande, in his top-selling book, *The Peacemaker*, provides conflict resolution solutions that focus on glorifying God, getting the log out of your eye, gently restoring, and experiencing reconciliation. This chapter explains how these principles can apply in a business setting.

Glorify God

The sovereign Lord of the universe is also a personal God who allows conflict to grow each of His followers. Conflict provides an opportunity for the believer to reflect God's character, serve others, and trust in the biblical passages about peacemaking. Biblical conflict resolution honors God by revealing the reconciling love and power of God, as made evident through the teachings of Christ and the grace of the Holy Spirit. As we draw on this grace, follow Christ's example, and put God's teachings into practice, we find freedom from the self-centered decisions that make conflict worse. Through our words, attitudes, and actions, we have continual opportunities to sow in righteousness and raise a harvest of peace.[3] We glorify God by displaying his presence and power in our lives under all circumstances.[4]

Get the Log Out of Your Own Eye

When attacked, we find it natural to counterattack. For example, if we receive a negative email, our first tendency is to send a rebuttal. Such rebuttals tend to focus on one person's view of the facts without fully considering the emotions or perspective of others involved in the email exchange. The safer solution is simply to respond to negativity by stating very briefly that there is a lack of agreement about the contents of the communication and to ask for a personal meeting to resolve differences.

Mature people value opportunities to resolve conflicts promptly. To encourage peacemaking, Jesus teaches us to face up to our own contributions to a conflict before we focus on what others have done to hurt us.[5] When we overlook the minor offenses of others and honestly admit our own mistakes, our opponents will often respond in kind. When we ask others to explain how we hurt them, this frequently opens up opportunities for sincere discussion, negotiation, and reconciliation.

Gently Restore

Jesus cautioned believers that they must first look at their own sin. In Matthew 7:3-5, the peacemaker first gets the log out of his own eye before confronting the speck in his brother's eye. When the time comes for believers to confront someone, they must focus on restoration.[6]

Too often a manager defends harsh statements by saying that he is trying to teach a valuable lesson. The intentions may be good, but the person targeted by the harsh words may wonder whether principles could be taught more clearly and graciously. Scripture teaches that peacemaking should be based on divine commands, and Galatians 6:1 encourages gentle correction when God's righteous standard is violated. When others are blind to how they have failed to honor principles or commitments, we sometimes need to graciously show them their fault. If they refuse to respond appropriately, Jesus calls us to seek involvement from Spirit-led friends, church leaders, or other individuals who know how to apply biblical teachings about repentance and conflict resolution.

Go and Be Reconciled

Since the early church, pastors have encouraged church members to resolve differences among one another in the spirit of love before taking communion. Commentators interpret Matthew 5:24-26 as promoting reconciliation as one of the highest acts of worship on earth.[7] Jesus exhorts, "Therefore, if you are offering your gift at the altar and there remember that your brother has something against you, leave your gift there in front of the altar. First go and be reconciled to your brother; then come and offer your gift."

Peacemaking involves a commitment to restoring damaged relationships and seeking Spirit-led agreement. When we forgive others as Jesus has forgiven us, we can be open to wise counsel from the Holy Spirit, Scripture, and mature elders who know how to discern the leading of the Spirit.[8] Such divine guidance helps conflicted parties find solutions that satisfy others' interests as well as their own.[9] This opens the door to genuine peace.

The above can work great in a church or family focused on glorifying God, but can it work in a secular organization? How can an individual develop skills to promote peace in a company? These questions are answered by examining how a Christian can reflect God's covenant through peacemaking. The Christian can see how God describes His covenant in terms of peace[10] as the Christian affirms these elements of divine character: 1) His revelation, 2) His purpose, 3) His call to repentance and servant leadership, as well as 4) relationship principles that result in 5) His blessing on communities with Christians who seek to enjoy 6) His expanding influence.

The above six elements of the covenant can be reflected by Christians even in secular circumstances. Such peacemakers, however, will encounter bullies. The workplace is full of self-interested individuals who seek to quietly further their interests through greed, pride, gluttony, laziness, anger, and other deadly sins that they do not want exposed.

These selfish business people operate in the dark and are threatened by a Christian reflecting God's character. These dark actors avoid and attack people who encourage teamwork and transparency. The attacks are often subtle and disguised, such as when the self-interested person ends healthy discussions with *tu quoque* arguments, *ad hominem* attacks, or other defensive behaviors based on bad logic or selfish premises. Anyone reading C. S. Lewis' *Screwtape Letters* can see how the dark behaviors in the workplace are from the devil and contrary to God's light.

Peacemaking involves reflecting the character of Christ, the Prince of Peace. The Christian worker who reflects the divine character knows that he can trust in the promises of Scripture and not take attacks personally, even when the hurtful attacks are intended to silence him. The believer knows that he can prayerfully cast anxiety upon the Lord and seek help from trained peacemakers in the church. Christians can band together in praying for the full armor of God[11] while trusting that God will keep in perfect peace those whose minds are centered on Him.[12]

A peacemaker can reflect the six elements of Christ's covenantal character, as explained in the following six sections. Peacemaking is seen through divine revelation, purpose, hierarchical leadership, ethics, outcomes, and legacy principles. Peacemaking is also observed in the practical situations summarized in the following paragraphs.

1. Revelation: Glorify God by reflecting grace and truth.

At Flow Motors, the peacemaking process is based on truth and grace.[13] The process involves bringing the conflicting parties together in one room and offering them space for apology and forgiveness. A facilitator follows a five-step process that emphasizes a) teaching the peacemaking principles, b) coaching parties to follow principles, c) counseling individuals when they are not able to ask forgiveness, d) disciplining behaviors that contravene company standards, and e) terminating employees who are not encouraging a culture of peace. Each step of the process is based on God's revelation in Scripture.

Peacemaking based on truth and grace is complemented by Flow's belief system that people bring their whole self to work, not just the part related to their job function. Therefore, when a technician at one store displayed anger in a way that threatened another employee, part of the process was to understand why the technician acted this way. Don Flow and Josh Benoit, the HR leader at Flow, discovered that the employee was modeling his father's behavior. Instead of firing him—the pragmatic solution—Don and Josh asked if the employee had ever seen his father apologize. Don and Josh decided that the employee could potentially grow in humility and patience by learning to apologize. Their hope was that this would be a more formative experience in the life of the employee than the pragmatic (and punitive) response of termination.

2. Purpose: Sow wheat and guard against the weeds so that God is glorified.

In Matthew 13:24-30, Jesus tells a parable to differentiate between the purposes of heaven and the purposes of the enemy. An owner of a field purposed to sow good seed in his field, but weeds were mixed with the good wheat. "The servants asked the owner, 'Do you want us to go and pull them up?' 'No,' he answered, 'because while you are pulling the weeds, you may uproot the wheat with them. Let both grow together until the harvest.'" The owner knew that the harvesters would burn the weeds but gather the wheat for storing in the barn. This story shows how believers should focus on the good in the midst of dark behaviors since the outcome is already assured for those who do.

3. Hierarchical leadership: Humbly get the log out of your own eye.

Mature peacemakers with authority in organizations know how to confess their own wrongs and model a lifestyle of repentance. Asking forgiveness of God and others helps a leader model humility and practice servant leadership.

Leaders may agree to consult a corporate chaplain, a Christian consultant, or another trained peacemaker. Involving an outsider helps a leader spot and confront gossip, heated words, unresolved conflict, or other sinful behaviors that undermine peacemaking. Wise consultants know how to conduct 360-degree reviews to spot problems festering beneath the surface in seemingly healthy organizations. In this way, managers trained in peacemaking know how teachings from Matthew can apply to organizations that appear professional while letting managers avoid accountability for inappropriate behaviors. Mature peacemakers will not tolerate "whitewashed tombs," which on the outside look beautiful but on the inside are full of everything unclean.

4. Ethics: Promote peacemaking through gentle correction.

Scripture abounds with peacemaking principles, all of which focus on healthy relationships. Ken Sande, author of *The Peacemaker*, writes,

> Harmful conflict is usually triggered by unmet desires. "What causes fights and quarrels among you? Don't they come from your desires that battle within you? You want something but don't get it" (James 4:1-2). Even good desires can evolve into controlling demands or idols that can lead us to judge others and then avoid or punish them until we get what we want (see Luke 10:38-42). This progression often starts with minor differences, but before we know it, we're sliding down a slippery slope of conflict that can drop off in two directions.

In the diagram below and at www.ReflectingGod.info/SlipperySlope, Ken shows how a person caught in conflict may be tempted to practice three types of escape responses (peace-faking) or three types of attack responses (peace-breaking). Scripture shows how these six approaches to conflict resolution do not honor God. Instead, Christians are called to practice the six peacemaking responses illustrated in the six sections on the top of the slippery slope pictured here.

Peacemaking is summarized by the six sections in brown on the top of the slippery slope. If there are negative emails, angry calls, or other negative behaviors in an organization, the offended party can overlook the offense or try to discuss and negotiate a solution according to established peacemaking principles. Such principles include the well-established guidelines in Ken Sande's book as well as more contemporary standards, such as those involving email communications.[14]

When peacemaking processes are respected, healthy organizations appoint corporate chaplains, mature managers, or qualified board members to confront dark behaviors while encouraging reconciliation. The confrontation rewards good behaviors and punishes bad behaviors, consistent with the fifth element of the covenant, discussed below.

All twelve conflict resolution methodologies on the Slippery Slope afford opportunities to confront and correct the behaviors of others. Gentleness and respect should guide these efforts. Galatians 6:1, says, "if someone is caught in a sin, you who live by the Spirit should restore that person gently." Likewise, Paul reminds Timothy that, "opponents must be gently instructed, in the hope that God will grant them repentance leading them to a knowledge of the truth" (2 Tim. 2:25).

5. Outcomes: Understand the blessings of peacemaking and curses of peace breaking/peace-faking as parties seek to be reconciled.

In the Sermon on the Mount reminds. Jesus reminds believers, "Blessed are the peacemakers, for they shall be called sons of God."[15]

At Turbocam, Mark, a senior organizational development leader, acts as the peacemaker when people are in conflict. Mark starts by asking, "Are you willing to sit down with the other person and hear what they have to say and just listen? Are you willing to share your side of the story completely?" After each side has said everything they want to say and heard everything the other party has said, Mark assesses whether there is a willingness on both sides to do what it takes to reconcile.

In cases where an employee sounds off toward his supervisor, Turbocam gives him an opportunity to leave. During a "decision leave," the employee stays home without pay for three days to make his decision: will he admit what he did, own his behavior, and do what it takes to repair a broken relationship? If he is willing to own his behavior and forgive, he is reinstated. If not, he leaves.

An effective process is built on truth and grace and involves a cycle of confession, redemption, forgiveness, and restoration. The conflicting parties have an opportunity to take responsibility, forgive, and grow, which is a transformational and empowering process. Accepting responsibility and forgiving empowers people on both sides of a conflict to experience the blessings of peacemaking.

Disregarding basic peacemaking principles can easily lead to passive "peace-faking" or aggressive "peace-breaking." Experienced peacemakers can recount many sad stories of leaders being criticized behind their backs while a small group of dissidents gains confidence that its position is right. Subversives may criticize existing leaders or contractual agreements until authority is undermined.

Usually, those sowing discord refuse to practice Matthew 18 by involving mature church leaders in resolving the conflict. In violation of Matthew 5:24, they go to the communion altar on Sundays without first trying to resolve conflicts. Leaders of the organization being criticized lose respect in the community and spend precious resources fighting the attacks coming from inside and outside the organization. Leaders of dissident factions seek to build a new organization apart from mature spiritual leadership and focus on serving their own selfish interests. Countless people are hurt and the Christian witness is tarnished. This pattern is repeated often wherever church leaders fail to shine light into darkness by not practicing peacemaking principles to address problems on and off the church campus.

If peacemaking is not taught and encouraged by churches, conflicts spill into the court system. Then, according to Paul, Christians are defeated: "If any of you has a dispute with another, do you dare to take it before the ungodly for judgment instead of before the Lord's people? The very fact that you have lawsuits among you means you have been completely defeated already."[16]

6. Succession: Developing peacemaking processes that can be replicated

Peacemaking within a company may reach people in dozens of different churches. The peacemakers helping the company should have opportunities to talk with pastors and elders at these churches about restoring unity among church members and within the community.

Beware of how churches may resist peacemaking. For example, a large megachurch in Southern California brought in a foremost peacemaking expert to speak to more than 600 people. The members hearing the training found great encouragement in the teaching and asked for more training. One of the main pastors resisted and ended all talk of additional training. Why? The speaker compared the leadership's fear of training laypeople as peacemakers to the medieval church's fear of giving people the Scriptures. Such aversion is contrary to 2 Corinthians 5 and related passages about equipping the saints for works of service.

2 Corinthians 5:17-21 offers hope of peacemaking that should extend around the world and across the generations:

> Therefore, if anyone is in Christ, the new creation has come: The old has gone, the new is here! All this is from God, who reconciled us to himself through Christ and gave us the ministry of reconciliation: that God was reconciling the world to himself in Christ, not counting people's sins against them. And he has committed to us the message of reconciliation. We are therefore Christ's ambassadors, as though God were making his appeal through us. We implore you on Christ's behalf: Be reconciled to God. God made him who had no sin to be sin for us, so that in him we might become the righteousness of God.

Conclusion

Peacemaking begins with a commitment to glorifying God, getting logs out of our eyes, gently restoring, and going to be reconciled. Peacemaking works when Christians are equipped to reflect what God communicates about His divine revelation, purpose, hierarchical leadership structures, ethics, outcomes, and succession principles.

At www.ReflectingGod.info/Survey, please indicate your level of
agreement with the following five statements:

My personal desire for money or assets (greed?) is not undermining my
relationships at work..

not true	1	2	3	4	5	*very true*
	○	○	○	○	○	

My personal need for control or stature (pride?) is not undermining my
relationships at work.

not true	1	2	3	4	5	*very true*
	○	○	○	○	○	

My conflicts about my personal desires do not manifest as anger (Jas.
4:1,.2; Proverbs 11:23) that undermines relationships.

not true	1	2	3	4	5	*very true*
	○	○	○	○	○	

My failure to achieve success seen by some of my peers does not manifest as envy.

not true	1	2	3	4	5	*very true*
	○	○	○	○	○	

My relationships have not been damaged by unwholesome talk (Eph.
4:29) in cases where I failed to forgive as Christ forgave me (4:32).

not true	1	2	3	4	5	*very true*
	○	○	○	○	○	

[1] Isiah 9:2,7

[2] John 3:19.

[3] James 3:18.

[4] 1 Corinthians 10:31.

[5] See, e.g., Matthew 7:5

[6] Galatians 6:1

[7] http://biblehub.com/commentaries/matthew/5-24.htm

[8] Ephesians 4:32

[9] Philippians 2:4-5

[10] Numbers 25:12, Ezekiel 34:25, Isaiah 54:20.

[11] Ephesians 6:10-18

[12] Isaiah 26:3

[13] Flow Motors equips managers to Teach, Coach, Counsel, Discipline, and Terminate. The process uses the key questions asked here:
   1. Teach – Have you taught them what they are expected to do?
   2. Coach – Have you coached them how to do it?
   3. Counsel – Have you counseled them that their behavior continues to be different from what they were taught and how they have been coached?
   4. Discipline – Have you told them, "If you continue to choose not to do what we have taught, coached, and counseled, you will be terminated"?
   5. Terminate

[14] See, e.g., www.ReflectingGod.info/Email10Commandments.

[15] Matthew 5:9

[16] See 1 Corinthians 6:1,7.

Section 5

Outcomes (KPI)

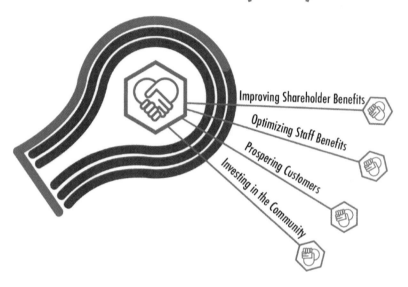

RESEARCH SHOWS HOW there can be financial rewards related to following biblical business management teachings.[1] Chapter 12 explains how these financial benefits enrich those who invest time, talent, treasure, and trust in a business. While these investments can provide great personal returns for anyone investing to gain a stake in a business, shareholders must not begin by focusing on benefiting themselves. They should begin by "doing everything unto the Lord," glorifying Him, and stewarding His resources.[2] Chapter 13 explains how a leader focused on God is empowered to equip, empower, train, and motivate staff members so that the whole team can benefit. The shareholders who serve staff can build a team that provides valuable products and services to customers and clients, as discussed in Chapter 14. The profits generated from serving others can then be invested in the community surrounding the business, as summarized in Chapter 15. Consultants can help companies implement strategic and operational initiatives that improve benefits in the four areas summarized in chapter 12 regarding shareholder benefits; chapter 13 regarding staff benefits; in Chapter 14 regarding client/customer benefits; and in chapter 15 regarding community benefits. Growing benefits can increasingly be tracked with financial statements, productivity metrics, and web-based dashboards. In this way, those involved with a company can monitor improvements in four areas as the company experiences improvement in the "Quadruple Bottom Line."

---

[1] www.ReflectingGod.info/CBSuccessMetrics

[2] See, e.g., Matthew 6:33 and 1 Corinthians 10:31.

Chapter 12

Improving Shareholder Benefits

> *But you shall remember the Lord your God, for it is He
> who is giving you power to make wealth, that He may
> confirm His covenant.*
>
> —DEUTERONOMY 8:18, NASB

"I REALIZE YOU HAVE compelling, even moral, reasons for considering that move," the longtime board member said to the board director. "But the numbers show that decision will cost us revenue. It'll negatively impact our bottom line."

"You actually mean it'll negatively impact *you*," the director responded. "There's more to this organization, you know, than making money. We have a responsibility to our vision and mission, and I'm convinced this move will fulfill both and better serve all our shareholders." He held his hand up before he could be interrupted yet again. "And if we do the right thing, God will honor it."

"Oh, don't spiritualize this," the board member retorted. "It *will* cost us revenue, and I will not support it!"

Most every organization has at least one—the influential board member who struggles to see anything beyond his or her personal bottom line. It's an unfortunate reality, and Christian organizations are not immune. Even more, such selfish mindsets are not confined to individuals in company leadership. It could just as easily come from the child of an owner, the spouse of a director, or an employee who feels entitled.

It is a common problem in organizations for somebody to undermine proposed company directives or teamwork within a business. Just as common is the fact that most cases of such behavior go unaddressed by the owner or management. When a greedy, proud, or self-interested person makes a stand, it can be hard to confront the problem.

However, this dysfunction cannot be allowed in a strong, growing, and functional organization. Thankfully, God's Word addresses seven principles that bring perspective to the issues of wealth, stewardship, returns, and benefits. These biblical insights will enable leaders to reflect God's character, uphold His righteous standards, and shine His light in response to those who exhibit selfishness or any of the other deadly sins identified in Scripture.

1. God *Owns* Everything

As we learned earlier in this book, God blesses everybody with abundant resources. For business owners, these resources allow him or her to build a team that can have productivity and success. But selfish individuals within the corporation can undercut teamwork by pursuing any array of the seven deadly sins (haughty eyes, a lying tongue, hands that shed innocent blood, a heart that devises wicked plans, feet that run rapidly to evil, a false witness who utters lies, and one who spreads strife among brothers) listed in Proverbs 6:16-19. These sins may seem innocuous or they may remain hidden; however, the sins fester in darkness until His light shines on them.

Psalm 24:1-5 declares,

> The earth is the Lord's, and all it contains,
> The world, and those who dwell in it.
> For He has founded it upon the seas
> And established it upon the rivers.
> Who may ascend into the hill of the Lord?
> And who may stand in His holy place?
> He who has clean hands and a pure heart,
> Who has not lifted up his soul to falsehood
> And has not sworn deceitfully.
> He shall receive a blessing from the Lord
> And righteousness from the God of his salvation. (NASB)

Only those who have been confronted about their sin and then choose to confess and repent of that sin can receive the blessing this psalm promises. It starts with an understanding of who owns the resources. They are His and His alone to give.

2. Shareholders Have *Wealth* from God

Shareholders—people vested with ownership, management, control, or cash flow rights—usually have wealth from God because they or people around them have followed principles from teachings throughout Scripture about covenant community. They live by the Bible passage, "Remember the Lord your God, for it is He who is giving you power to make wealth, that He may confirm His covenant" (Deut. 8:18 NASB). This shows how God confirms His covenant by bringing together people with a variety of skills who unite following biblical principles guiding teamwork and productivity.

Productivity leads to profits and wealth. Productivity is greatest when there is a team. That's why many passages in Scripture about wealth or material blessings are given to the covenant community, not to the individual. His promises that "you" will blessed are given to the *plural* "you" of covenant community members who remember the Lord. This wealth is provided to build up the community and give Him glory.

It is God alone who gives us the ability to produce wealth. The first and foremost precondition for us to do this is to put God first and not follow other gods. This includes not making wealth our god. However, the connection between our faithfulness and the wealth we receive is not direct and linear. Wealth is defined as "abundance of valuable material possessions or resources." These resources include rich relationships, favor with God and others, access to His revelation, and our talents. These are the resources needed to prosper spiritually, emotionally, financially, socially, and physically.

3. Wealth from God Must Be *Stewarded*

Whatever resources or wealth God grants us as members of the covenant community, we have a responsibility to be good stewards, as Paul explains,

> Instruct those who are rich in this present world not to be
> conceited or to fix their hope on the uncertainty of riches,
> but on God, who richly supplies us with all things to enjoy.
> Instruct them to do good, to be rich in good works, to be
> generous and ready to share, storing up for themselves the
> treasure of a good foundation for the future, so that they
> may take hold of that which is life indeed.
> (1 Tim. 6:17-19 NASB)

Wealth, says Paul, is taking hold of what is truly life, which equates to true success. True success comes from loving others as we love ourselves and in being a servant leader who brings new life and peace to individuals and the community. Applied to a business setting, the owner must be a good steward of what is invested: time, talent, treasure, and trust. Meanwhile, a shareholder is a steward over investments of capital, which include human, intellectual, and financial capital.

Often, though, the most important resource in a company is relationships built on trust. If customers do not receive value, their trust in the company is weakened. If staff members are not valued, their trust in the organization is eroded. Our employees must understand the importance of honoring commitments to customers and associates. Staff members need to realize that tending to the details is vital if strong trust is to be developed among co-workers and among customers.

An old idiom states, "The devil is in the details." The truth is, just as God is in the details, the covenant is in the details, too. When talking about stock options, liquidity events, pensions, and other types of shareholder wealth, is God even mentioned? Do wealthy shareholders see how God provides wealth and provides an opportunity to confirm His covenant?

4. Stewardship Involves Earning a *Return* for the Stakeholder

This principle may seem obvious, but it must be handled delicately. Why? Interestingly, many people, perhaps because of the deadly sin of envy, resent a Christian having capital and earning returns on it. Yet, we need to remember that those who possess capital have it because they likely stewarded the capital well in the past to accumulate capital according to what the Bible says about building wealth bit by bit (Prov. 13:11). It's good for Christians to have capital. It is what they do with that capital that matters.

All wealth needs to earn a fair return. There are various passages in Scripture about earning good returns. The most notable is Jesus' Parable of the Talents (Matt. 25:14-30), which culminates in verse 29 with this undeniable truth: "For to everyone who has, more shall be given, and he will have an abundance; but from the one who does not have, even what he does have shall be taken away" (NASB). This parable also makes it clear that a stakeholder not only has personal property rights, but a biblical mandate for earning a return on that property.

Applied further to business, stakeholderss have the freedom to use their property or to contract to share the property. These contracts to share may involve stock options, debt instruments, or other executive benefit programs. Employees are responsible to respect these agreements or opt to go to other companies. Regarding stakeholder investments of human capital, individuals contributing human capital deserve to be compensated for their time, while contributions of intellectual capital deserve to be compensated with royalties.

Any questions that arise about returns on capital can be resolved when the parties meet to read relevant scriptural passages and pray about application of marketplace principles from those passages. The

Holy Spirit can lead the parties to agreement. If necessary, Christian consultants can also help decision-makers reach an accord on returns.

5. Stakeholders Use Business Management Methods to *Track* Returns on Investment

Proverbs 27:23-27 teaches about the value of knowing the condition of the flock and warns, "For riches are not forever, nor does a crown endure to all generations." As stakeholders, complacency cannot be tolerated when it comes to tracking how our resources are generating returns. It's wise to have a digital dashboard to spot problems that might undermine profitability or productivity and to check it regularly.

In carrying out this responsibility, godly advisers are invaluable. Not only can they help manage resources, but often these advisers can provide cogent research, see potential red flags, and identify problems that stakeholders may not see. It's under the scrutiny of examination that we can discern where we have possibly failed to follow God's guidelines from Scripture.

6. Stakeholders Get *Non-Financial* Returns Such as Rich Relationships

Even though we use money and profits as a measure of success, the greatest indicator of success is rich relationships. It's so easy for money to become an idol, something that is so revered and even loved that we elevate it at the great expense of fostering relationships.

In a healthy business culture, Christ-centered and Spirit-led teamwork cemented by relationships is the fuel that drives the quadruple bottom line that produces profit and benefits for stakeholders, employees, customers, and the community. Another reward of relationships is seeing the fruits of the Holy Spirit—love, joy, peace, patience, kindness, goodness, faithfulness, gentleness, and self-control—manifested in our work and through our lives.

A wise stakeholder recognizes the extraordinary value in investing in a God-centered company and receives the short and long-term benefit of doing so in both financial and non-financial ways. Just as it makes sense to build a company on godly principles, it makes even better business sense to invest in one that does.

7. Stakeholders Must *Guard* Against Attacks on Their Returns

There's a real battle between light and darkness, between good and evil, within companies. Where there is money, people will try to undermine contracts to keep get their hands on it. They will lie, attacking those who try to confront them, and the lying tongue hates those it hurts (Prov. 26:28). Darkness hates the truth (John 3:19), yet light will vanquish the darkness when stakeholders stay focused on biblical principles, encourage relationships that honor God, and stay vigilant.

To protect rights to allocate or withdraw corporate capital, is a manager sending negative emails or talking behind a co-worker's back? Is a manager violating an agreement when using corporate resources? Are these behaviors known to the board or otherwise examined to expose greed, pride or other types of darkness? Anytime we see these sorts of abuses, we need to ask whether employees, managers, or outside consultants should do surveys or interviews to uncover and confront darkness.

Conclusion

In the end, the wealth, stewardship, returns, and benefits of our business are meant to be used to extend God's kingdom work. Everything we do, personally and professionally, is to be a legacy of our relationship with the living God that continues beyond our lifetimes—and even the lifetime of our organizations. When executed using biblical principles, and by taking a zero-tolerance approach to sinful behavior from the mailroom to the board room, the fruits will be manifested, even if the profits don't fully materialize in this generation.

Remember that success and impact are measured by far more than money. When we fulfill a God-honoring vision and mission, we will make a life-changing impact on everyone touched by our business.

At www.ReflectingGod.info/Survey, please indicate your level of agreement with the following five statements:

My power to make wealth is given to me by God so that He may con-firm His covenant (Deut. 8:18)

not true   1   2   3   4   5   *very true*
          O   O   O   O   O

My desire for wealth is focused on being rich in good works, being gen-erous and ready to share, storing up for treasure of a good foundation for the future (1 Tim. 6:17-19)

not true   1   2   3   4   5   *very true*
          O   O   O   O   O

My wealth is managed actively in keeping with the parable of the talents (Matt. 25:14-30)

not true   1   2   3   4   5   *very true*
          O   O   O   O   O

My success in managing wealth is monitored closely so that I know the details about all of my assets (27:23-27)

not true   1   2   3   4   5   *very true*
          O   O   O   O   O

My wealth is shared equitably with those who help contribute to the accumulation of the wealth (1 Cor. 9:9)

not true   1   2   3   4   5   *very true*
          O   O   O   O   O

Chapter 13

Optimizing Staff Benefits

JANE SEETHED INWARDLY as her supervisor Tom explained, "I expect you to process the claims accurately and efficiently, which involves identifying and correcting errors the first time. Our overriding goal is to meet the timelines and provide quality work. Currently, we have an unacceptable error rate of 13%. Let's shoot for a 50% decrease in errors in the next month."

Jane remained silent, thinking to herself, *This error rate has nothing to do with me. It's the other departments that don't give me what I need when I need it and cut corners just to get the job done. I am powerless to change them and am already compensating for their incompetency. Tom will just have to learn the hard way that they are to blame. I wouldn't receive this kind of foul treatment at our competitors in the next town.*

Engaging Staff

Jane and Tom are typical of two-thirds of employees in U.S. companies who are disengaged at work. Tom is disengaged because he fails to inspire Jane to achieve the larger purpose of the organization. His directions are vague, and he is not trying to help Jane diagnose the problem and provide her with appropriate resources to solve it.

Meanwhile, Jane is disengaged because she passively listens to the supervisor's charge but inwardly is rebellious. She blames others and is not a team player. She sees herself and functions as a victim rather than as a respected and valued person who makes positive contributions to the organization.

According to Gallup survey results, only 30% of employees in the U.S. are engaged, meaning they are enthusiastic about and committed to their work and workplace. The remaining 70% are not engaged, meaning they do the least they can to get by and/or actively undermine the organization's mission and values. These numbers have been consistent since 2000.[1]

Results from studies conducted by Gallup and Dale Carnegie suggest that engaged employees are more likely to be high performers and to have tenures of a decade or more in their organizations.[2]

Specifically, the Dale Carnegie study on over 1500 employees revealed that companies with engaged employees outperform those without by up to 202%. The Dale Carnegie study identified three key drivers of employee engagement: 1) relationship with the direct manager, 2) belief in senior leadership, and 3) pride in working for a company that makes a meaningful contribution to society.[3]

Driving Staff Engagement Through Servant Leadership

All three drivers identified in the Dale Carnegie study point to leadership qualities that honor God. Optimal leaders are servant leaders who have a God-honoring mission and values, relate to individuals with care and respect, and create high-performance cultures focused on serving other team members and the customers.

Consider how Jesus admonished his disciples to focus on serving others rather than on their own sense of self-importance.

> And Jesus called them to him and said to them, "You know that those who are considered rulers of the Gentiles lord it over them, and their great ones exercise authority over them. But it shall not be so among you. But whoever would be great among you must be your servant, and whoever would be first among you must be slave of all. For even the Son of Man came not to be served but to serve, and to give his life as a ransom for many. (Mark 10:42-45)

Leaders who are God's disciples are humble and demonstrate sacrificial love. They do what is best for the covenantal community which is the company as a whole rather than themselves. Their self-interest is subordinated to the interest of the whole. They feel a deep sense of responsibility for the well-being of each person whether a customer, employee, vendor, community member or owner.

Let's explore how company leaders have been modeling servant leadership in their companies. Common threads weave throughout the case examples below. The servant leaders who head these companies treat people with care and respect and relate to the whole person, believing that everyone is created in God's image (Gen. 1:27). They make mission and values meaningful and practical in day-to-day experience. They are "doers of the word and not hearers only" (James 1:22). They create the conditions for unified teamwork by building an environment of high support and high performance where team members serve one another as they pursue a shared mission and values in serving the customer. They develop people, hold them accountable, and reward them for a combination of character, teamwork, and productivity.

Building a Culture of Serving

HP, Flow Auto, Turbocam, and Capella Hotels and Resorts intentionally put programs and processes in place to develop and reward servant leaders. The servant leaders empower staff by giving them a meaningful purpose and equipping them to have a sense of accomplishment in completing tasks related to the fulfillment of the organization's mission. The intent is to pursue the task with a servant's heart, with excellence, and with a commitment to complete customer satisfaction.

At Flow Auto, the measure of success of leaders and staff is based on how well they "S.E.R.V.E." through character, competence, and relationships. Don Flow has developed the S.E.R.V.E. model, as explained here, and then equipped managers to explain the model through Teacher/Student, Coach/Player, Consultant/High-Performer, Equipper/Allstar roles explained below.

S = Show respect
E = Earn trust
R = Reach for perfection
V = Value input
E = Energize others

The managers serve individual staff members in different ways as the staff grow in competence and character through four stages of career progression:

1. **Teacher/Student:** The manager teaches the employee how to do his/her job.
2. **Coach/Player:** The manager plays a supportive and guiding role as the player performs.
3. **Consultant/High-Performer:** The manager fine tunes the work of the high performer who is given increased authority and responsibility.
4. **Equipper/Allstar:** The manager provides resources as needed to an employee who consistently executes the processes well. All stars are the pool for the next level of management.

At Turbocam, the head of Organizational Development builds servant leaders whose primary focus is to build self-awareness and relationship-awareness so they can serve the people around them. He considers work the best place for developing these leaders because it involves being with someone every day and experiencing life circumstances together. He facilitates regular discussions with small groups of emerging and current leaders that focus on how to apply biblical principles and the company's values to specific business situations. He views his approach to developing servant leaders as a lifestyle, which is unique among many other mentoring programs that focus specifically on the workplace context.

Building Community with Cross-Functional Teams

Peter clarifies that the role of servant leaders is to serve others by helping them to identify and use their individual talents to contribute to the community.

> Each of you should use whatever gift you have received to serve others, as faithful stewards of God's grace in its various forms. (1 Pet. 4:10)

On a practical level, this invokes each individual to share his gifts to serve others in the community from a heart of gratitude. As each person contributes his unique talents to achieve a shared purpose, the team becomes unified and strengthened. This outcome requires that the hiring, development, and placement of staff intentionally focuses on identifying individual God-given gifts and placing people in teams to complement one other.

At HP, job competence and character are intentionally developed at weekly company-wide training meetings led by the CEO or a senior leader. Team unity develops in an environment of mutual respect and idea exchange that fosters a positive culture. For example, at well-structured department meetings, employees discuss and brainstorm how they might be more productive and efficient.

At HP, cross-training among departments fosters mutual respect, appreciation, and shared goals. Across departments and geographies, workers help one another when called upon, even if it means temporarily subordinating their own goals and rewards. Their sense of solidarity transcends the conventional notion of teamwork.

At Turbocam, people work cross-functionally to make information flow smoothly and effectively across the shop. For example, an engineering manager at Automotive Production Systems involves IT people and representatives from other business-unit engineering groups who provide diverse input to arrive at more global solutions.

At Capella Hotels and Resorts, several of the 24 service standards refer to assisting each other in serving the customer, even when it means stepping out of a staff member's own primary duties.

Building Character Through Truth and Grace

Servant leaders also serve individuals by holding them accountable for their behavior and performance in an empowering way that fosters learning and character development. Paul explains that someone who is spiritually mature speaks openly and honestly in love to others so they can grow in character and God's image. In this way the whole community or team can grow in unity, love, and effectiveness.

> Instead, speaking the truth in love, we will grow to become
> in every respect the mature body of him who is the head,
> that is, Christ. (Eph. 4:15; see also John 1:17)

"Speaking the truth in love" is the catalyst to transform individuals, teams, and organizations. Caring about a person and speaking candidly to them without judgment, allows the person and the team to grow in competence and character. As they grow in competence and character, the team is more capable of becoming a high-support, high-performance team.

At Flow Auto, for example, an employee in one store displayed anger in a way that was threatening to another employee. When questioned by the senior director of the organization development department, the offending employee explained that his father would have behaved in a similar way. With a better understanding of the context for his behavior, the OD director realized that this was an opportunity for the employee to learn what forgiveness looks like so he could act differently the next time. This approach was driven by the belief system of the OD director and Don Flow, the CEO, that people bring their whole selves to work, so they should be regarded as whole people—not merely viewed as the functions they fulfill in the organization.

At Turbocam, if an employee talks abusively to his supervisor or co-worker, he is given a *decision leave*. On a decision leave, the employee stays home without pay and is required to make a decision. Will he admit what he did, own his behavior, and do what it takes to repair the broken relationship or not? If he comes back and says, "I am sorry," the relationship is reconciled and the job saved. If he is not genuinely sorry for his behavior, he must leave. This process combines grace and truth.

At HP's Monday morning meetings, servant leadership and humility are recognized as a means to build a spiritually positive culture.

All these processes of accountability based on grace and truth help to build godly character, a pre-condition for high-performing teams.

Meeting the Needs of the "Whole Person"

Servant leaders are stewards of the people whom God has entrusted to them. Therefore, they are called to invest in them spiritually, emotionally, financially, physically, and socially. Paul counsels fellow believers to be like Jesus by emptying themselves of their own self-interests so they can truly serve others.

> Do not be concerned about your own interests, but also be concerned about the interests of others. (Phil. 2:4)

A test for servant leaders is the extent to which their staff grow healthier, wiser, more secure, and become servant leaders to others at home and work. When making a decision and taking an action, the servant leader always asks, "how will this action fulfill God's law and positively affect all key stakeholders?"

In practical terms, our case examples demonstrate the comprehensiveness of the financial, housing, health, spiritual, and other benefits provided by the company. These benefits reinforce the organization's priority order of God first, family second, and work third.

For example, Flow Automotive has a college tuition scholarship available to the children of employees and an emergency assistance program led by a committee of employees to help employees in need.

Exceeding the traditional benefits within the construction industry, HP provides health insurance, a pension plan, and disability insurance for their employees.

Turbocam goes the extra mile in securing the jobs of employees during economic downturns and by supporting employees in new business ventures, within and outside of Turbocam.

All of these companies encourage religious freedom, celebrations, and observance of prayer for those who desire to express their faith in such ways. For example, Ralph Meloon, former CEO of Correct Craft, provided opportunities for employees to go to chapel as well as faith-based training to strengthen their families. Training topics included

Raising Kids God's Way and Dave Ramsey's *Financial Peace University.*[4] Several of these companies also sponsor humanitarian mission trips.

Conclusion

Staff benefits start with engaging employees. Engaged employees flourish in an environment of servant leadership. To significantly improve your quadruple bottom-line, be a servant leader, and develop servant leaders at every level of your company. Create and sustain policies, processes, and structure that reinforce a serving culture.

Servant leaders create an engaged and loyal staff by creating an environment of high support and high performance. For example, turnover rates of the case examples cited in this book, when compared to the general population of companies, validate this assertion. (For more comprehensive proof that Christ-centered leaders build companies with greater employee loyalty, see the research study by Nabil Ibrahim and John Angelidis at www.ReflectingGod.info/ChristianBusiness.)

Engaging staff fosters customer satisfaction and loyalty. Customer satisfaction and loyalty generate sustainable profits, which are used to grow the business, reward the staff, and serve the community. This is Christ's timeless and true path for creating and sustaining a quadruple bottom line.

At www.ReflectingGod.info/Survey, please indicate your level of agreement with the following five statements:

Quiz 13

My company serves the "whole" person including the financial, health, family and spiritual needs of the staff.

not true   1   2   3   4   5   *very true*
              ○   ○   ○   ○   ○

My company sees and treats all staff as created in God's image and deserving respect.

not true   1   2   3   4   5   *very true*
              ○   ○   ○   ○   ○

My company empowers staff by giving them an inspiring purpose, clarifying their role, giving them authority, and listening to their voice.

not true   1   2   3   4   5   *very true*
              ○   ○   ○   ○   ○

My company equips staff by developing servant leaders and building their competence.

not true   1   2   3   4   5   *very true*
              ○   ○   ○   ○   ○

My leadership team rewards staff who are high performers, team players, and committed to our core values.

not true   1   2   3   4   5   *very true*
              ○   ○   ○   ○   ○

[1] Annamarie Mann and Jim Harter, "The Worldwide Employee Engagement Crisis," *Business Journal* (January 7, 2016), http://news.gallup.com/businessjournal/188033/worldwide-employee-engagement-crisis.aspx.

[2] Jim Harter, "Companies are Maximizing only 5% of their Workforces," *Business Journal* (March 24, 2015), http://news.gallup.com/businessjournal/182087/companies-maximizing-workforces.aspx.

[3] Dale Carnegie Training, "Engaged Employees Infographic," http://www.dalecarnegie.com/employee-engagement/engaged-employees-infographic/

[4] Merlin Switzer, *Bold Leadership* (California: Public Policy Institute, William Jessup University, 2012), 29.

Chapter 14

Prospering Customers

TURBOCAM'S LONG-TIME CUSTOMER DEMANDED,

> I know that our initial agreement read that we would in-
> crease our volume each year and you would reduce the
> price of parts. However, we are in a jam, and although our
> volumes have decreased, we still expect you to reduce your
> price.

Knowing that a substantial amount of revenue was at stake, Marian, Turbocam's CEO and founder, prayed for God's guidance. With
clarity and confidence, Marian affirmed, "My posture is to keep my end
of the bargain."

Marian reduced the price of the parts even though he was not le-
gally bound to do so. The customer later decided to make his own parts
in-house.

Confronted with spiritual darkness when a customer unfairly demanded a price cut, Marian made his decision based on Turbocam's
foundational principle of building win-win relationships rather than
mere buy-sell, transactional relationships. Over time, God has revealed
His faithfulness by closing and opening the right doors to the right customers, enabling Turbocam to realize its goal of building long-term and

true customer partnerships. These are the customers who respect and share Turbocam's values.

The Turbocam case example demonstrates the reality that Christian CEOs are plunged into a playing field daily that pits spiritual light against darkness as they face constant competitive challenges. The character of the leader and the company either bears witness to Christ through their decisions and actions or negates Christ.

How can leaders navigate this great divide to reflect Christ accurately? How can they do so in a way that benefits the customer? It starts with the means of grace: prayer, preaching God's truth, and servant leadership under Christ's authority (with oversight from Spirit-led elders who encourage reflection of God's character).

Loving One's Neighbor Creates Win-Win Relationships

When Jesus was asked what the most important commandment is by a teacher of the Jewish Law, He replied,

> "Love the Lord your God with all your heart and with all your soul and with all your mind and with all your strength." The second is this: "Love your neighbor as yourself." There is no commandment greater than these. (Mark 12:30-31)

These commandments lay the foundation for truly serving others. In practical application, you cannot love your neighbor as yourself unless you love God first and put Him first. Only then can you love your neighbor in an unselfish rather than ego-centric way.

Loving your neighbor means creating win-win relationships not only with customers but with fellow employees, vendors, owners, customers, and the broader community. The win-win approach seeks cooperation, which is built on mutual influence and yields mutual benefits. When all shareholders benefit from the relationship, the customer thrives, and the relationship is sustainable over time because customer trust and loyalty is created.

In *The 7 Habits of Highly Effective People*, Stephen Covey includes win-win relationships as one of the seven critical success habits. The principle of Win-Win is fundamental to success in all our interactions, and it embraces five interdependent dimensions of life. It begins with character and moves toward relationships, out of which flow agreements. It is nurtured in an environment where structures, systems and processes are based on Win/Win.[1]

Win-win relationships, says Covey, begin with an individual's character. Character is reflected through healthy relationships and committed agreements. However, unless win-win relationships are reinforced by supportive processes and structures—such as recognition and reward systems—they will not be sustained. The following case examples illustrate how companies that reflect Christ make the principle of Win-Win practical and operational, fostering trust, customer loyalty, and long-term partnerships.

Cultivating Customer Loyalty Through Win-Win Relationships at Turbocam

In business, leaders are constantly tempted to put their self-interests first. It requires faith, courage, and discipline to give others equal or greater priority. Consider how Paul cautioned members of the churches in Galatia that they are given freedom to be others-centered rather than self-centered.

> You, my brothers, were called to be free. But do not use your freedom to indulge the sinful nature; rather, serve one another in love. (Gal. 5:13)

What differentiates the leaders who overcome the temptation to put their self-interest first is a genuine love in their hearts for God and people. This love is reinforced by their commitment to fulfill the commandment for building up the community in love. They also realize that their self-interest will be best served by doing the right things for the right reasons.

A Turbocam customer at Cummins Turbo Technologies once explained his predicament to Marian, CEO of Turbocam.

> Customer: Marian, I am being pressured by our customers on the price of the wheel for the turbocharger which you have so reliably provided us for years. Suppliers in low-cost countries are a serious price threat. Our long- term partnership is in grave jeopardy.

> Turbocam CEO: Bill, I don't know how yet, but I will find a solution.

Marian proceeded to do his own market analysis and discovered that he could not achieve that price level in his New Hampshire manufacturing facility because of labor costs. He prayed for wisdom to fulfill his mission to honor God through excellence. When he realized that the leverage he had was to process the part more quickly, he bought equipment that operated faster, developed more efficient processes, and leveraged his company's culture of high- performance teamwork . The result was a significant cost reduction that exceeded those of the suppliers in low- cost countries while still maintaining Turbocam's required profit margin.

Through this process, Turbocam was also able to deepen the level of trust with their customer by taking such an active role in addressing their problem. This same customer observed,

> When Marian makes an improvement in their facility to reduce costs or receives a cost reduction from one of his suppliers, he shares the cost reduction with us.

A representative from Peregrine Turbine Technologies, another Turbocam customer, said,

> We were in a conference room talking with people from Turbocam about parts to manufacture. A patentable idea came out of the discussion. I asked as a test, "Whose idea is that?"
>
> Tim, Marian's son, said, "Both of ours."
>
> I learned that Turbocam is fundamentally interested in technology and problem-solving and making sure they give the customer the best possible deal.

Building customer loyalty and trust also requires world- class performance based on exceptional service, quality, and value. When the employee is enthusiastic about his or her work and serving the customer with excellence, the customer feels important and cared for. In turn, loyal customers are created.

The best motivation for excellence is an outpouring of gratitude to a magnificent, good, and generous God. Paul directed his brothers in

Christ at Colossae to put their whole hearts into their work to honor God and not please men:

> Do everything as unto the Lord. (Col. 3:23)

Doing everything unto the Lord enables leaders and their people to make a difference by focusing on a greater purpose beyond themselves. This heart motivation leads to true employee and customer engagement to a level that can't be matched with mere techniques used to drum up engagement.

Marian, CEO of Turbocam, explained,

> If parts need to be within a certain tolerance, we narrow the margin even more. God is our standard. We do our best by improving processes and developing our people.

A Turbocam *customer at Cummins Turbo Technologies affirmed* this truth by saying,

> We measure delivery, quality, and cost reduction, and Turbocam is one of the highest scorers of all our suppliers for all of Cummins. They have controls in place and an infrastructure to meet and exceed our key measures and world- class performance.

Creating "Moments of Truth" for Exceptional Customer Service

Operationalizing a win-win approach and exceptional service requires customer-focused processes that make it easy for the customer to do business with the company and create a consistently positive customer experience.

Jan Carlzon, former CEO of SAS Airlines, built his turnaround strategy around the concept of "moments of truth." He measured the success of SAS by the quality of the contact between the individual customers and the SAS employees. Each of these contacts creates a "moment of truth" in which good or bad impressions are made and the company proves or disproves that they are the best alternative.[2]

Horst Schulze, former CEO of The Ritz-Carlton and current CEO of Capella Hotels and Resorts, was the leader of the first hospitality company to win the coveted Malcolm Baldridge National Quality Award. Horst revolutionized the hotel industry by delivering exceptional service and global consistency. He does this by creating positive moments of truth at the beginning, middle, and end of a customer's visit through efficient processes and the caring attitudes of the staff. The "Capella Canon" consists of 24 points with specific directions for how to treat customers and fellow employees in order to create exceptional service and value. The first item in the canon states why the company is in business.

> The Capella Group is in business to create value and unparalleled results for our owners by creating products which fulfill individual customer expectations.
>
> We deliver reliable, genuinely caring and timely service superior to our competition, with respected and

empowered employees who work in an environment of belonging and purpose.

We are supportive and contributing members of society, operating with uncompromising values, honor, and integrity.

Horst hires people to be part of a dream and part of a purpose—not merely to perform a function.

The Canon is operationalized in the form of 24 service standards that are embedded in daily work and focus the staff on excellence every minute of every day. Every day at the start of work, staff members at each hotel around the world meet together for 15 minutes to review one of the 24 standards. On the 25th day, the cycle is repeated.

Service, says Horst, means positively acknowledging customers in the first 10 seconds, complying with what they want in a caring and individualized way during their stay, and providing a warm farewell at the end of their stay. As an example of how this practice is communicated to the staff, number 8 of the 24 points is to "always recognize guests. Interrupt whatever activity you are doing when a guest is within 12 feet, greet them with a smile and offer of assistance."

The Capella Group was birthed by a prayer of the founders. Prayer in the workplace continues today on a daily basis for those who believe in the power of prayer. A different prayer is written for each of 20 days each month. The prayers recognize the lordship of Jesus Christ, seek to glorify God by reflecting the character of Christ, and unabashedly ask for God's abundant blessings over the hotel, the guests, the staff, and their families.

To create a "positive moment of truth," the Capella Group trains, develops, and inspires their employees on the front lines to provide personalized service to individual customers. Moreover, they are given the responsibility, authority, and resources to serve the customer well. For example, at the Cappella Group, service standard number 11 reads,

When a guest encounters any difficulty, you are responsible to own it and start the problem resolution process. You are empowered to resolve any problem to the guest's complete satisfaction.

For that purpose, staff members can use up to $2,000 at their own discretion to meet the expectations of guests.

Integrating Exceptional Customer Service into Policies and Processes

Flow Auto breeds customer loyalty and exceptional service based on a covenant with customers to do what is right. At Flow Auto, this means not advantaging themselves at the disadvantage of the customer and treating the customer like members of their own family. This paradigm sharply contrasts with the traditional transactional model in the automobile sales industry where both parties try to maximize their own position.

As referenced in Chapter 4, the staff at Flow Auto are steadfastly aligned around three principles:

- Covenant: A place that keeps promises
- Community: We work together toward a common vision.
- Commitment: We focus on the common good in every city where we do business.

Don Flow, the company's CEO, explained,

It all starts with a value proposition: if we create value for customers, they will reward us financially. That starts with being a place of trust and leads to creating enthusiastic customers for life.

Flow creates trust and loyalty through their sales and service processes. The pricing structure for used cars is set so there is no negotiating. Their pricing is competitive because they manage their costs better with their streamlined internal processes.

On the service side, there are unconditional commitments. Flow promises to repair a customer's vehicle correctly the first time, complete the repair at the time promised, and honor their cost estimate for repair. If they fail to fulfill these guarantees, Flow bears the cost of doing what it takes to make it right.

As a result, Flow is profitable and has enormous customer loyalty. Though Flow may retain slightly less than the average profit per vehicle than may be possible through traditional negotiation practices, they make up for it with higher productivity and process execution. Flow Automotive has also received numerous awards from many of the 20 auto manufacturers it represents, including being a 12-time winner of Honda's President Council.

Similarly, Correct Craft is a living testimony of a world-renowned company that builds the best wake and ski boats that provides unmatched service to customers. It also sets industry standards for quality, reliability, innovation, and integrity.

During World War II, General Eisenhower requested that Correct Craft build approximately 400 boats in 30 days. To accomplish this seemingly impossible task, Correct Craft created a new production process which produced the boats in record time. National Geographic dubbed this, "A Miracle Production," which solidified the company's reputation as being a reliable, quality boat manufacturer.[3] What makes this story more compelling is that Correct Craft stood firm about not working on Sunday even when they received tremendous pressure from the government to work seven days to meet the deadline. Even with the apparent handicap of working six days instead of seven, Correct Craft was the only boat manufacturer to meet the quota on time.

More recently, in February 2019 the National Marine Manufacturers Association (NMMA) awarded Nautique, a line of Correct Craft, the Customer Satisfaction (CSI) award for the 13th consecutive year. It measures outstanding customer service and continuous improvement to better serving the customer. At the same event Nautique also received the Marketing Innovation award for the launch of a brand-new boat which was showcased using a rich array of live events and digital media.

Conclusion

As a Christian CEO and a marketplace leader, your calling is to reflect Christ. In the case examples cited here, there are common elements in how the CEOs and their companies reflect Christ day-to-day which you can emulate.

1. Undergird your efforts in prayer.
2. Be a leader with a servant's heart who builds win-win relationships with all key stakeholders.
3. Focus on serving the customer with consistently exceptional service, quality, value, and integrity.
4. Align your processes, policies and practices to deliver on your promises in a defect-free, timely, and caring way.

5. Continuously improve based on foresight, creativity in problem-solving, and development of innovative processes and products.

6. Hire people who embrace your purpose.

When combined, these critical success factors will enable your company to grow profitably, set industry standards, develop loyal customers, build an extraordinary reputation, and be sustainable over the long term. This is the only way to reflect and glorify Christ so you can be a resounding witness for Him in the marketplace.

> Let your light so shine before men, that they may see your good works, and glorify your Father which is in heaven. (Matt. 5:16)

Successful businesses clarify how they can produce goods and services (good works) that glorify God. Production can be gauged by business analytics that monitor productivity. Ultimately, the business analytics need to show success in serving customers.

At www.ReflectingGod.info/Survey, please indicate your level of agreement with the following five statements:

My company relentlessly focuses on customer satisfaction.

not true   1   2   3   4   5   *very true*
○   ○   ○   ○   ○

Everyone in my organization maintains the highest standards of quality and service.

not true   1   2   3   4   5   *very true*
○   ○   ○   ○   ○

All work processes are designed to make it easy for our customer to do business with us.

not true   1   2   3   4   5   *very true*
○   ○   ○   ○   ○

We set the standard for the best customer service in our industry.

not true   1   2   3   4   5   *very true*
○   ○   ○   ○   ○

We build win-win relationships with our customers

not true   1   2   3   4   5   *very true*
○   ○   ○   ○   ○

[1] Stephen Covey, *The 7 Habits of Highly Effective People* (New York: Simon and Schuster, 2004), 227.

[2] Jan Carlzon, *Moments of Truth* (Pensacola, Florida: Ballinger Publishing Co., 1987).

[3] CorrectCraft.com, "Nautique-takes-top-honors-at-award-ceremony-during-miami-boat-show." Accessed October 24, 2017. https://www.correctcraft.com/nautique-takes-top-honors-during-award-ceremony-at-miami-boat-show

Chapter 15

Investing in the Community

HIS SCOWL COULD ALMOST be heard throughout the building as he stepped out from his office and screamed, "Am I the only one working this weekend?!" Those who heard him knew what he meant and began making calls to cancel family, community, and church activities they had planned for the weekend.

That senior manager had worked his way into a leadership position in the company but had lost his family, friends, and church affiliations in the process. His paycheck was large, but his contributions outside the office were insignificant and he expected everyone to join his misery.

Many secular companies are completely obsessed with the financial bottom line. Employees are given little or no time for community activities or interests. In many cases, outside activities and interests are discouraged, frowned upon, or at most, given lip service. Companies often look to their communities solely for what they can get *out of* them rather than for what they can invest *into* them. Employees are essentially slaves to the company, and the community is viewed only as a source of money, power, and prestige. In many cases, the community is even viewed as the *enemy* except as it relates to tapping into that money supply.

By applying God's principles of giving, we will multiply the money God entrusts to us tenfold. The business should focus on those who are least among us and give with a focus on purpose and dignity. The Bible says,

> But since you excel in everything—in faith, in speech, in knowledge, in complete earnestness and in the love we have kindled in you—see that you also excel in this grace of giving. (2 Cor. 8:7)

How a Company Should Invest in Its Community

What are some practical ways companies should invest generously into their communities?

First, employees should be encouraged to provide their time (may require paid time off), talent (could involve abilities developed in the company), and treasure (financial giving) to help charitable and community organizations.

Second, family activities should be encouraged and sponsored. Balance between spending time at work and spending time with family should be promoted.

Third, religious holidays and activities should be emphasized and promoted. This may include Christmas and Easter company celebrations.

Fourth, the company's leaders should model what it looks like to invest in their communities. They can take leadership positions in charitable organizations and encourage employees to participate and start charitable initiatives that are consistent with the company's values.

Benefits of Investing in the Community

As a result of investing in the community, the company's leaders and employees will be rejuvenated and refreshed by their spiritual activities outside the organization. When these community activities are sponsored by the company, they can create a spirit of cooperation and unity among the team. In addition, the company's employees will become even more proud to be part of an organization that does good works in the community.

By extension, the family members of the company's employees will become more supportive and understanding of the company's mission.

The community will also be grateful for the support. This goodwill often will be reciprocated through increased patronaged for the benefit of the company, thereby increasing profits and brand loyalty.

When the light of God's character is reflected through the company, the leaders will view service to the community, employees, and customers as redemptive. Jesus paid the price so we can live. Likewise, each of us must sacrifice for the benefits of others.

The giving should be relational. Speak to and touch the people being helped. Care about them in a way that opens the door to conversion and discipleship. The company can suggest and help guide employees to support genuine and worthy charities where God is glorified. When leaders serve with pure motivations, there are numerous signs and benefits.

The following are examples of companies who have demonstrated the value of investing in their communities.

Case Studies

HP

HP supports many local activities and charities. They sponsor a "mud run" at Camp Pendleton, and many of their employees participate. HP also sponsors numerous other local and national charities. They also invest in their communities by sponsoring paid time off for their employees to serve as volunteers in support of the charities they believe in.

Flow Motors

The goal at Flow Companies is to be a creator of societal value by contributing to the common good of the communities where they do business. The company's leaders believe that they are accountable to the community and to future generations, not only to replenish the cultural capital that they have drawn upon (e.g., social, intellectual, aesthetic, political, and economic) but also to be a creator of capital for the future. If the community is not growing and expanding, its future will be less prosperous than its past.

Flow does the work of replenishment and creation of cultural capital through the service of employees to non-profit organizations. For example, each dealership has projects in its community and gives paid time off for employees to participate in those and other community projects. Employees build Habitat for Humanity homes and are involved in dozens of United Way agency programs through which they serve.

From inner-city programs to universities, Flow Automotive Companies invests substantially in the educational system. Don Flow, the company's owner, has served as Chairman of the Economic Development Foundation in North Carolina where Flow Automotive's headquarters is located.

Overall, Flow contributes to the community in three ways: 1) by delivering unparalleled service to customers, 2) by enhancing the lives of their employees, and 3) by positively impacting the cities in which they operate. These ideals are balanced with one another and systematically related to teachings about covenants, commitment and community. These teachings are openly communicated before, during, and after the hiring of new team members (see, e.g., www.ReflectingGod.info/FlowCareers).

Turbocam

Turbocam's goal in community service is to empower people to be self-supporting and to create wealth. In the communities and countries where Turbocam does business, they focus on providing the three building blocks to support education, schools, and jobs:

1. Clean water
2. Structurally stable houses (especially during heavy rainfall seasons) – For example, the company designed pillars to elevate homes and prevent them from washing away. They also helped local people to start their own businesses to develop and sell the pillars, which were not available in Nepal.
3. Good nutrition – For example, the company supplies families with goats. Then, families sell goats and milk to other families to support themselves financially.

Turbocam has built several schools in Nepal and has brought in educators. For example, the automotive group donated from their bonus one year to build a school in Nepal. The idea was agreed to at a management team meeting and became an obligation for all employees. In addition, a woman in the quality control department initiated a year-long program to support education and the feeding of kids in Haiti.

The cafeteria at Turbocam is on the honor system. Employees pay for their food by putting money into one or more of 10 baskets that represent different charities.

It is estimated that 30-50% of employees volunteer in the community, and many more provide funds for various charitable causes.

While one Turbocam employee was visiting the company's plant in India, he visited a leper colony. The lepers had a box factory and made crates. One of the most striking things he ever saw was when his host asked an operator to take off his glove and he saw a club rather than a hand as a result of leprosy. The operator had no dexterity in his fingers. The Turbocam employee realized what it meant when Jesus asked a leper to stretch out his hand and Jesus cured him of leprosy (Luke 6:6-10). Turbocam partners with the leper colony and, with Turbocam's help, they are now earning income by making valves that they sell to an Indian car manufacturer.

As these companies demonstrate, there are many ways and views on how companies can invest in their communities, encourage charity, and reflect God's character through the business. There are many ways an organization can be charitable. The company can support and donate directly. This can be effective in smaller, closely held companies. A company can also support charitable works indirectly by paying employees generously and by providing paid time off to choose their own charities. Companies also can choose a combination of both direct and indirect investment in their communities.

Conclusion

Every business must decide where and how to give by supporting local churches and ministries without encroaching on their work. Business leaders should offer cooperation without intrusion. In most cases, it is better to help the local churches instead of diluting the focus of a business by asking a business to do the work given to the church. While businesses may be pressured to focus on the social gospel, and businesses may even be able to show quantitative success indicators based on charitable projects, business leaders must ask whether these charitable initiatives encourage gospel-centric living and discipleship as effectively as similar initiatives undertaken by churches. Ultimately, the real measure of success is the rate at which employees are converted by the godly culture that surrounds them. Development of a healthy culture very often requires collaboration between the business and the churches surrounding the business.

At www.ReflectingGod.info/Survey, please indicate your level of
agreement with the following five statements:

Quiz 15

My company encourages its leaders to provide leadership in charitable
organizations

not true   1   2   3   4   5   very true
○ ○ ○ ○ ○

The leadership team in my organization has the freedom to start new
ventures, including charitable organizations, when such initiatives are
consistent with the corporate vision and values

not true   1   2   3   4   5   very true
○ ○ ○ ○ ○

My company seeks to expand its influence through charitable activities
in the community

not true   1   2   3   4   5   very true
○ ○ ○ ○ ○

My company encourages staff involvement in philanthropic activities

not true   1   2   3   4   5   very true
○ ○ ○ ○ ○

My company is sensitive to how it can help staff members balance work
with family and religious community commitments

not true   1   2   3   4   5   very true
○ ○ ○ ○ ○

Section 6

Succession

Investing in the Future through Succession Planning

LEADERS CAN BUILD covenantal relationships with key stakeholders, staff members, clients, and the surrounding community by applying the biblical principles undergirding the six elements of the covenant. These covenantal principles are explained in the context of research conducted by Dr. Robert Clinton. Dr. Clinton studied 50 biblical leaders, 100 historical leaders, and 1,150 contemporary leaders. He observed that they (1) maintain a personal vibrant relationship with God, (2) learn continually how they can fulfill their life purpose, (3) manifest submission to the Spirit, (4) live out truth in their lives, (5) show fruit through lasting contributions, and (6) focus on fulfilling a destiny that extends beyond the leader's lifetime. In short, successful leaders reflect the covenantal character of God through their personal lives and through godly institutions.

Chapter 16

Investing in the Future Through Succession Planning

> *Therefore, since we have so great a cloud of witnesses surrounding us, let us also lay aside every encumbrance and the sin which so easily entangles us, and let us run with endurance the race that is set before us.*
>
> —HEBREWS 12:1, NASB

AS LEADERS, we can know God and grow personally through a covenantal relationship with our Creator. As we mature in our understanding of His divine character, we can enter covenantal relationships with our team members. As they develop more mature, covenantal relationships with God and each other, alignment of vision and values result. This results in unified teamwork and productivity.

While productivity is a key goal of business (and too often an idol), this book has tried to explain how sustainable productivity is based on teamwork reflecting divine character. It is never idolatrous to know and reflect the character of God while giving God the glory for the resulting productivity.

Great leaders have reflected how God communicates His character in the Bible, in history, and in modern culture but not all maintain commitment to divine character across time. Dr. J. Robert Clinton—author, speaker, and professor of leadership at Fuller Seminary—studied 50 biblical leaders, 100 historical leaders, and 1,150 contemporary leaders before concluding that less than one in three leaders *finish well.* He then asked, "What character qualities distinguish leaders who finish well?"

From that inquiry, Dr. Clinton developed six distinct "Finishing Well Principles" leaders can use to build covenantal relationships with key stakeholders, staff members, clients, and the surrounding community. This chapter draws on Biblical examples to show how these principles can be perpetuated across time as organizations grow.

Covenantal Principle 1: They maintain a personal vibrant relationship with God right up to the end.

Abram modeled finishing well when he was older and still with no heir. God told him that his offspring would be as numerous as the stars in the sky (Gen. 15:5), and that promise was fulfilled through his grandson Jacob's 12 sons.

Today, that communication of divine revelation through the patriarchs of the Old Testament is now proclaimed through Jesus: "So then faith comes by hearing, and hearing by the word of Christ" (Rom. 10:17, NASB). This gospel is "the power of God for salvation to everyone who believes" (Rom. 1:16 NASB), and we are born again by the preaching of the gospel (Rom. 10:6-17; 1 Pet. 1:23-25).

We need to understand the importance of sharing the gospel as well as the relevance of the gospel to business leadership. This is vital in that many leaders fall painfully short in exhibiting biblical characteristics of leadership. According to a survey of 1,000 Christian leaders across seven continents by the Lausanne Leadership Development Group, the worst characteristics are as follows: 1) being "prideful, always right, and always the 'big boss,'" 2) lacking integrity or being seen as untrustworthy, and 3) being harsh, uncaring, critical, and refusing to listen. According to the report, personal pride seems to be the primary cause of poor leadership—and all these characteristics are contrary to the servant leadership qualities Jesus exhibited.

Covenantal Principle 2: They maintain a learning posture and can learn from various kinds of sources—life especially.

Dr. Amanda Goodson is an engineer and pastor who worked for nearly 25 years at the National Aeronautics and Space Administration (NASA), and was the first African-American woman to serve as Director of Safety and Mission Assurance at the Marshall Space Flight Center in Alabama. A certified John Maxwell coach, Dr. Goodson uses her goal-setting and goal-getting expertise to help others develop as leaders—but many of her lessons of leadership came from trial.

Her team oversaw propulsion systems for the shuttle program with direct responsibility for launches when the Space Shuttle Columbia disaster occurred in 2003. Earlier in her career, she was part of the team that chose the new O-rings for NASA following the Space Shuttle Challenger accident in 1986. Dr. Goodson has used these experiences, along with obstacles she's overcome because of her race and gender, to develop specific leadership lessons that she plans to publish in 2018 in her latest book on leadership and faith principles.

Life indeed can be a great teacher for the Christian and is one of the reasons Proverbs 14:15 tells us that "the sensible man considers his steps" (NASB). Through his experiences, he has come to know his purpose and therefore examines all opportunities and threats in light of that purpose. He also considers his strengths and weaknesses when accepting or declining opportunities.

WOTS MOST IMPORTANT* is a strategic planning methodology that reviews weaknesses, opportunities, threats, and strengths (WOTS) to clarify the mission, objectives, strategies, and tactics (MOST) of organizations. Through this methodology, organizational leaders first examine external issues affecting the planning process, then look at several of the most important opportunities and threats. They then consider the response to those external issues in light of their company's internal strengths and weaknesses. After reflecting on the most important external and internal issues, organizational leaders are then positioned to clarify the plan by defining the company's mission, objectives, strategies, and tactics. The mission must be created in full view of the organization's vision and core values.

Covenantal Principle 3: They manifest Christ-likeness in character as evidenced by the fruit of the Spirit in their lives.

In his book *How I Pray*, Billy Graham told of a young company president who instructed his secretary not to disturb him because he had a vital appointment. The chairman of the board came in and said, "I want to see Mr. Jones." The secretary answered, "I'm terribly sorry, he cannot be disturbed; he has an important meeting."

This made the chairman angry. When he went to bang on the door of the president's office, though, it opened just enough for him to see Mr. Jones on his knees—in prayer. The chairman softly closed the door and asked the secretary," Is this usual?" She responded, "Yes, he does that every morning."

The chairman replied, "No wonder I come to him for advice."

Mature leaders seek a rich life of prayer that flourishes in the fertile soil that has been tilled and tended by Bible reading and study, and regular fellowship with other Christian believers (Acts 2:42). Through these spiritual disciplines, they receive godly vision and foresight, then fortify that using wise counsel from other mature leaders.

These leaders also focus on selecting, training, and empowering successor owners and managers, and they leverage their influence by raising up new believers in God. They reflect God's character, too, by investing in servant leaders through personal discipleship training.

Covenantal Principle 4: Truth is lived out in their lives so that convictions and promises of God are seen to be real.

In the New Testament, 2 Timothy 2:2 declares, "The things which you have heard from me in the presence of many witnesses, entrust these to faithful men who will be able to teach others also" (NASB).

Mature leaders learn from other trusted Christian business owners how to maintain their convictions and make biblical principles relevant to colleagues and customers. Lynsi Snyder (In and Out Burger), Truett

Cathy (Chick Fil-A), and David Green (Holly Lobby Inc.) are just three examples of these type of Christian business leaders who model values and reflect divine character in ways that inspire future generations.

In the case of David Green, his business courageously challenged a provision in the Patient Protection and Affordable Care Act in 2010 that mandated employers, regardless of their religious beliefs or moral convictions, to provide insurance that would pay for four embryo life-terminating drugs and devices. At risk of punitive fines of up to $1.3 million per day, Green refused to abide by the Act and took his case all the way to the U.S. Supreme Court, a ruling Hobby Lobby won in June 2014. Green and Hobby Lobby also boldly promotes the Christian meanings of Christmas and Easter and closes on Sundays (like Chick Fil-A) to allow their employees time every Sunday for family and worship.

Finally, these leaders are also careful to maintain fidelity to biblical principles at the board level where there is a danger that wolves in sheep's clothing could maneuver to get their hands-on corporate assets to further personal agendas.

Covenantal Principle 5: They leave behind one or more ultimate contributions.

In Acts 2, conversion is identified with the public hearing of the gospel, baptism, and being added to the church. These are obvious contributions that touch current and future generations. The work of all those in the early Christian church left behind a contribution of faith that extends into the present day and will continue until the day Christ returns to Earth.

Mature leaders can build covenantal relationships with key stake-holders, staff members, clients, and the surrounding community. While following Christ-centered principles can lead to blessings even in the lives of non-Christians (through common grace), the most effective leaders point to Christ as the source of the best principles.

A prime example is the common principle of work ethic excellence. Bible teacher D.L. Moody observed that "God has often called people to places of dignity and honor when they have busy and honest employment as their vocation. Saul was seeking his father's donkeys and David his father's sheep when they were called to the Kingdom. The shepherds were feeding their flocks when they had their glorious revelation. God called the four apostles from their fishing and Matthew from collecting taxes, Gideon from the threshing floor, and Elisha from the plows." Moody concludes, "God never called a lazy man. God never encourages idleness and will not despise persons in the lowest employment."

Covenantal Principle 6: They walk with a growing awareness of a sense of destiny and see some or all of it fulfilled.

Webster's dictionary defines the word "legacy" as "something handed on from those who have come before." The Bible tells us in Psalm 127:3 that our children are a gift of the Lord, a legacy that is a reward from Him. Joel 1:3 further explains: "Tell your sons of it, and let your sons tell their sons, and their sons the next generation" (NASB). Legacy is therefore passed on through the children of family business founders.

When it comes to legacy, mature leaders are challenged to follow the biblical case study of how Christ and the disciples spread Christianity to every corner of the world.

In the same way, leaders can create and sustain a legacy by:

- Building success across time and around the world through franchises, divisions, and other scalable operations.
- Adopting and nurturing a sustainable culture.
- Recording a legacy video or creating an ethical will that communicates core values to future managers by presenting emotionally engaging examples illustrating what it takes to maintain core values across time.
- Encouraging fidelity to the gospel across the generations with appropriate "dead hand control" in legal documents, such as through governance provisions

that help keep majority control in the hands of mature
Christians.

- Creating eternal fruit through evangelism efforts.

There is a story that when the famed English architect, Sir Christopher Wren, was directing the building of St. Paul's Cathedral in London, some of the workers were interviewed by a journalist who asked them, "What are you doing here?"

The first said, "I'm cutting stone for three shillings a day."

The second replied, "I'm putting ten hours a day in on this job."

But the third responded, "I'm helping Sir Christopher Wren build the greatest cathedral in Great Britain for the glory of God."

That worker understood legacy.

Conclusion

In his book *The Making of a Leader*, Dr. Clinton said, "A leader must have the ability to receive truth from God. This gift, receiving truth from God, is essential because it builds spiritual authority, which is the basis for a spiritual leader's influence. The right to influence comes from the ability to clarify God's truth to others. Clarifying truth from God is the essence of the cluster of spiritual gifts that I call the word gifts. Leaders always have at least one word gift along with others that make up their gift-mix. According to Clinton, the primary word gifts are teaching, prophecy, and exhortation. The secondary word gifts are apostleship, evangelism, and pastoring. Leaders will also use word gifts to discern guidance for the ministry."

As mature leaders cultivate these gifts, they are then enabled to equip followers to understand divine revelation, purpose, hierarchical leadership, ethical values, blessings of obedience, and succession plans. As these six elements of the covenant sequence are taught and modeled in a company, new employees and managers mature so that they can extend the influence of the company throughout the community and across the generations.

At www.ReflectingGod.info/Survey, please indicate your level of agreement with the following five statements:

My faith in God is vibrant and I plan to nurture my spiritual relation-ships actively throughout the rest of my life.

not true   1   2   3   4   5   *very true*
○ ○ ○ ○ ○

My commitment to learning helps me be like the sensible man who considers all his steps (Prov. 14:15)

not true   1   2   3   4   5   *very true*
○ ○ ○ ○ ○

My closest friend would say that my Christian practices and beliefs help me regularly experience the fruits of the Spirit (Gal. 5:22)

not true   1   2   3   4   5   *very true*
○ ○ ○ ○ ○

My spiritual insights are entrusted to reliable men and women (2 Tim. 2:2) who help me build a productive team.

not true   1   2   3   4   5   *very true*
○ ○ ○ ○ ○

My business practices can and should be passed from generation to generation (Joel 1:3)

not true   1   2   3   4   5   *very true*
○ ○ ○ ○ ○

Conclusion

BEHIND ALL STORIES about successful business practices, we can find God revealing Himself through covenants. This has been evident as He has reflected his love and holiness[1] 1) throughout the Hebrew Scriptures (Old Testament), 2) throughout the New Testament, 3) throughout the community of Christians, and 4) through discipleship along the path toward loving and holy relationships at work and elsewhere. The four brief sections of this Conclusion summarize these four topics.

1. Our Lord's Holiness and Love in the Old Testament

Our Lord reveals Himself as the sovereign Lord when He forms covenants with man (see, e.g., Gen. 3:14-19, 9:1-17, 15:1, etc.). He guides the humble in what is right and teaches them his way using covenants (Ps. 25:9-10). He describes covenantal relationships in terms of peace (Num. 25:12, Isa. 54:10, Ezek. 34:24, 37:26; Mal. 2:5). God shows how His revelation is actualized through purposeful leaders who obey Him. This results in prosperity for those who honor the divine covenant (Deut. 7:12-15; 8:18, 28:2-12). Before Christ, this prosperity was described not just in terms of wealth but also in terms of spiritual fruit (Lev. 26:4; Deut. 7:12-17)[2] and the loving fatherhood of God over people who have divine commands written on their hearts (Jer. 31:33). This law on their hearts unites believers in lovingkindness (Ps. 40:10).

Surrender to God comes before His people receive the blessings of the covenant. We see this when Moses reveals the Sinai covenant (Exod. 20 and Deut. 5) and then links blessings and curses to respect for the covenant (see, e.g., Deut. 7:12-15; 28:2-12) [3]. The blessings of respecting God's law are then emphasized throughout Scripture, which is seen in Psalm 1:

> Blessed is the one who does not walk in step with the
>   wicked...
> but whose delight is in the law of the Lord, and who med-
>   itates on his law day and night.
> That person is like a tree planted by streams of water,
>   which yields its fruit in season
> and whose leaf does not wither—whatever they do pros-
>   pers. (Ps. 1:1-3)

The Lord God calls his people to respect His law (be righteous) so that they may be people of the covenant and a light to the nation (Isa. 42:6). "'I will make a covenant of peace with them; it will be an everlasting covenant. I will establish them and increase their numbers, and I will put my sanctuary among them forever,' declares the LORD. 'Then the nations will know that I the Lord make [them] holy, when my sanctuary is among them forever'" (Ezek. 37:26-28).

God's light is a purifying light that fosters holiness (Isa. 60:1-4). Andrew Murray writes that, "The one purpose of His holy Covenant is to make us holy as He is holy. As the Holy One He says: "I am holy; be ye holy; I am the Lord which hallows you, which makes you holy." The highest conceivable summit of blessedness is our being partakers of the Divine nature, of the Divine holiness. This is the great blessing Christ, the Mediator of the New Covenant, brings." [4]

2. Our Lord's Holiness and Love in the New Testament

The covenants point toward the light of Christ. We remember his holy covenant... to enable us to serve God without fear in holiness and righteousness [and] to guide our feet into the path of peace" (Luke 1:68-79). Through covenants, God provides His light (Luke 1:78-79, John 8:12, John 12:35-36). The covenants provide an eternal lamp with light to guide believers before Christ and through Christ. Non-believers cannot see this light (2 Cor. 4:2), but for those who believe in Christ, God "[Lets His] light shine out of darkness" and [makes] His light shines in our hearts to give us the light of the knowledge of God's glory displayed in the face of Christ (2 Cor. 4:6).

Christ's light radiates and purifies. "The Son is the radiance of God's glory and the exact representation of his being, sustaining all things by his powerful word. After he had provided purification for sins, he sat down at the right hand of the Majesty in heaven" (Heb. 1:3). Through knowledge of Christ, believers can "contemplate the Lord's glory...being transformed into his image" (2 Cor. 3:14-18). Through this process, saved people reflect the Lord's glorious love and holiness (His character) to others, and at the same time are being transformed into his likeness.

Christ calls his followers to holiness and love (see, e.g., 1 John 1:5-7; 2 Cor. 4:6; 1 Pet. 2:9). Christ exhorts believers to "remember His Holy Covenant; ... serve Him without fear, in holiness and righteousness before Him, all our days" (Luke 1:68-75). Christ exhorts His followers to love by keeping the holy law. He says, "If you keep my commands, you will remain in my love, just as I have kept my Father's commands and remain in his love. I have told you this so that my joy may be in you and that your joy may be complete. My command is this: Love each other as

I have loved you" (John 15:10-12). In 1 John 5, we see a similar description of how Christians are to maintain loving and holy relationships,

> This is how we know that we love the children of God: by loving God and carrying out his commands. In fact, this is love for God: to keep his commands. And his commands are not burdensome, for everyone born of God overcomes the world. This is the victory that has overcome the world, even our faith. Who is it that overcomes the world? Only the one who believes that Jesus is the Son of God.
> (1 John 1:2-5)

To experience Christ's love and holiness, we are to be baptized into Christ (Rom. 6:3), united with Christ in his resurrection (Rom. 6:5), and seated with him in the heavenly realm (Eph. 2:6). Then Christ is formed in believers (Gal. 4:19) and He dwells in our hearts (Eph. 3:17). Upon conversion, the believer is in Christ (Rom. 6:11) and partakes of the divine nature (2 Pet. 1:4). Once we are united with Christ, we are justified (1 Cor. 1:30), sanctified by truth (John 17:17), and adopted so that God the Father loves us no less than he does his own eternal Son (John 17:23). Then we are competent as ministers of a new covenant (2 Cor. 3:6).

3. Our Lord's Love and Holiness Reflected Through the Community of Believers

Those who believe in Jesus as the Son of God respect divine authority (Rom. 10:9-13) and divine righteousness (Rom. 10:3-6). Such people come together in communities that reflect holy and loving relationships with one another. The apostle Paul writes, "Through Christ Jesus the law of the Spirit who gives life has set you free from the law of sin and death" (Rom. 8:2). "Such people have their minds set on what the Spirit desires. The mind governed by the flesh is death, but the mind governed by the Spirit is life and peace" (Rom. 8:5-6).

In community, Christ's followers see how Christ loves them as the Father loved Christ (John 15:9). Believers come together as the body of Christ (1 Cor. 6:15; 12:27) where Christ is in us (2 Cor. 13:5) and we are in Him (1 Cor. 1:30). In such a loving community, it is safe to confess weakness because then God is strong (2 Cor. 13:4, 9). In loving community, we do not have to rely in our own efforts to keep God's law, but we can instead obey from our hearts the pattern of teaching that leads to righteousness (Rom. 6:17-18). We then offer ourselves as slaves to righteousness leading to holiness and eternal life (Rom. 6:19, 22).

In community, Christ's followers experience not just love and holy faithfulness but other spiritual fruit as well. Jesus makes this clear in John 15:4-8 when he exhorts, "Remain in me, as I also remain in you. If you remain in me and I in you, you will bear much fruit; apart from me you can do nothing. If you do not remain in me, you are like a branch that is thrown away and withers; such branches are picked up, thrown into the fire and burned. If you remain in me and my words remain in you, ask whatever you wish, and it will be done for you. This is to my Father's glory, that you bear much fruit, showing yourselves to be my disciples."

In new covenant communities, we see a continuation of theocentric relationships guided by the commitment to ancient biblical covenants. The new covenant church fulfills the intention or goal of the Old Testament's promise of God's presence among his people. In churches committed to the establishment and maintenance of God's everlasting presence, there are abundant blessings described in 2 Corinthians 6:14-7:1, a section of Scripture with many passages tying back to parallel teachings in the Old Testament.[5]

Jesus exhorts churches to maintain His presence through communion which He defines as the new covenant in His blood (see, e.g., Luke 2:20, 1 Cor. 11:25.) The blood washes away sin as prayerful ministers of the Word teach about "repentance unto life"[6] and the Lord's Table.[7] Pastors invite to the Lord's Supper all who are believers in Christ, who are baptized members in good standing of an evangelical church, and who have been properly approved by church officers to take communion. Pastors may also remind those coming to the altar for communion that Jesus warns against participating in the Lord's Supper if there is unresolved conflict with a fellow Christian (see, e.g., Matt. 5:23-24). Effective leaders create a church culture where God's kindness leads to repentance (Rom. 2:4). Such kindness, when combined with warnings about sin and the disciplinary authority of Spirit-led elders, helps maintain the peace and purity of the covenant community church.[8]

When churches use preaching, prayer, and proper administration of the sacraments (the means of grace) to maintain the presence of Christ, leaders in the church see how they can similarly rely on prayer, teachings from God's Word, and discipline to extend Christ's presence beyond the Sunday worship service and beyond the church campus to the marketplace. As business leaders encounter sin in their organizations, they can encourage prayerful peacemaking, refer to relevant biblical teachings, and use various types of discipline to constrain behaviors that disrupt teamwork. Of course, a business is not the church and the business leader does not have the authority of church elders; however, a leader committed to the presence of Christ can learn much from how healthy churches maintain loving and holy relationships while encouraging unity.

4. Discipleship Along the Path to Loving and Holy Relationships

Despite the great promises made to those who remain in loving and holy community, we are far too prone to sin (see, e.g., Rom. 7). We are easily distracted from the true Gospel message.[9] We may be zealous for God, but that zeal may not be based on knowledge (Rom. 10:2). We may not know or submit to God's sovereignty and righteousness but seek to establish a righteousness of our own (Rom. 10:3). We may be saved, but we may not know how to enter into an intimate relationship with Christ and with mature believers. We may acknowledge Christ as Lord (Phil. 2:11-13), but they may need mature help in seeing how Christ's Lordship extends beyond the church campus and beyond Sunday morning service to the marketplace. In such cases, we need relationships that help us mature in faith, experience God's glory, and bear much fruit.

In his teaching about spiritual freedom, Jesus says, "If you hold to my teaching, you are really my disciples" (John 8:31). Christ tells his apostles to teach others to observe all that He has commanded (Matt. 28:20). The apostle Paul then describes how discipleship fosters maturity when believers invest their lives in one another. Paul writes, "We loved you so much that we were delighted to share with you not only the gospel of God but our lives as well, because you had become so dear to us (1 Thess. 2:8 NIV). Investing in one another is explained by Paul in 2 Timothy 2:2, "And the things you have heard me say in the presence of many witnesses entrust to reliable people who will also be qualified to teach others."

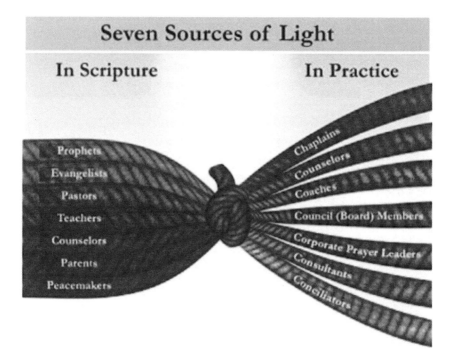

How do we find reliable people who are qualified to teach others? Above all also, we need leaders who are united with Christ and guided by the Spirit under the authority of the Father. How do we find such people who respect the Triune God? Christ gave us prophets, evangelists, pastors, and teachers. Christ shows us the perfect counselor (John 14:15-31). Christ also affirms the leadership roles of peacemakers (Matt. 15:9) and parents (Matt. 15:4).

These spiritual guides can be hard to find off the church campus. Moreover, when the Christian business leader goes to his/her church for guidance, the leader may find that the pastor and church elders know little about board governance, accounting standards, compliance burdens, personnel laws, strategic planning methodologies, stewardship of wealth not given to the local church, and other issues most distracting the business leader from a whole-hearted focus on Christ. Worse, leaders may find that church pastors and elders fail to keep confidences or focus too much on cultivating the business owner as a source of funding for the church.

How does a business leader find a spiritual guide who knows the Lord, knows the business leader, and knows the reality of the marketplace? How does a company owner find qualified consultants who know how to reflect God's character when establishing Christian business principles and practices?

Scripture shows us how prophets, evangelists, pastors, teachers, counselors, parents, and peacemakers can clearly provide much light when they know the Lord and reflect His character. When modern people in these roles lack knowledge of the business world or knowledge of the business person seeking counsel, a business person can turn to seven other sources of spiritual light. In the 21st century, corporate chaplains, business counselors and coaches, board (council) members, prayer partners, consultants, and peacemakers (conciliators) actively advertise their services within Christian circles. To view forty-seven of these services, visit http://www.reflectinggod.info/7LightSources/. At this link, you can see a grid which explains how the forty-seven services correspond to these seven roles: chaplains, counselors, coaches, council members, corporate prayer partners, consultants, and conciliators. You can see which of the forty-seven services you need and then choose which roles need to be filled as you seek guidance.

To further guide discussions about which advisers can reflect God's character and shine light into a business, this book includes five appendices with more information. Appendix 1 helps focus an adviser on building a Christian culture through personal discipleship and corporate consulting. Appendix 2 explains a strategic planning process that relates the traditional SWOT[10] analysis to the mission, objectives, strategies, and tactics of a business. Appendix 3 shows how success in fulfilling the mission and objectives can be monitored on web-based Key Performance Indicators (KPIs). Appendix 4 offers ideas about how a business leader might choose and evaluate a Christian consultant. A list of Christian business organizations, including those with consultants for hire, is in Exhibit 1. Appendix 5 includes ideas about how a business owner should focus on stewarding all of his/her assets throughout the consulting process.

Conclusion

Behind all stories about successful business practices, we can find God revealing love and holiness and other aspects of His character through covenants. Teachings in the ancient Scriptures are now made clear through Christ, the mediator of a new covenant, and through mature Christians who are competent as ministers of a new covenant. A proper understanding of Christ and His covenant community helps the business leader develop his personal relationship with Christ while building teams that reflect God's character. Business leaders all have weaknesses, but, in mature covenant communities, Christ is strong even when the leader is weak. This strength can be found through healthy churches and the types of consultants explained in the following appendices and exhibits.

---

[1] Throughout this book, we have emphasized that God is Holy and Loving. The holiness of God is closely related to God's character as the Just, Truthful, Wise, and Faithful God. The Love of God is closely related to God's character as the Good, Merciful, Gracious, and Patient God. All ten of these attributes of God are discussed well in a book by Jen Wilkin entitled, "In His Image: 10 Ways God Calls Us to Reflect His Character." See www.ReflectingGod.info/InHisImage

[2] www.ReflectingGod.info/OTFruit

³ https://tinyurl.com/ToWCovenantBlessings

⁴ www.ReflectingGod.info/HolyCovenant

⁵ www.ReflectingGod.info/NewCovenantTemple2Cor6-7

⁶ Repentance unto life is an evangelical grace. This doctrine is to be preached by every minister of the gospel along with preaching about faith in Christ. See Chapter 15 of the Westminster Confession of Faith at www.Covenant.net/WCF15.

⁷ For information about Protestant fencing of the communion table, see www.Covenant.net/CommunionFence. For parallel information about closed communion in Roman Catholic churches, see www.Covenant.net/RomanCatholicClosedCommunion.

⁸ For a very helpful summary of how a church can use church discipline to maintain peace and purity, see http://www.BiblicalPeace.com/RC.

⁹ Paul Washer warns that American Christians are often deceived into neglecting the repentance element of the Gospel; see www.ReflectingGod.info/GreatestHearsay. Ray Comfort warns that many people who make "decisions for Christ" never enter into a relationship with Christ; see www.ReflectingGod.info/DecisionsVsRepentance. Tim Keller warns that legalism and liberalism often distract us from a focus on the true Gospel; see www.Covenant.net/3ViewsKeller. H. Richard Niebuhr shows us how differing views of Scripture complete with one that emphasizes freedom in Christ and the transforming work of Christ; see http://www.covenant.net/5ViewsBusiness.

¹⁰ A business or business person should asses internal Strengths and Weaknesses in light of external Opportunities and Threats (SWOT). The SWOT process is also referred to as the WOTS process. To see how this assessment process relates to the Mission, Objective, Strategies, and Tactics (MOST) of a business, visit www.WOTSMOST.com.

Building a Culture That Honors God

*The first responsibility of a leader is to define reality.[1]
Culture is the creation of reality. The reality that is created
drives daily behavior and practices which produce specific
outcomes. Blanchard defines culture as "the
predominating attitudes, beliefs, and behavior patterns
that characterize an organization's functioning."[2]*

A CHRISTIAN LEADER should reflect love and holiness, two main attributes of God, to the culture in a distinctive way. Just like the Trinity is united, an organization needs to unite team members around beliefs that reflect God's truth and grace. Every employee has a sense of belonging within the company. They share a common goal to enhance and enrich the lives of four key groups: customers, employees, shareholders and the community—the quadruple bottom-line. They do so by providing superior products and services and by building trusting relationships.

This can only happen if the leader's heart has been transformed so that he himself is grounded in Christ's truth and grace. Tim Keller says, "Love is an active power and relational, not just a set of principles."[3] We love because He first loved us.[4] We love Christ by obeying all that He has commanded us.[5] By receiving God's love and reflecting it in a holy and principled way, a leader can overcome self-interest and focus instead on treating others as he would want to be treated.[6]

A leader can make the reality of Christ apparent to shareholders, employees, customers and the community through development of a Christ-centered corporate culture. This culture can drive daily behaviors and practices while producing specific outcomes. Key Performance Indicators can track improvement in attitudes, beliefs, and behavior patterns that characterize an organization's effectiveness in serving God and others. Effective service can result in great employee and customer satisfaction, improved profits, and more joy from knowing that Christ's character is being reflected through workplace experiences.

Following the leading of the Holy Spirit, a leader develops a plan based on the six essential steps we describe in this book. The leader begins with defining his or her personal plan. As the leader clarifies how God is working through him or her according to the six covenantal steps explained in this book, the leader can unite with other leaders to reflect divine character qualities throughout the organization. The following table explains how the covenantal planning process is developed at both the personal and corporate levels.

6 STEPS	PERSONAL COVENANTAL PLANNING PROCESS	CORPORATE COVENANTAL PLANNING PROCESS
Step 1: Discern Revelation and Resources	The leader, with the guidance of a spiritually mature prayer team, discovers God's revelation about his personal calling and purpose. He and the prayer team develop an understanding of how he can use personal strengths to pursue an opportunity while managing weaknesses and potential threats to achieve his purpose. (SWOT analysis) The leader and prayer team discern which non-financial resources can be developed to pursue his calling. Non-financial resources include emotional passions, spiritual insights, intellectual capital, physical talents, social networks, and professional skills.	The leader attracts other godly leaders who have prayed earnestly about their God-given purpose and who have sought out like-minded leaders who want to form a team. The leadership team is composed of people who are spiritually mature, show character, maintain godly personal values, and provide competencies to complement the strengths and weaknesses of other team members.
Step 2: Receive God's Vision and Mission	The leader reflects on God's revelation and available resources.	The leader communicates his personal SWOT to the leadership team. The team conducts an organizational SWOT analysis to identify strengths to build upon, weaknesses to overcome, threats to anticipate, and opportunities to leverage in pursuing the mission. The team members regularly evaluate internal strengths and weaknesses as well as external opportunities and threats.

6 STEPS	PERSONAL COVENANTAL PLANNING PROCESS	CORPORATE COVENANTAL PLANNING PROCESS
	The leader, after reflecting on his/her personal purpose and available resources, prayerfully develops an organization vision for using resources in full view of internal and external factors. The leader prays and seeks God's will: "Your Kingdom come, your will be done, on earth as it is in heaven."[7] The leader dedicates his/her company to maintaining Godly authority structures. The leader's vision should be coupled with a values statement that reflects God's unchanging law and the timeless spiritual truths of Scripture.[8] The model for leadership is Jesus, a servant leader who is led by the Holy Spirit.	The leader articulates the vision, mission, and values through words and actions to inspire team members with a compelling promise for the future. The team articulates a statement of vision, mission, and values that can guide the organization.
Step 2: Receive God's Vision and Mission	The vision and values guide development of a mission statement. The leader can explain his/her understanding of vision, values, and mission with hopes of uniting a team.	A compelling vision, mission, and core values provide the foundation for a strong, focused culture which facilitates unity and alignment.
	The leader pursues his/her personal purpose in the context of the organization's mission.	The leadership team consistently communicates the vision, mission, and values. In doing so, the needs of the whole supersede the needs of members' own departments. Leaders focus on goals and priorities that benefit the whole team.

6 STEPS	PERSONAL COVENANTAL PLANNING PROCESS	CORPORATE COVENANTAL PLANNING PROCESS
Step 3: Build a Unified Leader-ship Team	The leader develops a plan to change a culture with help from spiritually mature, competent managers and advisers.	Building a united team involves building trust through transparency and vulnerability and developing critical skills, such as conflict management and listening skills.
	The leader agrees to be accountable to God. This involves committing to daily prayer time and the spiritual disciplines.	Values are translated into specific behaviors and people are held accountable for living out the values. Senior managers and advisers commit to walking the talk and holding each other accountable to a visible change in behavior. People throughout the organization are held accountable for behaving and making decisions consistent with the service standards, vision, mission and values which the leaders have established.
	The leader articulates a consistent message to customers, employees, shareholders. and the community. The business case is persuasive and inspiring by emphasizing the urgency of the need for change.	The leadership team communicate a shared message in word and action.

6 STEPS	PERSONAL COVENANTAL PLANNING PROCESS	CORPORATE COVENANTAL PLANNING PROCESS
Step 3: Build a Unified Leadership Team	The leader reflects the character of other godly leaders who imitate Christ. The leader knows which great leaders from the past can provide the most inspiration.	The senior leadership team identifies culture heroes from among the employees who best reflect the vision and values and have credibility with their peers. They become the culture leadership team responsible for providing input into the change strategy and managing the day-to-day culture activities.
Step 4: Build the Plan Based on Clear Priorities and Principles	The leader focuses on achieving short-term measurable wins in the context of a longer-term culture change plan.	The senior leadership team in collaboration with the "culture leadership team" develops a plan to implement the strategy. The strategy builds on the vision, mission, values, SWOT analysis, customer and employee assessments. The plan identifies the current state, the future desired state, and the way to bridge the gap. The desired future state includes a picture of what leaders want the customer and employee experience to be. Bridging the gap involves identifying short-term initiatives to achieve results in 3-6 months. The plan includes how to communicate for buy-in, train, and mentor people, and measure progress using a dashboard based on the quadruple bottom-line.

6 STEPS	PERSONAL COVENANTAL PLANNING PROCESS	CORPORATE COVENANTAL PLANNING PROCESS
	The leader identifies the gap between the current state and desired future state.	The leadership team identifies what policies and processes are aligned and misaligned with the vision, mission, values, and strategy. Misaligned processes, structures, people systems, rewards, policies, and roles are redesigned to align with the new culture and reinforce the right behaviors.
	The leader emphasizes the importance of making the customer the organization's first priority, while providing superior products and an extraordinary customer experience.	The leadership team develops an inverted pyramid in which servant leaders engage, empower, and mentor the employees, particularly the frontline employees. Cross-functional teams are established around the initiatives to ensure seamless service for the customer.
Step 5: Execute to Realize Outcomes	The leader always asks, "Is it good for everyone concerned?" before making decisions. The leader identifies the indicators which best measure success. The leader tracks Key Performance Indicators and holds people accountable for achieving results which benefit customers, employees, shareholders, and the community.	The leadership team articulates and publishes Key Performance Indicators (KPI). Leaders implement specific goals and metrics, or KPI, to evaluate the impact of short-term initiatives and the value lifestyle. Employees and managers are rewarded for improving according to KPI reports and for demonstrating the right behaviors. Quadruple bottom-line measurements reveal the extent of the benefit to customers, employees, shareholders, and the community. Analysis will identify the critical success factors that generated the results.

6 STEPS	PERSONAL COVENANTAL PLANNING PROCESS	CORPORATE COVENANTAL PLANNING PROCESS
	Drawing on years of wisdom, the leader monitors success as well as failures to identify issues overlooked by less-experienced managers.	The dashboard provides a means for monitoring progress so that people can make course corrections in time. The dashboard monitors successes as well as failures. When results are sub-optimal, managers take corrective action.
Step 6: Prepare a Succession Plan	The leader reflects on Godly character qualities that should be reflected by successor managers and selects and develops successors accordingly.	The leadership team encourages activities to build bench strength, develop servant leaders, and equip a future CEO and managers. Leadership establishes processes to sustain gains and contribute to continuous improvement and innovation, such as systematically sharing and applying best practices and lessons learned. Leaders also document culture-building processes to make them replicable and scalable.

Conclusion

A leader proclaims the reality of Christ to shareholders, employees, customers, and the community by developing a Christ-centered corporate culture. This culture drives daily behaviors and practices which produce superior outcomes in customer satisfaction, employee engagement, community service, and profitability. In addition, a Christ-centered corporate culture provides fertile ground for discipleship and develops servant leaders so that God's character is reflected at an individual, team, and corporate level. This quadruple bottom-line can be scaled around the world and across time. These results are the eternal fruits of a Christ-centered culture.

---

[1] Max DePree, *Leadership Is an Art.*

[2] Blanchard, Ken. Leading at a Higher Level. New Jersey: Prentice Hall, 2007, p. 242.

[3] Tim Keller "Love, the Most Excellent Way." Sermon, What We Are Becoming: Transforming Love, May 1, 2016.

[4] 1 John 4:19

[5] John 14:15, 21

[6] Matthew 7:12

[7] Matthew 6:10

[8] Proverbs 29

Appendix 2

Strategic Planning

THE BIBLE STRONGLY ENCOURAGES strategic planning. This is clear in Luke 14:28–31 when Jesus says, "Suppose one of you wants to build a tower. Will he not first sit down and estimate the cost to see if he has enough money to complete it? Or suppose a king is about to go to war against another king. Will he not first sit down and consider whether he is able with ten thousand men to oppose the one coming against him with twenty thousand?"

The biblical planning process is based on assimilating abundant information. The business leader prayerfully discerns wisdom from divine teachings (Deut. 6:6), from wise counselors (Prov. 15:22), from data about resources (Prov. 24:3, Prov. 27:23), and from his or her own heart (Prov. 16:9).

Plans should be organized in written documents. Scripture abounds with examples of leaders following plans recorded in writing. The Lord instructs that a vision must be clarified in writing (Hab. 2:2). Rules were to be written, as in Deuteronomy 6:9 and 1 Samuel 10:25. 2 Chronicles 3:3 and Ezekiel 43:12 describe how the temple was built with written plans. Plans were written with necessary details, as in 1 Chronicles 28:19. The goal of biblical writers, such as Peter, was to record thoughts so that they could be read when the author was no longer around (2 Pet. 1:15).

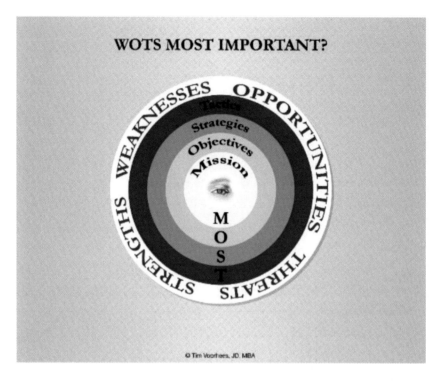

To follow teachings from Scripture and business books about writing plans, a planning process is needed. Business schools teach that a wise business leader should review Weaknesses, Opportunities, Threats, and Strengths (WOTS) to clarify the Mission, Objectives, Strategies, and Tactics (MOST). The leader should first examine external issues affecting the planning process while looking at several of the most important Opportunities and Threats. Then the leader should consider responses to external issues considering the company's internal Strengths and Weaknesses. After reflecting on the most important external and internal issues, the leader articulates a plan with a clear Mission, Objectives, Strategies, and Tactics.[1]

A Christian business leader will seek to build a plan around a clear vision and core values. Such values may include unchanging principles from Scripture as well as changing priorities based on available resources. The diagram at the right summarizes the different elements of a written plan based on a clear vision.

To test the validity of the plan, a business leader can circulate a draft plan among decision-makers to see if all will support the plan with "one voice," as in Romans 15:6. See the discussion of unified planning in Chapter 5 on Board Governance.

Once decision-makers agree to execute the plan, a budgeting process, project management system, employee education metrics, and marketing metrics are needed to track execution. Qualified advisers should prayerfully help the business owners and managers execute the plan so that daily tasks (tactics) are completed in full view of strategic priorities, periodic objectives, and the corporate mission. The goal is to have the daily details managed in harmony with a mission based on a carefully discerned vision statement.

The budgeting process is related to the Admin/Finance cornerstone of the business, the project management system is often related to the Production cornerstone, employee education metrics are related to the Training cornerstone, and marketing metrics are related to the Marketing cornerstone. The processes and systems are all linked to Key Performance Indicators (KPI) that track a company's effectiveness in tending to details related to periodic objectives, strategic initiatives, and specific tasks (tactics). The link between strategic efforts in seventeen areas and the four main cornerstones (Admin/Finance, Production, Training, and Marketing cornerstone) is summarized at www.ReflectingGod.info/4Cornerstones17Areas. These cornerstones can correspond to the quadruple bottom line discussed in Section 5 of this book and as illustrated here (see www.ReflectingGod.info/4XBottomLine):

BUSINESS CORNERSTONE	CONSTITUENCIES SERVED	KEY PERFORMANCE INDICATORS
Admin/Finance	Shareholders	QuickBooks Dashboard
Production/Service	Customers	Project Management and Customer Service Metrics
Training	Employees	Employee Engagement Metrics
Marketing	Community	Customers Acquired/Served

Modern cloud-based systems provide a variety of KPI reports that can help different constituencies review improvements. Executives and/or consultants can study a business to determine which performance indicators are most key to a company's success in realizing its vision and mission. Then consultants can help build reports that help executives track the execution of tasks to fulfill strategic goals in harmony with periodic objectives based on the mission. Such a process helps managers track how all team members tend to micro details while making necessary adjustments in full view of strategies, objectives, and the corporate mission.

The above process is explained in more detail at www.WOTS-MOST.com and in many books on Execution. For information about relevant books, visit www.ReflectingGod.info/Bibliography.

---

[1] The WOTS analysis is also referred to as SWOT analysis when planners look first at Strengths and Weaknesses followed by Opportunities and Threats. The WOTS MOST Process dovetails with values-based planning because planners are encouraged to ask continually "what's most important?" or "WOTS MOST Important?" See, e.g., www.WOTS-MOST.com.

Appendix 3

Focusing on KPIs as You Grow and Scale Your Business

THE 16 CHAPTERS of this book emphasize how reflecting God's character can enhance the quadruple bottom line. Divinely-guided teamwork can benefit shareholders, customers, employees, and the community. These four business stakeholders can all benefit when web-based dashboards track key performance indicators (KPI).

Tracking KPI helps business managers steward resources well. Managers committed to teachings about biblical stewardship (such as in the parable of the sower in Matthew 13 or the parable of the talents in Matthew 25) want accurate data that can guide them as they multiply what God has provided. Reliable KPI can help business owners know the condition of their flocks (their staff or other resources) in keeping with the teachings of Proverbs 27:23.

The best KPI reports shine a bright line into the performance of systems and staff. This sunlight acts as a powerful disinfectant as it reveals non-productive processes or people. More important, the KPI can help executives see which activities are most profitable. Monitoring KPI helps decision-makers allocate resources to the most promising ventures as they "leverage the best and ditch the rest" (to borrow a phrase from Ken and Scott Blanchard).

CRM and accounting systems provide a variety of KPI reports that can help different constituencies review improvements. Executives and/or consultants can study a business to determine which performance indicators are most key to a company's success in realizing its vision and mission. Then consultants can help build reports that help executives track the execution of tasks to fulfill strategic goals in harmony with periodic objectives based on the mission. The Admin/Finance, Production/Service, Training, and Marketing KPI can correspond to the Quadruple Bottom Line as metrics track success in serving shareholders, customers, employees, and the community.

BUSINESS CORNERSTONE	CONSTITUENCIES SERVED	KEY PERFORMANCE INDICATORS
Admin/Finance	Shareholders	QuickBooks Dashboard
Production/Service	Customers	Project Management Metrics
Training	Employees	Employee Engagement Metrics
Marketing	Community	Customers Acquired/Served

People served by a business will focus on what the company measures in the four cornerstone areas discussed in Appendix 2. For example, shareholders can use KPI reports to track administrative and financial variables. Focus groups of customers may look for improvements in metrics related to the quality of products or services, and employees may focus on variables that track training and career advancement. The community surrounding a company may know the company mostly by its marketing messages, so marketing executives may focus on KPI tracking positive responses to print and media advertisements. The loyalty and satisfaction of customers is related to teamwork and productivity, which is tracked using measures of growth and consistent excellence, as well as engagement and retention of *employees*. Productivity should result in profits for *shareholders* and enhanced participation in, or donations to, *community* activities. [1]

To grow a business in harmony with a God-inspired vision, business owners work with consultants to develop KPIs that focus on bringing in clients (marketing), producing products and services with quality (production), maintaining profitable administrative support (Admin/Finance), and equipping staff to work in profitable teams (training). Given the critical importance of attracting and engaging customers and clients, business owners often start with KPI reports focused on marketing.

Before creating any marketing KPI reports, a business owner needs a clear vision for maintaining world-class systems to serve clients. A business must build and refine reliable systems first because failure will create a negative compound effect on customer service and returns. Worse, lack of reliability will adversely affect reputation. Proverbs 22:1 says, "A good name is to be chosen rather than great riches." A good name will generate much good will among shareholders, customers, employees, and the community. This creates positive word-of-mouth referrals, which is the best form of marketing.

When client fulfillment systems are fine-tuned to provide exceptional value, a business can then focus on marketing to attract clients and grow. This is best done with a Client Acquisition System that focuses managers on 1) Lead Generation System KPIs, 2) Lead Warming System KPIs, and 3) Lead Closing System KPIs. The remainder of this appendix will focus on these topics while closing with a summary of how 4) KPIs can be linked to the strategic plan.

Marketing systems and client acquisition systems are essentially "selling systems." Such systems are built around clear messages to three different types of prospects. The business owner needs to sell to the Colds, the Warms, and the Hots.

1. The "Colds" don't know you and have some level of interest in what you are selling but are not ready to commit to much action.
2. The "Warms" may or may not know you, but they have a higher level of interest in solving their problem and are looking for possible solutions.
3. The "Hots" may know you, but they have a burning hot desire to solve their problem and are ready to take action.

When the business person sells in person, she can pivot and adapt quickly. If she is using the internet to get leads, the system needs to filter and handle each type of prospect. To manage web traffic, a turnkey selling system should:

- Filter out the tire kickers while locating promising leads with a Lead Generation System
- Nurture the Colds and educate them until they become Warm
- Heat up the Warms with a Lead Warming System until they become Hot
- Close the Hot prospects with a Lead Closing System
- Document a scalable process
- Maintain a measurable process
- Leverage a profitable process
- Keep the business owner focused on freeing up more time for family, church involvement, or other meaningful relationships.

To explain the above bullet points another way, the Selling System is composed of three main systems:

1. Lead generation system for the Colds
2. Lead warming system for the Warms
3. Lead closing system for the Hots

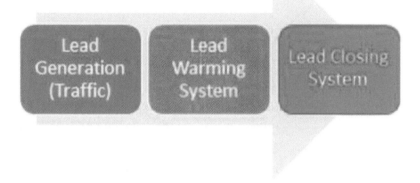

Lead Generation System KPIs

For Lead Generation using the internet, the business owner should measure the following:

1. Impressions – the number of times an advertisement is shown
2. Clicks/Sessions – the number of times someone clicks on an advertisement and follows prompts to go to the designated website
3. Actions – the number of specific actions taken, such as opt-ins or forms filled out to receive a special report, white paper, webinar, or a request for a consult or meeting

The KPIs below are taken from Google Ads (formerly Google Ad-Words). It was unknown whether this traffic source would work or not, so, as with all good marketing, the business manager started with "precision targeting." The goal was to "Aim Small, Miss Small." Starting with a very controlled process allows marketers to prove viability before spending much money. Once marketing is proven, it can be scaled to the extent the business can move new leads through the sales funnel.

The following example is from a project where the client was able to prove out a new concept, double sales, and slash their acquisition costs by 93.5% (or just under $2 million). The client focused initially on impressions and clicks until the conversion data started coming in. When getting started, there were benchmarks for each industry that the client wanted to track. It is important to compare results to benchmarks until custom benchmarks are established for a particular situation.

The goal of the lead generation system is to establish client acquisition costs and cost per lead. Once these numbers are determined, a business can "gamify" the process, using modified variables to try to beat the benchmarks. The same principles apply regardless of whether the traffic source is LinkedIn, Google, YouTube, Facebook, direct mail, magazines, radio, TV, trade shows, email marketing, or any other form of marketing.

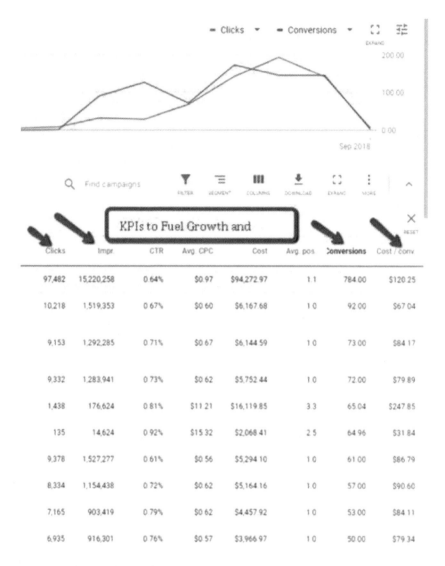

Clicks	Impr.	CTR	Avg. CPC	Cost	Avg. pos.	Conversions	Cost / conv.
97,482	15,220,258	0.64%	$0.97	$94,272.97	1.1	784.00	$120.25
10,218	1,519,353	0.67%	$0.60	$6,167.68	1.0	92.00	$67.04
9,153	1,292,285	0.71%	$0.67	$6,144.59	1.0	73.00	$84.17
9,332	1,283,941	0.73%	$0.62	$5,752.44	1.0	72.00	$79.89
1,438	176,624	0.81%	$11.21	$16,119.85	3.3	65.04	$247.85
135	14,624	0.92%	$15.32	$2,068.41	2.5	64.96	$31.84
9,378	1,527,277	0.61%	$0.56	$5,294.10	1.0	61.00	$86.79
8,334	1,154,438	0.72%	$0.62	$5,164.16	1.0	57.00	$90.60
7,165	903,419	0.79%	$0.62	$4,457.92	1.0	53.00	$84.11
6,935	916,301	0.76%	$0.57	$3,966.97	1.0	50.00	$79.34

Graphics help track the number of people who see a web-based advertisement (impressions), the number of clicks, the "click through ratio," and the cost per conversion. Graphics show the relationship between clicks and conversions as well as the cost for each new customer. Such tracking of KPIs helps a manager prudently spend on advertising to fuel growth and scale up the size of a business.

Lead Warming System KPIs

The KPI chart and table below is from Google Analytics. This incredibly powerful tool allows you to track all activity throughout your website. You can see what is going on now and where the opportunities lay. When we start sowing seeds, some will fall on hard ground, some will grow small roots, and some will become a harvest. It's important to know what sources produce the harvest and then optimize them.

The following graphics help a business owner track success with attracting high net worth individuals, with the ultimate goal of booking a meeting and making a presentation. Tracking this data helps a manager create and test new advertisements, change the words and the imagery in ads, and test different offers.

As indicated by the pie chart and bar charts below, advertisements posted to the web are tracked with a pie chart indicating whether people view an ad as a result of a paid search, display ad impression, direct email advertisement, referral from a forwarded ad, social media posting, or organic (e.g., Google) search. Web metrics track each of these channels to count the number of new web-viewing sessions, new users, and pages viewed. As indicated by the red arrows, KPIs focused on maximizing sessions, especially new sessions, are connected to KPIs focused on conversion rates. By linking these data to financial data, it is possible to place a value on achieving goals. (To see a larger version of the following graphic, please visit www.ReflectingGod.info/Dashboard2.)

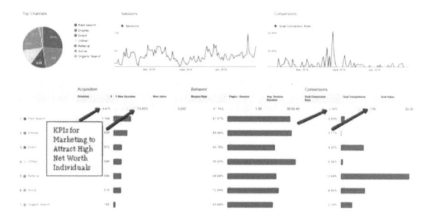

When developing KPIs like those above, the goal is to determine 1) client acquisition cost—how much it costs to acquire a new customer by each channel—, and 2) cost per lead—how much it costs to get a new lead. With these two numbers established, the manager can easily determine the profitability of the campaign. From there, the manager can discern which activities are profitable or not. When spending is profitable, the manager can discern what can be done to be even more profitable. Conversely, when profits are not evident, the manager can look at the gap between actual and desired results while possibly eliminating non-productive spending on dubious traffic sources.

World-class marketing uses a concept that engineers call "Kaizen," which stands for continuous and ongoing improvement. Managers focus on a steady improvement until they hit the point of diminishing returns. When profitability drops in one area, the managers use data to spot other Areas of Highest Opportunities (AOHOs). Astute managers constantly look for AOHOs. Every business has them. There are three to four main AOHOs in any business. Managers who focus attention on AOHOs while tracking KPIs can have remarkable success, God willing.

Lead Closing System KPIs

This example of a Lead Closing System is based on data from a law firm that measures the effectiveness of a marketing strategy. The system tracks the number of incoming calls from different traffic sources for specific campaigns. The goal is to determine 1) if calls could be generated and 2) the acquisition cost and profitability of those calls.

The chart below was generated by call tracking software that monitors KPI with "Call Tracking Metrics." Many wonderful software and phone services can integrate with various systems to create similar reports for any industry or specific situation. In the graph below, managers track the number of incoming calls and track each back to specific individuals to see if they become clients and generate profits. Managers can see the increasing trend where more resources were devoted after getting through the initial viability phase. The goal is to invest more resources (time, money, and energy) where it makes sense.

Lead Closing System graphics track calls from high-net-worth prospects. The colored layers of the mountain charts show the source of the calls as well as data about the number of unique callers. (Please see www.ReflectingGod.info/Dashboard3 to see a larger version of the following graphic.)

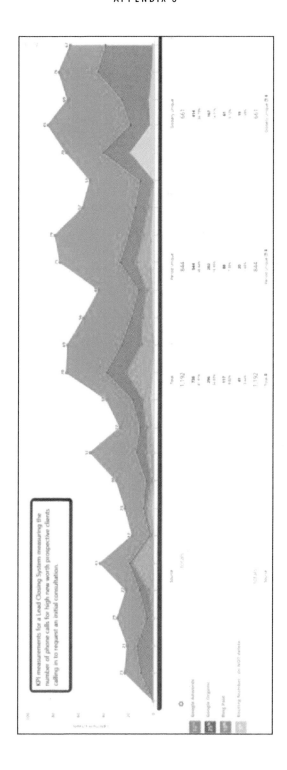

KPI measurements for a Lead Closing System measuring the number of phone calls for high new worth prospective clients calling in to request an initial consultation.

KPIs Linked to the Strategic Plan

When building a Client Acquisition System, the manager must focus on a sequence of Goal > Strategy > Tactics. As explained in Appendix 2, the goals are linked to quarterly objectives, the strategies are linked to job descriptions, and the tactics are related to specific next actions or "to dos" or tasks. Marketing KPIs are, therefore, linked to objectives, strategies, and tactics based on the business vision and mission.

Tracking fulfillment of specific tasks results in fulfillment of the corporate mission and vision. This appendix has focused on marketing KPIs. The same process for tracking, reporting, and using marketing KPIs can be used and refined to make wise decisions in other parts of an organization.

KPIs for the client acquisition system (marketing) can be linked to parallel KPIs for the client fulfilment system (production), staff education systems (training), and shareholder profitability systems (e.g., financial statements produced with help from web-based accounting systems such as QuickBooks). Marketing, Production, Training, and Financial KPIs work together to help executives measure how well business executives service clients, retain clients, and generate long-term profits and/or positive client satisfaction results.

The following graphic provides one example of how proposals sent as part of a client acquisition system (marketing) are linked to revenues tracked as part of the shareholder profitability (financial) systems. Additional gauges can be added to the following dashboard to focus managers on all variables that most influence the success of a business. (To see a larger version of the following graphic, please visit www.ReflectingGod.info/Dashboard4.)

Data from working with hundreds of business owners, and interviewing thousands more, show that a very small percentage of business owners track KPIs successfully. If they are Christian business owners, they are called to steward assets in accordance with a God-honoring vision and strategic plan, as described in Appendix 2. The objectives, strategies, and tactics in Appendix 2 can be linked to KPIs described in Appendix 3 to track important details. Tracking details and stewarding all resources is important because, as Jesus reminds us in Luke 16:10, "He who is faithful in a very little thing is faithful also in much."

Our friend Michael Gerber, who wrote the phenomenal book, *The E-Myth Revisited*, says that most business owners are really technicians who started a business and don't understand all the issues related to running a business. His point is that virtually everyone starting a business is good at working in the business, but proficient technicians do not understand all the aspects of working on a successful business. If you are an attorney, consultant, doctor, or financial adviser, do not assume you are good at running a business. If you make green juices, bake cookies, or do anything else you are good at doing, do not assume this qualifies you to run a business well. You need to use established systems for marketing, advertising, and selling. You need to link marketing systems to other systems to fulfill goals in your plan. (If you have not read Gerber's book, you can click the link referenced above to buy it. The book sold millions of copies and is on the top 10 list of books that billionaires read.[2])

The good news is that a business person can start applying Gerber's ideas even if broke, with nothing but the God-given resources described in Chapter 2 of this book. With whatever knowledge and resources are available, the ideas in Appendices 2 and 3 can, over time, establish a road to growing a business like few would imagine possible.

Growth takes commitment to clarify a vision and mission, as described in Chapter 3, and then follow through. Visions are fulfilled when there is imagination. Imagine having a website where people lose sleep because they're in wide-eyed amazement, marveling at how you're exactly what they've been yearning for and are spending every waking moment on it and referring everyone they know—a site so wonderful, so magical, that it multiplies profits exponentially faster than money can be spent. Imagine web-based solutions that forever solve all business problems.

The good news is that a business leader can create something truly wonderful that will make life much easier. It is possible to have a turnkey selling system that will take people with varying degrees of interest and meet them where they are, filter good leads, and warm leads according to individual needs. The system can produce hot prospects ready and wanting to do business. Creating this client acquisition system takes an investment of time, money, and energy, but abundant examples now exist to prove what is possible when leveraging web-based systems to fulfill a vision.

The key is setting up a client acquisition system, measuring the KPIs, and using wisdom and discernment to improve upon them. Marketing systems need to be linked with related web-based business systems so that each business manager can have a web-based dashboard with all relevant metrics automatically updated. Then the business can track how all team members tend to micro details while making necessary adjustments in full view of strategies, objectives, and the corporate mission.

Conclusion

Following the above steps helps a business develop a powerful selling system (client acquisition system). Once the system is set up, the business manager can actively measure results and look for potential enhancements. Examining profitability related to different variables gives the manager a vitally important data feedback system, which is made up of custom KPIs. The KPIs tell the manager how well the system is, or is not, performing. Reliable data makes it clear where a business should focus to grow.

Managers want a positive Return on Investment (ROI). Managers want every dollar invested to turn into two dollars, or three dollars, or five dollars, or ten dollars, or whatever the number is for a particular business. It is important to note that, when starting out, it is quite common to have a negative return while learning and fine-tuning systems. Depending on the product or service, that can be a normal part of growth. If you can measure it, you can improve it.

Anyone reading this appendix must be cognizant of the many challenges that may arise while trying to implement the seemingly simple process described in the following paragraphs. The possible obstacles and solutions are summarized in endnote 3.

So what should a manager measure? We should look at the KPIs for the 1) Lead Generation System, 2) Lead Warming System, and 3) Lead Closing System. We should link marketing systems to production, training, and financial systems so that owners and managers can have 4) KPIs clearly linked to the mission and objectives in the strategic plan. The KPIs help business leaders tend to details linked to the realization of strategic initiatives, periodic objectives, and a corporate mission based on the company's vision. Shareholders, customers, employees, and members of the community can then see how resources are stewarded by staff members who delight in serving others while glorifying and enjoying God.

Source: Chris Goegan is the source of KPI charts and much content used in this appendix. Chris is a highly sought-after marketing consultant, speaker, and entrepreneur. He has worked with hundreds of business owners in 100+ industries around the world, but he's really a simple guy. He loves his work, loves his clients, and loves his family. He works with well-known thought leaders and professionals while also working with start-ups, friends, and small business owners.

Chris started as an engineer building high-volume manufacturing lines and then got into sales and marketing. He struggled at many times and had wonderful people give him wisdom and assist him at every stage. Now he wants to do the same for others.

Chris now builds high-volume manufacturing lines, but instead of manufacturing engines like he did at Ford Motor Co., he now manufactures high-volume marketing and sales systems for business owners who want to grow to an entirely new level.

If you are struggling or frustrated or irritated or annoyed because you need more leads, or need more sales, or need systems working for you, then Chris can help. Chris can show you how to build automated sales and marketing systems that generate more leads and sales so you can free your mind (and time) while focusing on growing and scaling your business. Please visit www.ChrisGoegan.com/Scale for special free resources.

---

[1] This appendix focuses on marketing Key Performance Indicators (KPIs) because business owners of all sizes can typically justify spending money to build selling systems that drive marketing. Nonetheless, business consultants can create a myriad of additional KPIs to track how a business improves production, financial performance, or employee training and engagement. For examples of employee engagement KPIs, see www.ReflectingGod.info/EmployeeEngagement and www.ReflectingGod.info/EmployeeEngagementMetrics.

[2] See www.ReflectingGod.info/10BillionaireBooks.

[3] A wise leader inquires thoroughly (Deut. 17:4), seeks to be informed about the whole situation (Col. 4:9), consults wise men who understand the times (Esth. 1:13), and considers well his steps (Prov. 14:15). Applying these passages to 21st-century business, a corporate executive needs to heed the unprecedented competition in the marketplace.

According to the America Marketing Association, "studies show that the average consumer is exposed to up to 10,000 brand messages a day. As marketers leverage more and more channels to reach their customers, the number of marketing messages grows daily. Consumers switch between screens up to 21 times an hour according to a British study, which correlates with Microsoft's claim that the average person's attention span is now just eight seconds." A 2018 study showed that the average person touches, swipes, or clicks their phone 2,617 times a day. The top 10 percent do so 5,427 times a day, and it's probably only going to get worse. Consumers face crazy levels of distraction.

Even crazier is how business owners market their business to try to get around this distraction. They push their message harder. They make more phone calls. They up their advertising budget. They try new traffic sources. They go to more networking events. They throw more mud at the walls. To get more leads, business owners spend more time and money on the latest traffic technique promising lower costs. They push, and then if the pushing does not work, they push the advertising and traffic sources harder. This is the traditional (old school) way of marketing.

In the new school of marketing, it is not about "getting your message out there" (although you do need to get your message out there). It is not about the latest traffic fad or how many impressions you get (although traffic and impression metrics matter). Why?

Most old school marketing does not work because the strategy is completely wrong. The strategy focuses too much on traffic – getting leads from Facebook, or

Google, or LinkedIn, or YouTube, or whatever the latest online or offline source is. While traffic is good, starting with traffic metrics is counterproductive. Good business managers waste months or even years trying to figure out how to get their marketing and the internet to work for them. Instead, they should be spending time helping more people; leveraging time, talents, and treasures, and growing the business.

Appendix 4

Consulting

THE CONSULTANT HELPS a business discern "what is" and "what ought to be." Seeking "what is" can be difficult because of people's tendencies to flatter themselves too much to detect or hate their sin (see, e.g., Psalm 36:2 and 2 Corinthians 10:12). Seeking "what ought to be" is difficult because people with differing values and perceptions need to build unified teams in order to maximize productivity, fulfill objectives, and realize the corporate mission while respecting the company's vision and core values. If a company struggles in the above areas, consultants can help. For more information, see www.ReflectingGod.info/Consulting.

Appendix 5

Stewarding Wealth for God's Glory

BUSINESS OWNERS MAY SPEND more than half of their wealth on taxes. Three months of each year are spent doing work to pay money to the state treasury departments. An additional three months may be spent paying capital gains, alternative minimum, estate, gift, IRD, sales, or other taxes. Money directed to taxes is spent on projects deemed important to the government. Christian purposes are often ignored. As Jesus reminds us in Mark 9:38–41, what is not spent to further the cause of Christ is against Christian causes.[1]

In America, a portion of lifetime income and transfers to beneficiaries must be allocated for the good of the community. Every taxpayer is either a voluntary or involuntary philanthropist. Christian tax advisers can use all their wealth to fund Christian causes. The process begins with choosing between voluntary philanthropy and involuntary philanthropy:

- Taxpayers are **involuntary philanthropists** if they do nothing and give to the state and federal treasuries through taxes. As an involuntary philanthropist, an individual must usually sit back and let the government make decisions about spending his or her wealth.

- Alternatively, taxpayers can be **voluntary philanthropists**. Congress allows Americans to use a variety of charitable trusts to direct their would-be tax money to their favorite charities. Taxpayers can send their voluntary tax money to foundations that then redirect those funds to a broad array of causes close to their hearts. Through active involvement in philanthropic planning, individuals can control—and feel good about—the portion of their wealth that must go to the community.

Voluntary philanthropy may involve gift annuities, charitable remainder trusts, charitable lead trusts, donations of company stock, gifts of intellectual property, and numerous other techniques. Skilled wealth advisers can integrate these tools into plans involving clients' existing planning instruments, such as their retirement plans or living trusts. Competent advisers can show their clients how to control not just their personal wealth but their community wealth as well. For example, a wealth adviser can structure family foundations with boards composed of family members who gain great influence in the community as they fund favorite charitable causes with money that would have been wasted in taxes.

Understanding tax planning techniques helps business owners integrate non-charitable business planning with charitable planning. In this way, business owners can control all their wealth. They not only manage their businesses, but they also manage how favorite charities receive funds that would have gone to taxes. At www.ReflectingGod.info, readers can learn how advisers can choose, customize, and integrate planning instruments to help business owners apply biblical stewardship principles to personal wealth as well as business wealth.

Personal Wealth | Community Wealth

Effective advisers can give their clients much guidance in deciding what portion of their wealth will be consumed by them or transferred to their charitable or non-charitable beneficiaries. Furthermore, advisers can help their clients redirect tax money to foundations that fund a variety of favorite charities. In this way, clients can use all their personal and community wealth to fund the people and causes who carry on the values that are most important to them. As shown in the following diagram, taxpayers can perpetuate their values by allocating wealth to any of the four "buckets." Personal wealth can be 1) consumed or 2) transferred to beneficiaries. Community wealth can be 3) gifted to charities or 4) directed to the Treasury Department as tax payments.

As summarized here (and explained in materials at www.ZeroTax-Counsel.info), individuals can give a large portion of their assets to charity without reducing what is available for their retirement and/or family. Each person can control all his or her wealth and effectively "disinherit" the IRS. In addition to directing their personal wealth to worthwhile causes, individuals can redirect wealth from involuntary philanthropy to voluntary philanthropy. Instead of letting the government choose who receives their hard-earned money, donors can direct wealth through their preferred charities and causes that uphold their vision and values.

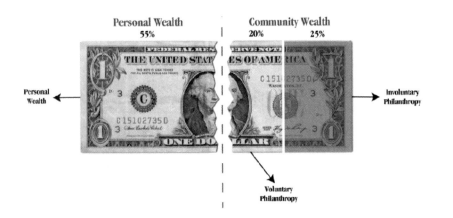

The above diagram shows a win-win-win outcome with more for family, more for favorite charities (voluntary philanthropy), and less for taxes (involuntary philanthropy). Experienced planners can enhance this outcome to show more for retirement and little or nothing for taxes.

Even simple tax planning tools can direct taxes to charity without reducing what is available for retirement or family. More advanced tools can provide greater benefits and even zero-out taxes. As might be expected, the more sophisticated plans may involve more risk, complexity, or expense. Nonetheless, experienced advisers can normally show how the planning benefits far outweigh the costs.

As individuals take control of their capital, they should see that they have far more wealth available to fund their vision. They can use wealth in their non-charitable trusts for retirement, transfers to family, or a wide array of investments that build value. They can use wealth in their charitable trusts for investments and/or charitable gifts. They can confidently use all their charitable and non-charitable wealth to support causes that are probably much more consistent with their values than those the government funds with their tax money.

---

[1] The Tax Foundation publishes an annual "Tax Freedom Day." For 2017, the Tax Freedom Day was April 23. The foundation used average compensation and tax rates to calculate that Americans would work 113 days from January 1 to April 23 to pay federal, state, and local taxes at a combined rate of 31%. If budget deficits were funded through taxes, Tax Freedom Day would be extended into May. If wealthy individuals calculated tax freedom dates at their higher marginal rates and included transfer taxes (including estate, gift, and GST taxes), "freedom" may not occur until the second half of the year. Using other methodologies that consider the cost of government as a percentage of the Gross Domestic Product,

researchers conclude that Americans worked until July 15th in 2012 to pay the annual cost of government.

For more information, please visit taxfoundation.org/tax-freedom-day-2017/ and www.costofgovernment.org/files/files/COGD2012_hi%20res.pdf.

Exhibit 1

Marketplace Ministries

Type of group	Name of group	Website
CEO Groups	C12	http://c12group.com
CEO Groups	Convene	http://convenenow.com
CEO Groups	Fellowship of Companies for Christ	http://fcci.org
CEO Groups	CBMC Forums	http://cbmc.com
CEO Groups	Truth at Work	http://truthatwork.org
Chaplains	Corporate Chaplains of America	http://chaplain.org
Chaplains	Marketplace Chaplains	http://mchapusa.com
City-Centric Worklife Networks	Center for Faith + Work Los Angeles	http://faithandworkla.com
City-Centric Worklife Networks	Faith and Work Life (Orange County)	http://faithandworklife.org
City-Centric Worklife Networks	Dallas Business Forum	https://dallasbusinessforum.org/
City-Centric Worklife Networks	Chicago Christian Business Fellowship	https://christianbusinessfellowship.org
City-Centric Worklife Networks	Redeemer Center for Faith and Work (NYC)	https://faithandwork.com/
Community	Full Gospel Business Fellowship	http://http://fgbmfi.org/
Community	CBMC	http://cbmc.com
Community	Marketplace Leaders	http://marketplaceleaders.org
Community	4word	http://4wordwomen.org
Community	Alpha in the Workplace	http://alphausa.org/workplace
Community	At Work on Purpose	http://atworkonpurpose.org

REFLECTING GOD'S CHARACTER IN YOUR BUSINESS

Community	Work Matters	http://workmatters.org
Community	Worklife	http://worklife.org
Community	Legatus	https://legatus.org/
International	Marketplace Advance	marketplaceadvance.com
International	Call2Business	http://call2business.org
International	Partners Worldwide	http://partnersworldwide.org
International	Global Advance	http://globaladvance.org
International	NewVo BAM Network	http://newvobusiness.com
Leadership Training	Master's Program	http://themastersprogram.org
Leadership Training	Lifework Leadership	http://lifeworkleadership.org
Leadership Training	Lead Like Jesus	http://leadlikejesus.com
Leadership Training	Halftime	http://halftime.org
Leadership Training	Nehemiah Project	http://nehemiahproject.org
Leadership Training	Primemovers	http://primemoversonline.com
Legal	Christian Business Legal Defense Association	http://ReflectingGod.info/CBLDA
Legal	Pacific Justice Institute	http://pacificjustice.org
Legal	Christian Legal Society	http://clsnet.org
Seminary Training	Theology of Work Project	https://www.theologyofwork.org
Seminary Training	Institute for Faith Work & Economics	https://tifwe.org
Seminary Training	Gospel Coalition	http://thegospelcoalition.org
Seminary Training	Foundations for Laity	https://issuu.com/laityrenewal
University	Intervarsity MBA Ministry	http://ivmba.org
Web Resources	Theology of Work Project	http://theologyofwork.org
Web Resources	Right Now Media	http://rightnowmedia.org
Web Resources	Two Ten Magazine	http://twotenmag.com
Web Resources	The High Calling	http://thehighcalling.org

EXHIBIT 1

Web Resources	Patheos	http://patheos.com
Women	4word	http://4wordwomen.org
Women	PURE	http://thepureconference.com
Women	Women Doing Well	http://womendoingwell.org
Work and Culture	Centurions	http://centurionsprogram.org
Work and Culture	Pinnacle Forum	http://pinnacleforum.com
Work and Culture	Barnabas Group	http://barnabasgroup.org
Work and Culture	New Canaan Society	http://newcanaansociety.org
Work and Culture	Salt & Light Leadership Training	http://sallt.com

Exhibit 2

80 Questions to Assess Your Commitment to Christ-Centered Business

At www.ReflectingGod.info, please indicate your level of agreement with the five statements corresponding to each of 16 chapters of *Reflecting God's Character in Your Business*.

Chapter 1	My leadership team seeks to use God's word to shine light into darkness.
Chapter 1	My advisers help me apply God's law to confront pride, greed and other deadly sins.
Chapter 1	My managers learn how people in covenant community identify resources, pursue a mission, respect authority, uphold ethical precepts, encourage blessings, and extend the Kingdom.
Chapter 1	My company encourages managers to develop leadership skills, following Biblical patterns, in family, church, and/or government roles.
Chapter 1	My key advisers seek wisdom through God's word and prayer in church communities that administer sacraments to maintain peace and purity.

Chapter 2	I choose prayer partners who are spiritually-mature and wise advisers.
Chapter 2	My prayer partners help me see and leverage my God-given non-financial resources, starting with God's calling on my life and work.
Chapter 2	My prayer partners guide me in developing a personal SWOT and Spirit-led plan.
Chapter 2	My plans are tested against Scripture to confirm that they are in line with God's plans for developing resources.
Chapter 2	I am committed to being a servant leader who enhances the well-being of all key stakeholders.
Chapter 3	My mission and vision are articulated in written statements and embedded in strategy, leadership practices and company culture.
Chapter 3	My leadership team agrees on ranked and time-bound goals based on our vision and mission.
Chapter 3	My leadership team and key stakeholders are aligned around a shared corporate vision and mission.
Chapter 3	My vision and core values are articulated in written statements and embedded in strategy, leadership practices and company culture. (Deuteronomy 6:4–9)
Chapter 3	My mission and vision are a revelation from God and reveal His Character and Word.

EXHIBIT 2

Chapter 4	My company's statement of core values is based on proven principles of the founders and timeless spiritual truths.
Chapter 4	My leadership team fosters trust by demonstrating character and competence.
Chapter 4	My leadership team makes decisions and behaves consistently with our core values.
Chapter 4	My leadership team aligns our corporate culture with our core values.
Chapter 4	My leadership team members hold one another accountable and enforce accountability throughout the whole organization. .
Chapter 5	My board members affirm our core values and maintain accountability to a church which embraces the historical and literal interpretation of scripture.
Chapter 5	My board members affirm a statement of faith, mission statement, and core values based on scripture
Chapter 5	My board members govern with one voice based on a shared understanding of God's revelation, purposes, and authority structures.
Chapter 5	My board has third party audits and annual reviews of board members to ensure accountability to core values.
Chapter 5	My board confronts and terminates board members or executives who disregard the mission, core values and statement of faith.

Chapter 6	My business has clear roles for each member of the C-Suite.
Chapter 6	My business has clear goals for each member of the C-Suite.
Chapter 6	My business has clear workflows so that all projects are completed by the right person by the right date, with details in documents that are properly named, organized, and easily accessed.
Chapter 6	My business has complete cash flow statements so that managers can confirm activities are profitable.
Chapter 6	My business managers and compliance consultants have clear controls to verify that work is done properly.
Chapter 7	My company has a clear understanding of the spiritual authority process.
Chapter 7	The managers in my company listen to employees while showing principled concern for all.
Chapter 7	My company trains groups of employees to reflect timeless character principles.
Chapter 7	My company identifies and mentors existing and new leaders.
Chapter 7	My company provides opportunity to disciple employees one-on-one.
Chapter 8	My calendar shows that I have set aside regular time for activities that glorify God.

EXHIBIT 2

Chapter 8	My resume shows that I am using my talents to pursue my calling and steward resources for God's glory.
Chapter 8	My checkbook registers show that I am spending money to build God-glorifying businesses, families, and churches
Chapter 8	My employee and client satisfaction surveys show that I am fulfilling commitments and maintaining trust.
Chapter 8	My pastor and/or spiritual advisory board would agree that I am guarding against idols that undermine stewardship
Chapter 9	My company gives opportunities to people to influence decisions that affect them.
Chapter 9	My company helps each staff member discover, develop, and use his/her natural gifts on the job.
Chapter 9	My company provides training to help all staff members develop their competence and character.
Chapter 9	My company has e-mail policies in place to help ensure positive communications with staff members, vendors, and clients.
Chapter 9	My company respects and honors employees with time off and encourages family time and celebration of religious holidays.
Chapter 10	My business hires compliance consultants and/or maintains compliance procedures to help confirm that we follow all government regulations, even when we disagree with them.

Chapter 10	My company helps executives provide for their families by funding trusts outside of the taxable estates.
Chapter 10	My business managers count costs through a careful budgeting process before undertaking new projects (Luke 14:28-30).
Chapter 10	My strategic planning process does not presume upon tomorrow but instead develops realistic projections and contingency plans (James 4:13-15).
Chapter 10	My strategic planning process involves wise counselors who can help me assess risks and respond appropriately (Proverbs 15:22).
Chapter 11	My personal desire for money or assets (greed?) is not be undermining my relationships at work.
Chapter 11	My company rewards staff members when customers share stories of their excellent service.
Chapter 11	My personal need for control or stature (pride?) is not undermining my relationships at work.
Chapter 11	My conflicts about my personal desires do not manifest as anger (James 4:1,.2; Proverbs 11:23) that undermines relationships
Chapter 11	My relationships have not been damaged by unwholesome talk (Ephesians 4:29) in cases where I failed to forgive as Christ forgave me (4:32).
Chapter 12	My power to make wealth is given to me by God so that He may confirm His covenant (Deuteronomy 8:18).

EXHIBIT 2

Chapter 12	My desire for wealth is focused on being rich in good works, being generous and ready to share, storing up for treasure of a good foundation for the future (1 Timothy 6:17-19).
Chapter 12	My wealth is managed actively in keeping with the parable of the talents (Matthew 25:14-30).
Chapter 12	My success in managing wealth is monitored closely so that I know the details about all of my assets (Proverbs 27:23-27).
Chapter 12	My wealth is shared equitably with those who help contribute to the accumulation of the wealth (1 Corinthians 9:9).
Chapter 13	My company serves the "whole" person including the financial, health, family and spiritual needs of the staff.
Chapter 13	My company sees and treats all staff as created in God's image and deserving respect.
Chapter 13	My company empowers staff by giving them an inspiring purpose, clarifying their role, giving them authority, and listening to their voice.
Chapter 13	My company equips staff by developing servant leaders and building their competence.
Chapter 13	My leadership team rewards staff who are high performers, team players, and committed to our core values.
Chapter 14	My company relentlessly focuses on creating a positive customer experience.

Chapter 14	Everyone in my organization maintains the highest standards of quality and service.
Chapter 14	All work processes are designed to make it easy for our customer to do business with us.
Chapter 14	We set the standard for the best customer service in our industry.
Chapter 14	We build win-win relationships with our customers.
Chapter 15	My company encourages its leaders to provide leadership in charitable organizations.
Chapter 15	The leadership team in my organization has the freedom to start new ventures, including charitable organizations, when such initiatives are consistent with the corporate vision and values.
Chapter 15	My company seeks to expand it's influence through charitable activities in the community.
Chapter 15	My company encourages staff involvement in philanthropic activities.
Chapter 15	My company is sensitive to how it can help staff members balance work with family and religious community commitments.
Chapter 16	My faith in God is vibrant and I plan to nurture my spiritual relationships actively throughout the rest of my life.
Chapter 16	My commitment to learning helps me be like the sensible man who considers all his steps (Proverbs 14:15).

EXHIBIT 2

Chapter 16	My closest friend would say that my Christian practices and beliefs help me regularly experience the fruits of the Spirit (Galatians 5:22).
Chapter 16	My spiritual insights are entrusted to reliable men and women (2 Timothy 2:2) who help me build a productive team.
Chapter 16	My business practices can and should be passed from generation to generation (Joel 1:3).

Glossary

Please visit www.ReflectingGod/info/Glossary to see a more complete glossary.

Alignment	Alignment results from team members agreeing on first principles and priorities (e.g., core values). In business, goals should be linked to cash flow projections that have support of team members. When members of a team share commitment to core values and goals, they have reason to contribute to the success of one another, thereby enhancing productivity and increasing the likelihood of fulfilling the mission.
Calling	A person identifies calling using the process at www.covenant.net/BiblicalPurpose. The process relies on results from tests, such as those at www.covenant.net/Calling
Covenant Sequence	A covenant defines bond of love in which the parties of the covenant solemnly swear to devote themselves to seek the blessing of the other party. The covenant is the formal expression of the mutual commitment of love among Father, Son, and Spirit. In the Triune God's relationship with man, the covenant is the formal commitment to reflect divine love and grace to man. This unconditional expression of care elicits reciprocation. Man therefore loves his Creator by, 1) seeking to know His revelation, 2) pursue his purposes, 3) respect Godly leaders, 4) obey divine commands, 5) encourage the blessings of obedience, and 6) build covenant communities that can grow and be replicated. These 6 responses are part of deeper 6-element covenant sequence developed and explained by Meredith Kline, Ray Sutton, Vern Poythress and other theologians committed to a covenantal view of the God-honoring relationships. The 6-elements of the covenant sequence can be observed in personal communion with God as well as in covenant communities patterned after those in Scripture.

Mission	The shared purposes of team members form a mission. This mission should be defined in full view of the vision (described below). Clarifying the mission involves prayerfully discerning how God's wisdom applies to the opportunities and strengths given to a family, church, or other organization. Because these opportunities and strengths will change, the mission can/should evolve. Even if the mission evolves, part of the mission may be based on non-changing (transcendent) Biblical principles or transcendent purposes from Scripture that remain constant.
Prosperity	God prospers the faithful! Prosperity comes in the form of rich relationships. The rich relationships are enjoyed most in covenant community. When a member of the covenant community focuses too much on personal property or material wealth, this is a sign of the greed, pride, envy, gluttony, laziness and other deadly sins that can easily undermine teamwork and prosperity. When a pastor preaches prosperity, he should focus on how the promises of blessings are often made to YOU as a plural "you" referring to members of the covenant community. Pastors frequently misappropriate these verses to promise blessings to you (the singular person interested in autonomous freedom and blessings apart from the covenant community.)
Purpose	A person's purpose statement is based on the unique calling given to each individual. The calling is refined into a statement of purpose that can be shared with others, especially leaders who know how to build teams. Some purposes described in Scripture, such as glorifying God, are constant and therefore deemed transcendent.

Quadruple Bottom Line	To drive economic progress, enabling profitable economic enterprise has been a primary responsibility of governments in free countries and governance boards in successful companies. Recently, however, growing numbers of companies have looked beyond profits to consider people, the planet, and progress. These 4 Ps provide a framework for sustainable prosperity with continuous and competitive innovation. Individuals and their communities can flourish when resources are optimized in these 4 areas. Ideally, the resource optimization should be tracked with Key Performance Indicators ("KPIs") that focus stakeholders on successful implementation of new combinations of innovations by entrepreneurial shareholders committed to profitable service to employees, customers, and the community.
Stakeholders	Anybody with an interest in the success of a business. See https://en.wikipedia.org/wiki/Stakeholder_(corporate)
Stewardship	Fundamentally, stewardship is about exercising our God-given dominion over His creation, reflecting the image of our creator God in His care, responsibility, maintenance, protection, and beautification of His creation. See http://www.ReflectingGod.info/Stewardship/
Vision	Vision is developed as part of God's revelation. Divine revelation reveals the immutable character of God as well as His unchanging law. See, e.g., Proverbs 29:18. Because the vision is closely linked to God's unchanging revelation, authors of strategic planning books frequently write that vision must remain constant. Vision can be discerned through prayer by men and women who seek the leading of the Holy Spirit; in such cases, the vision may be referred to as a "spirit-led vision."

Bibliography

Anyabwile, Thabiti M. *What Is a Healthy Church Member?*, Wheaton, IL: Crossway, 2008

Auerbach, Justice Jerold. *Without Law? Non-legal Dispute Settlement in American History* 22 (1983)

Bachelder, Cheryl. *Dare to Serve*. Oakland, CA. Berrett-Koehler Publishers, 2015.

Barrett, Lois. *Doing What Is Right: What the Bible Says about Covenant and Justice*, Harrisonburg, VA: Herald Press, 1989

Bellah, Robert N. *The Broken Covenant: American Civil Religion in Time of Trial*, Chicago, IL: University of Chicago Press, 1992

Birch, Bruce and Ronald E. Vallet. *The Steward Living in Covenant: A New Perspective on Old Testament Stories*, Grand Rapids, MI: Wm. B. Eerdmans Publishing Company, 2001

Blanchard, Ken. *Leading at a Higher Level*. Upper Saddle River, NJ: FT Press, 2006

Blanchard, Kenneth and O'Connor, Michael, *Managing by Values*. Blanchard Family Partnership and O'Connor Family Trust, 1995.

Boa, Kenneth. *Conformed to His Image: Biblical and Practical Approaches to Spiritual Formation*, Grand Rapids: Zondervan, 2009

Boice, James Montgomery and Philip Graham Ryken, R. C. Sproul. *The Doctrines of Grace: Rediscovering the Evangelical Gospel*, Wheaton, IL: Crossway, 2009

Brueggemann, Walter. *The Covenanted Self: Explorations in Law and Covenant*, Minneapolis, MN: Fortress Press, 1999

Cahill, Thomas. *How the Irish Saved Civilization*, Flushing, MI: Anchor Books, 1996

Calvin, John and James B. Jordan. *The Covenant Enforced: Sermons on Deuteronomy 27 and 28*, Tyler, TX: Institute for Christian Eco-nomics, 1990

Cameron, Kim. S. and Quinn, Robert E. *Diagnosing and Changing Organization Culture*. San Francisco, CA. Jossey-Bass, 2011.

Chapman, Gary. *Covenant Marriage: Building Communication and Intimacy,* Nashville, TN: B&H Publishing Group, 2003

Clinton, Dr. Robert. *The Making of a Leader: Recognizing the Lessons and Stages of Leadership Development.* Colorado Springs: Nav Press, *2014.*

Cloud, Henry. *Integrity.* New York, New York. Harper, 2006.

Collins, Jim. *Good to Great.* New York: Harper Business, 2001

Covey, Stephen M.R. *The Speed of Trust.* New York, New York. Press, 2006.

Covey, Stephen R. *Principle-Centered Leadership.* New York., New York. Summit Books, 1991.

Denison, Daniel R. *Corporate Culture and Organizational Effectiveness.* Daniel R. Denison, 1997.

Dever, Mark and C. J. Mahaney. *The Gospel and Personal Evangelism (9Marks),* Wheaton, IL: Crossway, 2008

Dever, Mark and Joshua Harris. *Nine Marks of a Healthy Church,* Wheaton, IL: Crossway, 2004

DeYoung, Kevin L. and Jerry Bridges. *The Good News We Almost For- got: Rediscovering the Gospel in a 16th Century Catechism,* Chicago, IL: Moody Publishers, 2010

Donegan, Susan. *ADR in Colonial America: A Covenant for Survival,* 14, 16 Arbitration Journal June 1993

Drucker, Henry F. *Managing for Results.* New York, New York. Harper & Row Publishers, 1964.

Elkouri, F. and E.A Elkour. *How Arbitration Works,* Washington, DC: Bureau of National Affairs, 1973

Engelsma, David J. *Reformed Education: The Christian School as Demand of the Covenant, Jenison,* MI: Reformed Free Publishing Association, 2000

Ferguson, Sinclair. *In Christ Alone: Living the Gospel Centered Life,* Sanford, FL: Reformation Trust Publishing, 2007

Flanders, Henry Jackson and David Anthony Smith. *People of the Covenant: An Introduction to the Hebrew Bible,* New York, NY: Oxford University Press, 1996

Frangipane, Francis. *The Power Of Covenant Prayer: Christian Living,* Lake Mary, FL: Charisma House, 1999

Gerber, Michael. *The Most Successful Small Business in The World: The Ten Principles*, Hoboken, NJ: Wiley, 2010

Gerstner, Jonathan N. *The Thousand Generation Covenant: Dutch Reformed Covenant Theology*, Leiden, Netherlands: BRILL, 1991

Gibson, Scott and Warren Wiersbe. *Preaching with a Plan: Sermon Strategies for Growing Mature Believers*, Grand Rapids, MI: Baker Books, 2012

Gill, L. *God's Covenant Blessings for You*, Tulsa, OK: Harrison House, 1998

Goldberg, Steven. *Dispute Resolution*, Boston, MA: Little, Brown & Co. 1985

Harris, Jim. *Our Unfair Advantage*. Houston, TX: High Bridge Books, 2015

Henry Horwitz and James Oldham (1993). *John Locke, Lord Mansfield, and Arbitration During the Eighteenth Century*. The Historical Journal, 36, pp 137-159. doi:10.1017/S0018246X00016149.

Hill, Craig and S. *Marriage: Covenant or Contract*, Fort Washington, PA: Harvest Books, 1992

Horowitz, Morton. *The Transformation of American Law*, 1780-1860" 145 (Cambridge: Harvard University Press, 1977)

Horsley, Richard. *Covenant Economics: A Biblical Vision of Justice for All*, Louisville, KY: Westminster John Knox Press, 2009

Horton, Michael. *Gospel Commission: The: Recovering God's Strategy for Making Disciples*, Grand Rapids, MI: Baker Books, 2011

Horton, Michael. *Introducing Covenant Theology*, Grand Rapids, MI: Baker Books, 2009

Horton, Michael. *The Gospel-Driven Life: Being Good News People in a Bad News World*, Grand Rapids, MI: Baker Books, 2009

Hunt, Susan. *Heirs of the Covenant: Leaving a Legacy of Faith for the Next Generation*, Wheaton, IL: Crossway, 1998

Ibrahim, Nabil and John P. Angelidis. *The Long-Term Performance of Small Businesses: Are there Differences Between "Christian-Based" Companies and their Secular Counterparts?*, Journal of Business Ethics, Spring 2005, 58:187–193 Springer 2005

Jordan, James. *Law of the Covenant: An Exposition of Exodus 21-23*, Tyler, TX: Institute for Christian Economics, 1984

Jung, Joanne. *Godly Conversation: Rediscovering the Puritan Practice of Conference*, Grand Rapids, MI: Reformation Heritage Books, 2011

Karlberg, Mark. *Covenant Theology in Reformed Perspective*, Eugene, OR: Wipf & Stock Publishers, 2004

Keller, Timothy J., *Center Church: Doing Balanced, Gospel-Centered Ministry in Your City*, Grand Rapids, MI: Zondervan, 2012

Keller, Timothy, D. A. Carson, et al. *The Gospel as Center (The Gospel Coalition)*, Grand Rapids, MI: Zondervan, 2013

Kelley Varner. *Whose Right It Is: A Handbook of Covenantal Theology*, Shippensburg, PA: Destiny Image Publishers, 1995

Kingsley, Fletcher. *The Power of the Covenant: The Key to Secure and Lasting Relationships*, Ventura, CA: Gospel Light Publications, 2000

Kline Cebuhar, Jo. *So Grows the Tree–Creating an Ethical Will–The Legacy of Your Beliefs and Values, Life Lessons and Hopes for the Future*, West Des Moines, IA: Murphy Publishing, 2010

Kline, Meridith. *By Oath Consigned: A Reinterpretation of the Covenant Signs of Circumcision and Baptism*, Grand Rapids, MI: Eerd- mans, 1968

Kline, Meridith. *The Structure of Biblical Authority*, Eugene, OR: Wipf & Stock Publishers, 1997

Kotter, John, P. *The Heart of Change*. Boston, Mass. Harvard Business School Press, 2002.

Kouzes, James M. *Credibility*. San Francisco, CA., Jossey-Bass, 1993.

Kouzes, James M. *Leadership Challenge*. San Francisco. Jossey-Bass, 2007.

Lothrop, Samuel Kirkland. *The Mature Christian Ripe for the Harvest*, Boston, MA: J. Wilson and Son, 1861

Machen, Gresham. *The Doctrine of the Atonement: Three Lectures*, Amazon Digital Services,

Mann, Bruce H. "Formalization of Informal Law: Arbitration before the American Revolution, The." *NYUL Rev.* 59 (1984): 443.

Mann, Bruce. *Law, Legalism, and Community Before the American Revolution*, 1415 Michigan Law Review 84 Mich. L. Rev. 1415 June, 1986

Marshall, Walter. *The Gospel Mystery of Sanctification*, Seattle: WA: Amazon Digital Services, Inc., 1692

Maxwell, John C. *Developing the Leader Within You*. Nashville, Tennessee. Thomas Nelson Publishers, 1993.

Mendenhall, George E. *Law and Covenant in Israel and the Ancient Near East*, Pittsburgh, PA: Biblical Colloquium, 1955

Miller, Brad. *Church Health and Growth Primer*, Amazon.com, ChurchTech Press, 2010

Monter, E. William, *Calvin's Geneva*, Malabar, FL: R. E. Krieger, 1975

Moore, T.M. *I Will Be Your God: How God's Covenant Enriches Our Lives*, Phillipsburg, NJ: Presbyterian & Reformed Publishing Company, 2002

Murray, Andrew. *The Two Covenants*, Whitefish, MT: Kessinger Publishing, 2012

Murray, John. *The Covenant of Grace: A Biblico-Theological Study*, Phillipsburg, NJ: Presbyterian & Reformed Publishing Company, 1987

Nee, Watchman. *Better Covenant*, Richmond, VA: Christian Fellow- ship Publishers, 1982

Packer, J. I. *An Introduction to Covenant Theology,* Largo, Maryland: FIG Publishing, 2012

Pierce, Chuck and Rebecca Wagner Sytsema. *Possessing Your Inheritance: Take Hold of God's Destiny for Your Life*, Ventura, CA: Regal Books, 2009

Poirier, Alfred. *The Peacemaking Pastor: A Biblical Guide to Resolving Church Conflict*, Grand Rapids, MI: Baker Books, 2006

Powell, Edward. *Settlement of Disputes by Arbitration in Fifteenth- Century England*, 24, 25 Law and History Review Riemer, Jack and Nathaniel Stampfer. *So That Your Values Live On*, Windsor, VT: Long Hill Partners, Inc, 2009

Rienow, Rob, *Limited Church: Unlimited Kingdom*, Nashville, TN Randall House, 2013

Robertson, O. Palmer. *The Christ of the Covenants*, Phillipsburg, NJ: Presbyterian & Reformed Publishing Company, 1981

Rodes, Robert E. "Secular Cases in the Church Courts: A Historical Survey" Catholic Lawyer 301-309 Vol. 32, No. 4, pages 306-09

Rudolph, Sarah. *Blackstone's Vision of Alternative Dispute Resolution*, 280 Memphis State University Law Review Vol. 22 (1992)

Ryken, Philip Graham. *City on a Hill: Reclaiming the Biblical Pattern for the Church in the 21st Century*, Chicago, IL: Moody Publishers, 2003

Sande, Ken. *Peacemaking for Families*, Colorado Springs, CO: Focus on the Family, 2002

Sande, Ken. *The Peacemaker: A Biblical Guide to Resolving Personal Conflict*, 3rd edition, Grand Rapids, MI: Baker Bookhouse, 2004

Schein, Edgar H. *Organizational Culture and Leadership*, second edition, San Francisco, CA, Jossey-Bass, 1992.

Senge, Peter. *The Fifth Discipline*. New York: Random House, 2010

Shepherd, Norman. *The Call of Grace: How the Covenant Illuminates Salvation and Evangelism*, Phillipsburg, NJ: Presbyterian & Reformed Publishing Company, 2000

Sinek, Simon. *Leaders Eat Last*. New York, New York. Penguin Group, 2014.

Sinek, Simon. *Start With Why*. New York, New York. Penguin Group, 2009.

Smeaton, George. *The Apostles' Doctrine of the Atonement,* Carlisle, PA: Banner of Truth, 1991

Stackhouse, Max. L. *Covenant and Commitments: Faith, Family, and Economic Life*, Louisville, KY: Westminster, 1997

Sutton, Ray R. *That You May Prosper: Dominion by Covenant*, Tyler, TX: Institution for Christian Economics, 1987

Voorhees, Tim. *The Best Zero Tax Planning Tools: How to Maximize Tax-Efficient Lifetime Income*, Transfers to Heirs and Gifts to Favorite Charities, Costa Mesa, CA: Wealth Strategies Counsel, 2012

Vos, Geerhardus. *Biblical Theology: Old and New Testaments*, Eu- gene, OR: Wipf & Stock Pub, 2003

Vos, Geerhardus. *The Doctrine of the Covenant in Reformed Theology*, Phillipsburg, NJ: Presbyterian & Reformed Publishing Company, 1980

Vos, Geerhardus. *The Mosaic Origin of the Pentateuchal Codes*, Bos- ton, MA: Hodder & Stoughton, 1886

Walton, John H. *Covenant : God's Purpose, God's Plan*, Grand Rapids, MI: Zondervan, 1994

Whitney, Donald S. and James Montgomery Boice. *Spiritual Disciplines within the Church: Participating Fully in the Body of Christ*, Chicago, IL: Moody Publishers, 1996

Whitney, Donald S. *Spiritual Disciplines for the Christian Life with Bonus Content* (Pilgrimage Growth Guide), Colorado Springs: Nav- Press, 2012

Whitney, Donald S. *Ten Questions to Diagnose Your Spiritual Health*, Colorado Springs: NavPress, 2001

Wilson, Douglas. *For Kirk and Covenant: The Stalwart Courage of John Knox*, Nashville, TN: Cumberland House Publishing, 2000

To see additional books consulted during the development of this book, please visit www.ReflectingGod.info/Bibliography.

Topic Index

T

V

W

Scripture Index

Reflecting God's Character in Your Business refers to more than 400 Bible verses, which are listed below in order from Genesis to Revelation. To see page numbers where the verses appear, please visit the more complete index at http://www.ReflectingGod.info/ScriptureIndex.

Deuteronomy 8:18

Joshua 1:8

1 Samuel 10:25

1 Samuel 18:3

1 Samuel 8:6-21

1 Kings 3:10

1 Chronicles 28:11-12

1 Chronicles 28:19

2 Chronicles 16:9

2 Chronicles 1:8

2 Chronicles 3:3

Nehemiah 1:5-11

Nehemiah 2:11-16

Nehemiah 2:16

Nehemiah 2:17

Nehemiah 2:18

Nehemiah 2:19

Nehemiah 2:4-6

Nehemiah 2:5

Nehemiah 2:7-8

Nehemiah 3:1-32

Nehemiah 4:16-18

Nehemiah 4:6

Nehemiah 5:1-6

Nehemiah 5:5

Nehemiah 7:1-4

Nehemiah 7:2

Nehemiah 7:3-5

Nehemiah 7:4

Nehemiah 7:70-72

Esther 1:13

Psalm 1

Psalm 1:1–3

Psalm 119:105

Psalm 127:3

Psalm 15

Psalm 15:4

Psalm 16:11

Psalm 24:1-5

Psalm 25:9-10

Psalm 36:2

Psalm 40:10

Psalm 66:18

Psalm 73

Psalm 74:20

Psalm 74:20

Psalm 89:7

Psalm 90:2

Prov 3:4

Proverbs 11:23

Prov 13:11

Proverbs 13:20

Proverbs 14:15

Proverbs 14:15

Proverbs 14:15

Proverbs 14:15

Proverbs 15:1-2

Proverbs 15:4

Proverbs 15:22

Proverbs 15:29

Proverbs 16:3

Proverbs 16:9

Prov 20:12

Matthew 5:24	John 10:10
Matthew 5:24-26	John 10:10
Matthew 5:8-9	John 10:14
Matthew 5:9	John 10:27
Matthew 6:10	John 10:27
Matthew 6:10	John 12:26
Matthew 6:20	John 12:35-36
Matthew 6:33	John 14:15
Matthew 7:12	John 14:15
Matthew 7:12	John 14:15, 21
Matthew 7:3-5	John 14:15-31
Matthew 7:3-5	John 14:21
Matthew 7:5	John 14:21
Mark 10:42-45	John 14:21
Mark 12:30-31	John 15:10-12
Mark 12:31	John 15:4-8
Mark 14:33	John 15:9
Mark 3:14	John 17:17
Mark 5:37	John 17:23
Mark 9:38-41	John 21:8
Luke 1:68-75	John 3:19
Luke 1:68-79	John 3:19
Luke 1:78-79	John 3:19
Luke 10:1	John 3:19
Luke 10:38-42	John 3:19
Luke 14:28	John 3:19
Luke 14:28-30	John 3:19
Luke 14:28-30	John 4:7
Luke 14:28-31	John 5:30
Luke 16:10	John 5:30
Luke 2:20	John 8:12
John 1:17	John 8:31

Ephesians 3:20	1 Thessalonians 2:8 NIV
Ephesians 4:11-13	1 Timothy 6:17
Ephesians 4:15	1 Timothy 6:17
Ephesians 4:3	1 Timothy 6:17-19
Ephesians 4:29, 4:32	1 Timothy 6:17-19
Ephesians 1:21-22	1 Timothy 6:17-19
Ephesians 1:21-22	2 Timothy 1:7
Ephesians 2:6	2 Timothy 2:1-26
Ephesians 3:16-19	2 Timothy 2:2
Ephesians 3:16-19	2 Timothy 2:2
Ephesians 3:17	2 Timothy 2:2
Ephesians 4:29	Hebrews 1:3
Ephesians 4:29	Hebrews 1:3
Ephesians 4:3	Hebrews 1:3
Ephesians 4:32	Hebrews 10
Ephesians 4:32	Hebrews 11:37-38
Ephesians 5:1	Hebrews 11:39
Ephesians 5:1	Hebrews 11:6
Ephesians 6:10-18	Hebrews 12:1
Ephesians 6:5-7	Hebrews 12:14
Ephesians 6:6	Hebrews 13:7
Philippians 2:11-13	Hebrews 4:15
Philippians 2:2	Hebrews 4:15
Philippians 2:4-5	James 3:18
Philippians 3:10-12	James 4:1
Philippians 2:4	James 4:1
Colossians 1:17	James 4:13-15
Colossians 1:18-20	James 4:13-15
Colossians 1:18-20	James 4:2
Colossians 3:23	James 5:16
Colossians 4:1	James 1:22
Colossians 4:9	1 Pet 4:10